THE END FROM THE BEGINNING

(The Origin of Western Civilization)

Clayton Willis

[handwritten inscription: 09/03/2018 FOR JOANN Thanks for the Christian friendship. May God bless you + yours. Clay Willis]

Table of Contents

FORWARD – A CAVEAT

If you are opening this book on your Kindle or in hard copy format for the first time, and if you are a Bible scholar or a person who reads the Bible avidly, I respectfully request your patience with the first four chapters as some of this material may be well known to you.

However, there are many who have never actively studied the scriptures – especially the Old Testament – and in order to understand the last six chapters the background information presented in the first four chapters is vital.

My major impetus for writing this book is to demonstrate for Christians as well as unbelievers with open minds and hearts that there is a direct connection between the scriptures and our world as it is today in 2018 when this work was finished. In fact, our world would be drastically different but for *the Hand of God* guiding the Israelites – both genetic and spiritual Israelites.

In those last six chapters there are many new concepts about the growth of the Christian church as well as the development of Western Civilization. I sincerely believe that it will be worth your time to read the chapters in sequence so the whole, beautiful panorama of God's plan up to the present time will be displayed for your consideration.

* * *

Acknowledgement

In the period from November 30, 2016 – May 18, 2018, the author was greatly blessed to make the acquaintance of Dr. Harold Raymond Booher and to become as close friends as one can be with e-mail correspondence. I answered a question from Hal that was sent to the website www.biblestudy.org. He liked my answer and our correspondence began. He eventually asked about my own writing.

About 25 years ago, I did the basic research and composition of a paper called *The Hand of God*. Much of that material is incorporated in this book. Hal read the paper and began to urge me to write a book. He wrote this comment, and many others, in the paper (*I've added italics to certain lines*):

> It appears to me with all the research you have done on this topic that you may be the best qualified to do a scholarly work on this topic. Since it can't be proven like one would like. There is enough circumstantial evidence to make a case. From a biblical prophecy point of view, you have a strong biblical link. What you need is a strong historical argument that does not rely on some the deficiencies of the literature. May I humbly suggest my approach of "best of all alternatives"? Starting with the last point we know where the 10 tribes were concentrated outline the most likely scenarios (alternatives) for movement to next areas. Set up criteria which if true would give great confidence that Israel and the scepter passed through there. Evaluate the best alternative based on the criteria. *Anyway, a book that tackled this would be an incredible contribution to Scripture and History. I'm so excited about it that I might be talked back into work.* What I am good at is making up Book outlines and challenging questions which takes you looking into details. Etc   Could you get fired up about such a project or do you think it next to impossible to make a better case than has been made already?

Hal did *extensive* editing of the first 8 chapters. About two weeks before his death he wrote:

> I don't know if I have said it enough times because I am as you see a tough editor. But you have done some incredible research and I am truly amazed at what you have found. Jack[1] seems more informed on Ancient

4

history than I do may be more amazed at some of these discoveries. *For when I read your stuff it is my first exposure to them so have no predisposed ideas to have to overcome. But I assure you Jack is totally right about your contribution to Western Civ. In fact, it does seem you are being led. There is no way you could go each step on faith and have so many doors open just as you need them. It is amazing how you seem to just plow ahead into these areas and pull out so much that has been overlooked. How do you do it?*

I found Hal's death on May 18, 2018 to be a devastating experience. Not only did I lose a magnificent editor but also a brother in Christ and a true friend and mentor. Without his encouragement and assistance, I would likely have never attempted to write this book.

With love and affection, I dedicate this book to Hal. *R. I. P.*

HAROLD BOOHER

Dr. HAROLD RAYMOND BOOHER

The first Senior Executive Director of Manpower and Personnel Integration (MANPRINT) for the Department of the Army, died on May 18, 2018 in Baltimore, MD. He was 81. He received degrees from Depauw University (BA), Rose Polytechnic Institute (BS Electrical Engineering), George Washington University (MA Experimental Psychology) and The Catholic University of America (Human Factors Engineering). His career in federal government spanned service with the U.S. Patent Office, Department of the Navy, Nuclear Regulatory Commission, National Highway Traffic Safety Administration, ending his career with the Department of the Army. He edited two books on MANPRINT and Human Systems Integration. Dr. Booher was a fellow of the Human Factors and Ergonomics Society. He is survived by his wife Anne Terzian Booher; his four children and their spouses, Dr. Catherine Booher-Price (Christopher), Alice Johnson, Susanna Clay (Andrew), John Booher (Kimberly); eight grandchildren; siblings Homer and Donald Booher and Shirley Hodge. A memorial service will be held on June 16, 2018 at 1 p.m. at the Cathedral of the Incarnation in Baltimore, MD.

$$* \; * \; *$$

---

[1] "Jack" was Jack Hiller, a friend of Hal's who also contributed some editing and commentary.

PREFACE

[10] I make known the end from the beginning, from ancient times, what is still to come. I say, 'My purpose will stand, and I will do all that I please.' Isaiah 46:10 (NIV)

What is the Bible? It most certainly is neither a history of the universe nor this planet; nor is it a history of the human race. If God inspired the writing of the Bible, He chose to tell us very little about our origin. He told us the earth was in a state of devastation – "without form and void"[2] – before He changed this world into habitable form for life. He then placed our planet, the sun and the moon into their positions. He created the flora and fauna and last He created man. In terms of origins, that's essentially all the Bible tells us.

Only the first 11 chapters of Genesis, the first book of the Bible, are devoted to that creation. That text must be understood as being allegorical[3]; it is a story handed down orally over hundreds of generations before it was committed to writing.

Those who interpret the time spans given in the first 10 chapters of the Bible – using the genealogy recorded in Genesis chapter 5 for instance – find themselves at odds with science and secular and archeological history. Those who attempt to extrapolate or justify those time lines to fit with science create more problems than they solve. The Bible tells us that a "day" with God is "as a thousand years"[4]. This too is allegory and informs us that the human concept of measured time is meaningless to an immortal being.

God did not give us historical specifics; instead, He gave mankind intelligence and a sense of curiosity. In our search for such origins, man came to realize our relative individual insignificance in this universe. We came to understand that there

---

[2] Genesis 1:2 KJV
[3] having hidden spiritual meaning that transcends the literal sense of a sacred text
[4] II Peter 3:8

are things we probably will never know and things we seem incapable of comprehending, no matter how advanced our knowledge and science becomes.

Albert Einstein wrote, "science without religion is lame, religion without science is blind ... a legitimate conflict between science and religion cannot exist."[5]

The wise man who wrote the book of Ecclesiastes expressed the humility engendered by this knowledge:

> I have seen the burden God has laid on men. He has made everything beautiful in its time. He has also set eternity in the hearts of men; yet they cannot fathom what God has done from beginning to end. I know that there is nothing better for men than to be happy and do good while they live. NIV[1] Ecclesiastes 3:10-12

Our curiosity about our origins and the quest for understanding of the origin of the universe led the belief in a Creator. The ubiquitous nature of religion throughout all cultures and civilizations shows that man has always had an innate sense of powerful, intelligent forces at work that we cannot fully comprehend. Religions were developed to offer explanation.

The first 10 chapters of the Bible deal with this enigma with a brief description and little explanation. That a Creator exists, that He communicates with mankind, that He created mankind for a purpose, that He gave us laws and that He influences or directs what happens to mankind are all matters of faith and not science. The Bible makes no pretense of being scientific.

However, the accumulation of proven, scientific knowledge tends to strengthen the faith of we who believe in the Creator.

Most of the 11th chapter of Genesis traces the genealogy of Noah after the great flood to the time of a man called Abram and the rest of the Bible is devoted to his descendants. The only time other nations and people are mentioned or described in the Bible is a result of their contact with Abram's descendants.

Three major religions – Judaism, Christianity and Islam – sprang from the events that transpired with Abram. The Bible defines the religions of Judaism and Christianity. The writings included in the canon were completed before the end of the 1st Century A.D. while Islam originated in the 7th Century A.D.

---

[5] Einstein 1940, pp. 605–607

Though neither Judaism nor Christianity have ever held sway over a majority of the earth's population, secular history shows that these religions are interwoven into almost every major event in the last 4,000 years. Western Civilization is the result of the combination of the influences of Judaism and Christianity. Our world today would be drastically different but for the underpinning of the tenets of these religions.

Christianity and Judaism not only affected the moral character of the people of Western Civilization but also were the basis of the legal and social foundations of its institutions, political character and governments. The common law of the nations comprising Western Civilization can be traced to laws given in the Old Testament and continued in the New Testament with the teaching of Jesus and His disciples and apostles.

While adherents to both religions have done some bad things, the basic beliefs of these religions have had profound effect upon the nations in which those adherents dwelt.

Islam, which traces its origins to Abraham in its sacred writing, the Quran, is in the news today and much of the current friction and armed conflict is a result of the actions of radical, militant adherents to that religion. The conflict between the Islamic nations and the nation of Israel and the nations of Western Civilization can be traced to events that happened 4,000 years ago. The current Middle Eastern conflicts are a direct result of the Israelite claim to the land of Palestine and the Islamic denial of that claim.

It is important to understand the Biblical origin of the Israelites and the other descendants of Abram – who is better known as Abraham. This book will trace the interaction between God and those descendants – especially the Israelites – to help us understand how the *hand of God* shaped the history of the last 4,000 years and how we came to be where we are today in that history.

God's interactions with the Israelites did not stop in the 1st Century AD but formed the world as it is today. Truly understanding the Bible, the headlines in our newspapers and the massive data available on the Internet is impossible without this knowledge.

If the Bible is, as I believe, truly the word of God, what has happened over the last 4 millennia is the result of God's guidance and direction of the fate of Abraham's descendants.

This is neither to dismiss the actions and history of the Oriental people or the Indian people or the African people as inconsequential nor is it to suggest that God may not have *also* dealt with those people in His own way. Those dealings are, however, not recorded in the Bible.

The Bible presents a vista of 2,000 years in which it is apparent that there were forces in play that were not human in origin. The Bible traces select portions of the history of Abraham's descendants and those forces are displayed down to the time of Jesus and the New Testament.

We begin on a solid foundation using the scriptures as our guide. This narrative begins *from the beginning* with God's call to Abraham, the Covenant between God and Abraham and the bequeathing of the blessings of that Covenant down through the generations to the time of Jesus. The *hand of God* is evident as we follow the Israelites' history through the scriptures and see some of the Covenant blessings bestowed. The greatest of all those blessings was the birth of God as the "son of man" in the person of Jesus.

Yet, very important parts of that Covenant did not reach fruition in Biblical times. Assuming the Bible to be true, we insist that those forces have continued in play since that time as well; that God kept His part of the Covenant with Abraham and delivered the promised blessings to the Israelites and that delivery is responsible for our world as it is today.

It is my belief, and a major tenet of this book that, from the beginning, God planned and guided Abraham's descendants' movements and actions that eventually led to the establishment of Western Civilization!

However, we will not have guidance from the scriptures to show us the work of the *hand of God* over the past 2,000 years. We must rely upon the history written by men and we cannot assume that their writing was inspired by God.

Without God's inspiration, historians are subject to their personal biases and the influence of the cultures in which they lived when they recorded their histories. Their narrative of events and their descriptions of the actions of people reflect those biases and cultural influences. Discerning those biases and influences is made more difficult because the discerner is subject to his own biases and beliefs as well as the contemporary cultural influence.

Therefore, it was necessary for us in writing this book to return to the ultimate *Source* and use that *beginning* and that *end* to anchor this narrative. We asked God to guide our understanding and to help us transcend the holes in the fabric of secular histories; to help us find the information needed from myriad sources to identify the *real, continuing history of Abraham's descendants over the past 2,000 years.*

From the beginning with Abraham, God had already laid out His plan for Western Civilization.

To discern *the end from the beginning*, we start with the patriarchal father of Israel – Abraham.

* * *

PART I

Biblical and Secular History of Israel

CHAPTER 1
The Patriarchs

The story of how God formed Israel[1] begins with his calling a single individual, Abraham, and initiating a covenant with him which passed through him to his son Isaac and then to Jacob the son of Isaac. These three are known as the patriarchs of Israel.

Israel was unique in the civilizations of the ancient world for two reasons. First, it is the only nation directly created, sustained, formulated and guided by God. Second, it is the only ancient nation with a written record from its beginning to the dispersion of its people. [2]

The Bible is the sole source of the oral and written record of this story. It alone reveals the origin of the Covenant between God and Israel. It follows the fulfillment of the promises God made in that Covenant and explicitly details how God sustained the nation Israel until the time of Jesus. Jesus was and is the culmination of the most important Covenant promise: He fulfilled His role as the Son of God – God "born in the flesh" and savior of all mankind.

The Call of Abraham and God's Covenant

God's Covenant was first made with one individual – Abraham, who was born in Ur[6]. Abraham's ancestry is traced in the Bible through 9 generations to Noah's son Shem, whose recognized descendants today are called Shemites or Semites.

God first spoke to Abraham (then called Abram) when he was 75 years old and living in Harran[3]:

> [1] The LORD had said to Abram, "Go from your country, your people and your father's household to the land I will show you. [2] "I will make you into a great nation, and I will bless you; I will make your name great, and you will

---

[6] A city in Mesopotamia near the junction of the Tigris and Euphrates Rivers – Iraq on today's maps

be a blessing. 3 I will bless those who bless you, and whoever curses you I will curse; and all peoples on earth will be blessed through you." Genesis 12:1–3 (NIV)

From the very first promise we see God had in mind ultimately a relationship not only with Israel but also the entire world. Through Abraham all the world would be blessed.

At God's command to "go from your country" Abraham and his wife Sarah (first named Sarai) set out from Harran accompanied by their nephew Lot 4, their household servants, possessions and livestock to travel to an area in Canaan called Shechem5. The rest of Abraham's Shemite clan remained in Harran when Abram left and later became known as Arameans.6

At Shechem, God made a specific promise to Abraham:

> 7 The LORD appeared to Abram and said, "To your offspring I will give this land." So, he built an altar there to the LORD, who had appeared to him. Genesis 12:7 (NIV)

"This land" was Canaan, the land settled by Noah's grandson Canaan, son of Ham. The Canaanite clans were living there when Abraham arrived.

Because there was a famine in Canaan, Abraham, Sarah, Lot and their entourage soon traveled into Egypt where there was plentiful food. Canaan tended to be dry country experiencing drought frequently. By comparison, Egypt was able to tap the waters of the Nile if there was not enough rainfall and so seldom suffered famine.

The Bible implies that Sarah was both beautiful and unusual looking. Perhaps her half-brother Abraham's physical appearance was like Sarah's – the Bible does not say – but it is likely that these Aramaic Semites were either red-haired or blonde with blue or green eyes.7 Sarah's beauty was so unique that the Bible relates two incidents in which an Egyptian king (Pharaoh) and later a Canaanite king decided they *had* to have her. God intervened.8

Abraham and Sarah returned to Canaan and once again God made promises to Abraham:

> 14 The LORD said to Abram after Lot had parted from him, "Look around from where you are, to the north and south, to the east and west. 15 All the land that you see I will give to you and your offspring forever. 16 I will make your offspring like the dust of the earth, so that if anyone could count the dust, then your offspring could be counted. 17 Go, walk through the length

and breadth of the land, for I am giving it to you." ¹⁸ So Abram went to live near the great trees of Mamre at Hebron, where he pitched his tents. There he built an altar to the LORD. Genesis 13:14–18 (NIV)

This was the "promised land" – Canaan – that God bequeathed to Abraham with a promise of innumerable descendants. Yet at this time, after decades of marriage, Sarah remained barren – unable to conceive Abraham's child.

God then promised Abraham a son – Abraham's own flesh and blood – to be Abraham's heir. God repeated the promise of innumerable descendants:

⁵ He took him outside and said, "Look up at the sky and count the stars—if indeed you can count them." Then he said to him, "So shall your offspring be." Genesis 15:5 (NIV)

The Bible records an important theological point[9] for future generations – Abraham's faith in God was considered by God to be the equivalent of Abraham being "righteous" – in complete compliance with God's laws:

⁶ And he believed in the LORD; and he counted it to him for righteousness. Genesis 15:6 (KJV 1900)

When Abraham was about 85 years old, God made a Covenant with him abiding by the human customs[7] at that time – ritually using the bodies and blood of certain animals as symbols of and surety for the Covenant. This was a serious, meaningful and portentous ritual ceremony that bound both parties in the only legal terms of that time.

To finalize their Covenant, both Abraham and God passed between the divided carcasses of sacrificed animals.[8] In this manner the Covenant was sealed (legitimized) by the human standards of that day. In this Covenant, God incorporated all the previous promises He had made to Abraham. (**see Figure 1**)

Figure 1
Covenant of Special Promises to Abraham and Descendants
1. God would make Abraham's name great
2. Abram's descendants would become a great nation
3. God would bless Abraham
4. God would protect Abraham
5. Through Abraham all the nations of the world would be blessed
6. God would give Abraham's descendants the land of Canaan

---

[7] Genesis 16:3
[8] God appeared as a "firepot" and a burning candle.

7. Abraham would have innumerable descendants

Within the terms of this formal Covenant God added these prophecies and promises:

8. Abraham's descendants would spend 400 years in slavery
9. God would punish the nation that held them in slavery
10. Abraham's descendants would come out of that slavery with great wealth
11. Abraham would die at "a good old age"
12. In the fourth generation Abraham's Covenant children would return to Canaan
13. God gave Abraham's descendants all the land from the Euphrates River to the "river of Egypt"

Important: God placed no conditions on any of these promises made to Abraham.

The Covenant promises to Abraham like the one of "give to you and your offspring forever" – Genesis 15 and the Fig. 1. (6, 12) – in a patriarchal system of blood line inheritance depended on the line not being broken[10].

Two major challenges appeared to threaten the line of inheritance.

The First Challenge to the Inheritance Bloodline

The first – Abraham's line was in trouble from the beginning. He was already 75 when God first called and Sarah was only a few years younger. Still later, at age 85 and after decades of marriage, Sarah remained barren – unable to conceive Abraham's child.

With thoughts of creating a family a different way, Sarai suggested that Abraham sleep with Hagar – Sarai's Egyptian maid. Abraham complied – promptly impregnating Hagar. Hagar then became haughty and despised Sarah for being unable to bear children.[11] Even though the liaison was Sarah's idea she reproached Abraham. She asked for and received permission to drive the pregnant Hagar out from the household – essentially a death sentence because of the arid, desert territory surrounding them – and she did so.

God intervened directly with Hagar, telling her to return, submit to Sarah and have the child. He made promises to Hagar about the child she would bear and foretold that child's name and his future:

> [11] The angel of the LORD also said to her: "You are now with child and you will have a son. You shall name him Ishmael, for the LORD has heard of your misery. [12] He will be a wild donkey of a man; his hand will be against

15

everyone and everyone's hand against him, and he will live in hostility toward all his brothers." Genesis 16:11–12 (NIV84)

Ishmael

Abraham was 86 years old when Ishmael was born. Abraham loved Ishmael.

When Abraham was 99 years old and Ishmael was 13, God made another covenant with Abraham. This was the "covenant of circumcision" which came to be the most important identifying physical characteristic of Abraham's offspring. The circumcision covenant had special conditions. (See Figure 2)

Figure 2
Circumcision Covenant
1. Abraham must walk before God and be blameless
2. Abraham's descendants must be circumcised
3. Members of the household whether genetic family members or not were to be circumcised
4. Those who failed to be circumcised would be cut off from their people

At the same time, God changed Abram's name to Abraham[12] and Sarai to Sarah[13] while adding more promises to the Covenant with Abraham (**see Figure 3**).

Figure 3
Covenant of Special Promises Continued

14. Abraham would be the father of many nations
15. Kings would come out of his descendants
16. God would be Abraham's God and the God of Abraham's descendants
17. Nations and kings would come from Sarah
18. God would give Abraham a son by Sarah
19. God named their future son Isaac and confirmed he would be the Covenant son – not Ishmael – and he would be born in one year from that day
20. God placated Abraham, who loved Ishmael, by promising to bless Ishmael, making him into a great nation with territory and the father of 12 kings

When God told Abraham and Sarah they would have a son in one year, Abraham doubted and Sarah laughed. When the child was born at the precise time God had promised, Sarah laughed again and named her son Isaac.[9]

Abraham was 100 years old and Sarah 90 years old at Isaac's birth. The Bible affirms Isaac's good character and confirms that the Covenant birthright was passed from Abraham to Isaac:

---

[9] *Yitzchak* (Isaac) – means "he laughs"

² The LORD appeared to Isaac and said, "Do not go down to Egypt; live in the land where I tell you to live. ³ Stay in this land for a while, and I will be with you and will bless you. <u>For to you and your descendants I will give all these lands and will confirm the oath I swore to your father Abraham</u>. ⁴ I will make your descendants as numerous as the stars in the sky and will give them all these lands, and through your offspring all nations on earth will be blessed, ⁵ because Abraham obeyed me and kept my requirements, my commands, my decrees and my laws." Genesis 26:2–5 (NIV84)

After Isaac was born, Hagar and Ishmael were disinherited and sent away – but God protected them as He had promised Abraham. The Bible says of Ishmael and his descendants:

¹⁷ Altogether, Ishmael lived a hundred and thirty-seven years. He breathed his last and died, and he was gathered to his people. ¹⁸ His descendants settled in the area from Havilah to Shur, near the border of Egypt, as you go toward Asshur. <u>And they lived in hostility toward all their brothers.</u> Genesis 25:17–18 (NIV84)

God gave what is today called the Arabian Peninsula to Ishmael and his descendants. They intermarried with the descendants of Lot's sons (Ammon and Moab) and with descendants of Isaac's son Esau (who was dispossessed by his twin brother Jacob) and with the descendants of Abraham's children by Keturah, whom Abraham married after Sarah died. The most famous of Keturah's sons was Midian, whom the Israeli judge Gideon routed from oppressing Isaac's descendants.[14]

The Second Challenge to the Inheritance Bloodline

God tested Abraham some years later, when Isaac was still a young man – perhaps in his late adolescence or his early teen years. God appeared to Abraham and instructed him to travel to Mount Moriah and there to offer Isaac as a sacrifice to God. As Abraham always did, he obeyed, took Isaac and two servants and the wood for a burnt offering and traveled for three days to reach Mount Moriah.[15]

It is nowhere implied that Isaac offered any objection to Abraham's actions. Isaac carried the wood for the sacrifice leaving the two servants behind as he and his father traveled on for an additional three days. When they reached the spot God had told him about, Abraham built an altar, placed the wood upon it and then bound Isaac (without recorded objection from Isaac), placed him on the altar, drew his knife and started to kill his son.[16]

Why would Abraham agree to kill the son that God had clearly said would be his heir and the source of the innumerable progeny of the Covenant?

Sarah was well beyond the normal child bearing years when Isaac was born. They considered this miraculous but it was still a human function to have children and *could* have happened naturally. The writer of Hebrews explains why Abraham was willing to obey God without question and kill that son through whom the covenant was to be kept.

> [17] By faith Abraham, when he was tested, offered up Isaac, and he who had received the promises offered up his only begotten *son*, [18] of whom it was said, *"In Isaac your seed shall be called,"* [19] concluding that God *was* able to raise *him* up, even from the dead, from which he also received him in a figurative sense. Hebrews 11:17–19 (NKJV)

When it was apparent that Abraham's faith was so strong that he would obey God and kill his only son simply because God told Him to, God stopped Abraham at the last minute, declared Abraham had passed the test and then swore by Himself (there is no higher authority to swear by) to keep the Covenant promises:

> [15] Then the Angel of the LORD called to Abraham a second time out of heaven, [16] and said: "<u>By Myself I have sworn</u>, says the LORD, because you have done this thing, and have not withheld your son, your only *son*—[17] blessing I will bless you, and multiplying I will multiply your descendants as the stars of the heaven and as the sand which *is* on the seashore; and your descendants shall possess the gate of their enemies. [18] In your seed all the nations of the earth shall be blessed, because you have obeyed My voice." Genesis 22:15–18 (NKJV)

Perhaps the most important result of that test was that God then made the Covenant between God and Abraham, all the promises – spiritual and physical – *unconditional.* No promises or vows were extracted from Abraham – it was only God who made promises and He "swore by Himself". (See Fig 4)

In the future, it would not matter what Abraham's descendants did or how evil they might become, or where they might be located; *God had now obligated Himself to bestow those covenant blessings.*

Also, of great importance, there was a *new* promise made at this time: Abraham and Isaac's descendants would "possess the gates of their enemies."[17] (See Figure 4)

Isaac

Later, after Abraham and Isaac returned to their home, Sarah died at age 127 and was buried in Hebron in Canaan[10].

When Isaac was 40 years old, Abraham sent his chief servant – the head of his household, possibly Eleazar – back to Harran in Aramea where Abraham's original clan had settled with the charge to find a wife for Isaac.

Through miraculous means[11], God chose Rebekah (Abraham's brother Nahor's granddaughter[18]) to be Isaac's wife. Rebekah was in the mold of Sarah, a stunningly beautiful woman who – also like Sarah – was barren for many years of their marriage.

Abraham's relatives consented to send Rebekah to be Isaac's wife and the oral history records their blessing:

> 60 And they blessed Rebekah and said to her: "Our sister, may you become the mother of thousands of ten thousands; And may your descendants possess the gates of those who hate them." Genesis 24:60 (NKJV) [19]

After several years without children, Isaac prayed to God that Rebekah would conceive and she did conceive – twins. These twin boys "struggled" in her womb which troubled Rebekah so she asked God to explain. He did:

> 23 And the LORD said to her: "Two nations *are* in your womb, Two peoples shall be separated from your body; *One* people shall be stronger than the other, And the older shall serve the younger." Genesis 25:23 (NKJV)

At birth, the first born was covered with red hair so was named Esau (hairy); the other twin was born holding on to Esau's heel so they named him Jacob (heel-catcher).[20]

These two were at odds even before birth. Esau, as the firstborn, should have received the physical and spiritual birthright blessings of the Covenant God made with Abraham and passed to Isaac. But, the oral history records, Esau "despised his birthright" best illustrated by his selling that birthright to Jacob for a bowl of stew.[12]

---

[10] Abraham, Isaac, Jacob, Rachel, Leah and Joseph were all buried in the cave at Machpelah in Hebron

[11] Genesis 24:1–67

[12] Genesis 25:27–34

At 40 years old, Esau alienated Rebekah and grieved Isaac by marrying two Hittite women. Their families worshipped pagan gods and had other practices that were anathema to the patriarch and his family.

Isaac loved Esau but Rebekah loved Jacob and remembered the prophecy God had given her while she carried the twins in her womb.

As Isaac grew old his eyesight began to fail; he became essentially blind. He called Esau and asked him to hunt for some wild game that Isaac particularly loved as a celebratory meal. This was in preparation for giving Esau the official birthright blessing that would pass Abraham's Covenant to Esau.

Rebekah overheard and sent Jacob to acquire a young goat. She knew how to make a stew from that goat that would fool Isaac; in addition, she covered Jacob's hands and neck with the goatskins to simulate the hairy skin of Esau. She then sent Jacob and the stew in to Isaac so Jacob would receive the official birthright blessing.

Isaac was fooled. However, there is no condemnation of either Rebekah or Jacob in the oral history. Rather, the story is told as the natural outcome of God's prophecy given to Rebekah before the twins were born.

Isaac passed the Covenant birthright to Jacob:

> [28] Therefore may God give you Of the dew of heaven, Of the fatness of the earth, And plenty of grain and wine. [29] <u>Let peoples serve you, And nations bow down to you.</u>[21] Be master over your brethren, And let your mother's sons bow down to you. Cursed *be* everyone who curses you, And blessed *be* those who bless you!" Genesis 27:28–29 (NKJV)

Esau came back from the hunt to find he had been *supplanted* by Jacob. Isaac explained that Jacob had received the blessing from God and that he, Isaac, could not undo it. When Esau demanded a blessing, Isaac gave him a lesser one:

> [39] Then Isaac his father answered and said to him: "Behold, your dwelling shall be of the fatness of the earth, And of the dew of heaven from above. [40] By your sword you shall live, And you shall serve your brother; And it shall come to pass, when you become restless, That you shall break his yoke from your neck." Genesis 27:39–40 (NKJV)

This proved to be graphically prophetic of Esau's future.[22]

Jacob

Since Esau was threatening to kill Jacob for his duplicity, Rebekah and Isaac sent Jacob back to Harran to Rebekah's father Bethuel and her brother Laban. This was not only to distance him from Esau's threats but also to help him find a wife among his kin as did Isaac.

Before Jacob left, Isaac pronounced further blessings upon him:

> ³ May God Almighty bless you and make you fruitful and increase your numbers until you become a community of peoples. ⁴ May he give you and your descendants the blessing given to Abraham, so that you may take possession of the land where you now live as an alien, the land God gave to Abraham." Genesis 28:3–4 (NIV84)

As Jacob traveled to Harran, God gave him a vision as he slept – the famous "stairway to heaven" dream – in which God re-confirmed to him the blessings of Abraham:

> ¹³ There above it stood the LORD, and he said: "I am the LORD, the God of your father Abraham and the God of Isaac. I will give you and your descendants the land on which you are lying. ¹⁴ Your descendants will be like the dust of the earth, and you will spread out to the west and to the east, to the north and to the south. All peoples on earth will be blessed through you and your offspring. Genesis 28:13–14 (NIV84)

As Jacob approached Harran he saw Laban's daughter Rachel with whom he immediately fell in love. After being welcomed by his relatives and spending a month with them, Jacob agreed to work 7 years for the right to marry Rachel.

When the 7 years were up, Jacob was tricked by his future father-in-law, Laban, into marrying Leah, his oldest daughter, rather than Rachel. Laban sent her to Jacob's tent in the dark of night after the revelry of the marriage feast. Jacob, perhaps inebriated, did not know it was Leah until the sun rose the next day. By custom, that legitimized the marriage.

Laban allowed Jacob to marry Rachel also, but only after Jacob spent the first week with Leah "sealing" the marriage. He had to agree to work another 7 years for Rachel. He later agreed to work an additional 6 years to accumulate possessions, servants and flocks of animals that would form the dowry for the daughters. From Jacob's two wives and their servant girls came 12 sons. ²³

After leaving Laban, on the way back from Harran to Bethel in Canaan Jacob had an encounter with God in which Jacob wrestled all night with what appeared to be a man. Somehow, Jacob knew better and withstood the other person's efforts to subdue him. He refused to loosen his hold until the "man" told him His name and blessed him.

God then changed Jacob's name to Israel removing the stain of the name "the heel catcher – the supplanter". God gave him a name that is a combination of the Hebrew words *'el* (God) and *Sarah* (the masculine form means "prince") which means, "one who prevails with God" or "a prince before God".

God also reiterated His Covenant with Abraham and Isaac and expanded it slightly:

> [11] Also God said to him: "I *am* God Almighty. Be fruitful and multiply; a nation and a company of nations shall proceed from you, and kings shall come from your body. [12] The land which I gave Abraham and Isaac I give to you; and to your descendants after you I give this land." Genesis 35:11–12 (NKJV)

The expanded promise to Jacob projected: A nation and a company of nations would come out of Jacob. This promise of becoming "a nation and a company of nations" coupled with the previous promises of "possession of the gates of their enemies" and "nations will bow down to you again confirms the promise of political and economic hegemony on a large scale at some point in their future.[24]

Joseph

The story of Jacob's son Joseph is well known to readers of the Bible. Joseph was envied by his 11 brothers because Jacob loved him more than the others as the child of his true love Rachel. His jealous brothers saw an opportunity to rid themselves of him and sold Joseph into slavery with slave-traders headed to Egypt.

God kept watch over Joseph and he eventually found favor with Pharaoh because of God interpreting dreams for various Egyptian officials and eventually for Pharaoh. The dreams predicted a coming famine. Joseph's ideas on how to survive the famine made Joseph second in authority only to Pharaoh.

Canaan again experienced famine and Jacob's time in Canaan ended. He then moved with his 11 sons and their wives and children --the whole clan, 70 persons[13] in all – to Egypt where Joseph's position in the government allowed them to settle the Egyptian land of Goshen.

That territory was considered to have little value to the Egyptians who were cosmopolitan for their day and disdained shepherds.[25] However, it was the perfect

---

[13] Genesis 46:26–27

location for the children of Israel to grow and become a nation. It was protected by the might of the Egyptian army and for many years by Joseph, the second most powerful person in Egypt.

Jacob lived his last years in peace and comfort[14] and his family prospered.

When Jacob knew he was dying he passed the blessings and prophecies of Abraham's and Isaac's Covenant to the next generation as God led him.

Jacob's firstborn, Reuben – the customary prime inheritor – and the second and third-born sons Simeon and Levi, had disqualified themselves[26]. The fourth in line was Judah. Jacob passed the right of royalty – the actual line from which kings would come and from which Jesus eventually came – to Judah.

However, Jacob gave the physical birthright – all the promises of land, wealth, and political power to his first-born from Rachel, his son Joseph. He did so by passing that birthright to Joseph's sons (from Joseph's Egyptian wife) Ephraim and Manasseh.

Therein lies a most critical shift in the status of Abraham, Isaac and Jacob's *unconditional* Covenant with God. *Before this time, both physical and spiritual birthrights were held by one person; Judah now held the spiritual birthright and Ephraim/Manasseh held the physical birthright.* (See Fig 4)

Ephraim, Manasseh and Judah

The Bible does not tell us exactly why the *physical* birthright went to Joseph, who was the firstborn of the wife Jacob loved – Rachel. Perhaps it was Jacob's right to make that choice; perhaps it was because of Joseph's exalted position as a result of his rise in the Egyptian government and his saving of his whole family from famine; but it is somewhat logical if romantic to think it was because of Jacob's great love for Rachel. But above all else, it was obviously the will of God.

Furthermore, Jacob chose to "adopt" Joseph's two sons, Ephraim and Manasseh, and passed the physical birthright to them while elevating their legal status from grandsons to sons for inheritance purposes and *gave them his name – Israel*. The Bible recounts the story:

> Sometime later Joseph was told, "Your father is ill." So he took his two sons Manasseh and Ephraim along with him. When Jacob was told, "Your

---

[14] Genesis 46:31–47:12

son Joseph has come to you," Israel rallied his strength and sat up on the bed.

Jacob said to Joseph, "God Almighty appeared to me at Luz in the land of Canaan, and there he blessed me and said to me, `I am going to make you fruitful and will increase your numbers. I will make you a community of peoples ["company of nations"], and I will give this land as an everlasting possession to your descendants after you.'

"Now then, your two sons born to you in Egypt before I came to you here will be reckoned as mine; Ephraim and Manasseh will be mine, just as Reuben and Simeon are mine. Any children born to you after them will be yours; in the territory they inherit they will be reckoned under the names of their brothers.

As I was returning from Paddan, to my sorrow Rachel died in the land of Canaan while we were still on the way, a little distance from Ephrath. So I buried her there beside the road to Ephrath" (that is, Bethlehem).

When Israel saw the sons of Joseph, he asked, "Who are these?"

"They are the sons God has given me here," Joseph said to his father.

Then Israel said, "Bring them to me so I may bless them." Now Israel's eyes were failing because of old age, and he could hardly see. So Joseph brought his sons close to him, and his father kissed them and embraced them.

Israel said to Joseph, "I never expected to see your face again, and now God has allowed me to see your children too."

Then Joseph removed them from Israel's knees and bowed down with his face to the ground. And Joseph took both of them, Ephraim on his right toward Israel's left hand and Manasseh on his left toward Israel's right hand and brought them close to him. But Israel reached out his right hand and put it on Ephraim's head, though he was the younger, and crossing his arms, he put his left hand on Manasseh's head, even though Manasseh was the firstborn.

Then he blessed Joseph and said, "May the God before whom my fathers Abraham and Isaac walked, the God who has been my shepherd all my life to this day, the Angel who has delivered me from all harm --may he bless these boys. May they be called by my name and the names of my fathers Abraham and Isaac, and may they increase greatly upon the earth."

When Joseph saw his father placing his right hand on Ephraim's head he was displeased; so he took hold of his father's hand to move it from Ephraim's head to Manasseh's head. Joseph said to him, "No, my father, this one is the firstborn; put your right hand on his head."

But his father refused and said, "I know, my son, I know. He too will become a people, and he too will become great. Nevertheless, his younger brother will be greater than he, and his descendants will become a group of nations ["company of nations" - KJV]."

He blessed them that day and said, "In your name will Israel pronounce this blessing: `May God make you like Ephraim and Manasseh.'" So, he put Ephraim ahead of Manasseh. NIV Genesis 48:1-20

After the physical birthright had been passed to Ephraim and Manasseh, Jacob extended his final blessings (actually God's unconditional blessings) upon all 12 of his sons. He then explained that Reuben (the firstborn of Leah) had disqualified himself by incest with one of Jacob's servant wives and likewise Simeon and Levi (also Leah's sons) had been disqualified as excessively violent people.

The first three could not receive the *spiritual* blessing of royalty and leadership he was to bestow upon the eldest qualified son. That blessing fell therefore to the fourth son – Judah. Jacob made this "birthright" vow to Judah:

> 8 "Judah, your brothers will praise you. You will grab your enemies by the neck, and your brothers will bow down to you. 9 Judah is like a young lion. You have returned from killing, my son. Like a lion, he stretches out and lies down to rest, and no one is brave enough to wake him. 10 Kings will come from Judah's family; someone from Judah will always be on the throne. Judah will rule until Shiloh comes, and the nations will obey him. Genesis 49:8–10 (NCV)

In this way the *spiritual* blessing of God's Covenant promises first made to Abraham was bequeathed to Judah:

> The scepter shall not depart from Judah, Nor a lawgiver from between his feet, Until Shiloh comes; And to Him shall be the obedience of the people. Genesis 49:10 [NKJV]

"Shiloh" in this context can be translated as "Prince of Peace" [Isaiah 9:6] and is almost universally agreed by Bible scholars to be a reference to Jesus[27], who was a physical descendent of Judah.[15]

Another scripture verifies the two Covenant promises – spiritual and physical – were given by God to two different descendants of Abraham, Isaac and Jacob. The physical and spiritual birthrights were divided on those lines for the rest of the existence of Israel:

> Now the sons of Reuben the firstborn of Israel, (for he was the firstborn; but forasmuch as he defiled his father's bed, his birthright was given unto

---

[15] Matthew 1:1–16

the sons of Joseph the son of Israel: and the genealogy is not to be reckoned after the birthright. For Judah prevailed above his brethren, and of him came the chief ruler; but the birthright was Joseph's: KJV 1 Chronicles 5:1-2

Figure 4
Covenant Promises Continued

21. God made the Covenant *unconditional*
22. Descendants will possess gates of enemies; be a company of nations; people will serve and nation's bow down
23. Ephraim and Manasseh bore the name of Israel
24. Manasseh would become a great nation
25. Ephraim would be greater still and become a company of nations
26. Judah was promised the scepter until Shiloh (Jesus) comes

The Great Mystery of Israel's Disappearance

How can it be explained that over a thousand years after the time of Jacob and Joseph – in about 721 BC – the physical birthright holders (descendants of Ephraim and Manasseh), the Kingdom of Israel and all the tribes other than Judah, Benjamin and Levi (the Kingdom of Judah) disappear from the pages of the Bible without receiving most of those physical birthright promises? They leave almost no trace in secular history.

This has troubled Bible scholars for many years. Some of the "founding fathers" of the USA refused to accept much of the Bible because of this fact.

The path of the spiritual birthright promises of royalty and blessings can be traced with the preservation of Judah (the Jews) and the birth of Jesus. The teaching of Jesus and His followers has truly bestowed great blessings *upon all who have believed in Him*, but does that truly fulfill the promise: "Through your descendants *all the nations of the world* would be blessed"?

Throughout history have there not been millions – even billions – of people who have known little or nothing about Jesus and His teaching. What blessing have the promises of the spiritual side of the Covenant brought to those people?

Jesus never sat on a throne on this earth and never ruled over Israel or any other nation. Yet that throne was said to be His forever.

> [10] The scepter shall not depart from Judah, Nor a lawgiver from between his feet, Until Shiloh comes; And to Him *shall be* the obedience of the people. Genesis 49:10 (NKJV)

God preserved Judah (the Jews) as a nation till 70 AD. when Judah ceased to exist as a nation. Yet the Jews are still with us and know who they are and to some extent the Kingdom of Judah has been back in existence since 1948 AD.

Did God stop guiding the fate of *all the rest of the Israelites* who disappeared in 721 BC – the ones holding the physical birthright? He promised that they would be "sifted among all nations" but that He would not destroy them completely nor would He forget them:

> 8 "Behold, the eyes of the Lord GOD *are* on the sinful kingdom, And I will destroy it from the face of the earth; Yet I will not utterly destroy the house of Jacob," Says the LORD. 9 "For surely I will command, And will sift the house of Israel among all nations, As *grain* is sifted in a sieve; <u>Yet not the smallest grain shall fall to the ground</u>. Amos 9:8–9 (NKJV)

Did God fail to keep His Covenant promises? Impossible!

So, what happened to the rest of God's *unconditional* Covenant promises? This book addresses that question through the perspective of the history of the past 2000 years and the tracing of blessings that have befallen those affected by the grain sifted among the nations.

Because of Israel's sinful nature after being freed from slavery, at Mt. Sinai God made another *conditional* covenant with the children of Israel to insure the continued existence of the nation of Israel *until the spiritual blessings were completed*. The penalty for failure to keep that covenant was a lengthy punishment that would *delay* the fulfillment of many of the physical birthright promises from the Covenant made with Abraham after the faith he had shown with the willingness to sacrifice Isaac. *Delay – not destroy or negate.*

One should note that this Covenant that we are tracing, the sum of all the promises made to Abraham, was both *physical and spiritual*: the spiritual parts are the *spiritual* blessings God bestowed upon Abraham and his descendants and through them the whole world – this was fulfilled with the advent of God born in the person of Jesus. The physical parts of the Covenant are the innumerable descendants, the territory given and the political power implied – "possess the gate of their enemies".

This Covenant was reaffirmed with Isaac and with Jacob and with Joseph's two sons, Ephraim and Manasseh. Abraham, Isaac and Jacob made no promises to God concerning this Covenant – promises were not necessary since God had made the Covenant *unconditional*. No matter whether those descendants were good or bad people; no matter if they violated God's laws; no matter where they were on this earth, those promises would be kept by God. See **Table 1** for complete list of God's promises to Israel.

It is important to understand that this demonstrates how closely God guided the bloodlines to reach the intended end *on the spiritual side*: Abraham being loyal for decades to Sarah who could not bear him children and an heir; Isaac chosen by God as Abraham's heir keeping that bloodline passing from Sarah as God wanted it; Jacob chosen by God over his firstborn twin brother; Joseph and Judah chosen to preserve the bloodlines of the Covenant through Rachel and Leah. Later the bloodline continues through Rahab (the Canaanite harlot and mother of Boaz), through Boaz and Ruth (a Moabitess and grandmother of King David) – through a total of 42 generations[16] preserved and guided by God to produce the perfect human mother (Mary) for Jesus of Nazareth, the Son of God.

There were many promises made under an *unconditional* Covenant with and guaranteed by the Creator of this universe. Only a few of those have been kept. See Table 1.

In later chapters we'll attempt to solve the great mystery of Israel's disappearance.

Table 1. Covenant Promises and Bible Verse Sources

Covenant Promises	Sources
1. God would make Abraham's name great	Gen 12:2
2.Abraham's descendants to become a great nation	Gen 12:2
3. God would bless Abraham	Gen 12:3; 13–15
4. God would protect Abraham	Gen 12:3; 28:13–15
5. All nations of the world blessed through Abraham	Gen 12:3; 22:15–18; 28:13–15
6. Abraham's descendants to have the land of Canaan	Gen 12:7; 13:14–15; 17:8; 28:3–4; 13–15; 35:11–12; 48:3–4; 50:24–25; Ex 3:6–8; 16,17
7. Abraham would have	Gen 13:16; 15:5;

---

[16] Matthew 1:17

innumerable descendants	22:15−18
8. Abraham's descendants spend 400 years in slavery	Gen 15:13
9. God to punish the nation that held them in slavery	Gen 15:14; Ex 3:18−22
10. Abraham's descendants to bring great wealth from slavery	Gen 15:14; 50:24−25; Ex 3:6−8; 16,17, 18−22
11. Abraham would die at "a good old age"	Gen 15:15
12. In the fourth generation Abraham's Covenant children would return to Canaan	Gen 15:16; Ex 3:6−8, 16,17
13 Abraham's descendants to possess all land from the Euphrates River to the "river of Egypt"	Gen 15:18
14. Abraham would be the father of many nations	Gen 17:5−6
15. Kings would come out of his descendants	Gen 17:5−6
16. God would be Abraham's and his descendants God	Gen 17:7,8
17. Nations and kings would come from Sarah	Gen 17:16
18. God would give Abraham a son by Sarah	Gen 17:19; 18:10
19. God named their son Isaac and confirmed he would be the Covenant son	Gen 17:19, 21; 18:14
20. God promised to bless Ishmael, making him into a great nation	Gen 17:20; 21:12, 13; 25:12−18
21. God made the Covenant unconditional	Gen 22:15−18
22. Their descendants to "possess the gates of their enemies"; become a	Gen 22:15−18; 24:60; 27:27−29; 35:11−12; 48:3−4

"company of nations;" and nations to bow down to them	
23 Ephraim and Manasseh would bear the name of Israel	Gen 48:5,6, 15,16
24 Manasseh would become a great nation	Gen 48:17–20; 49:22–26
25 Ephraim would be greater still and become a company of nations	Gen 48:17–20; 49:22–26
26. Judah was promised the scepter until Shiloh (Jesus) comes	Gen 49:8–10

* * *

CHAPTER 2

The Twelve Tribes of Israel

When Jacob moved to Egypt with his 11 sons and their wives and children and reunited with Joseph the "children of Israel" totaled only 70 people including Joseph's two sons Ephraim and Manasseh. So long as Joseph lived, there were no problems between the Israelites and the Egyptians.

The Israelites fecundity[17] is displayed throughout the Bible. Pharaoh noted the increasing population and began to fear insurrection. He enslaved them, placed harsh taskmasters over them and used their labor to work on farms and to build at least two large cities.[18] The Bible says they were worked "ruthlessly".

One reason God allowed Abraham's descendants to experience slavery for so long is that it was a safe place to grow in numbers and become a true nation. As slaves in Egypt – the most powerful nation in the area with the largest standing army – the Israelites were oppressed but they were relatively safe and able to breed freely and to accumulate some wealth.

Nevertheless, as the 400 years of slavery were drawing to a close, it was time for God to speak again, to fulfill His promises and to now deal with and rescue the children of Israel who had been born into slavery.

In Chapter 1 we saw that God placed no conditions on the Covenant promises other than telling Abraham to leave Harran and travel to Canaan. He never predicated His promises on the behavior of Abraham, Isaac or Jacob. Then, when Abraham was willing to kill his Covenant son because his faith was so profound, God *swore by Himself (as the highest authority) to fulfill the Covenant promises.* God would uphold those Covenant promises *unconditionally* – the physical and spiritual promises – regardless of Israel's behavior.

In this chapter, shortly after the Israelites – one million+ strong – come out of Egypt, God introduces an additional Covenant – this one is *conditional.*

---

[17] The ability to produce an abundance of offspring or new growth; fertility.
[18] Exodus 1:8–14

God broke His 430 years of silence by calling His next chosen leader – Moses.

Moses

After Joseph died, the Egyptians became increasingly worried because of the fecundity[28] of the Israelites. In their Egyptian province of Goshen in the safety of Joseph's protection they produced children and filled that land with more and more children of Israel. Even when the new Pharaoh placed slave masters over them, their numbers increased rapidly.

> [8] Then a new king, who did not know about Joseph, came to power in Egypt. [9] "Look," he said to his people, "the Israelites have become much too numerous for us. [10] Come, we must deal shrewdly with them or they will become even more numerous and, if war breaks out, will join our enemies, fight against us and leave the country." Exodus 1:8–10 (NIV84)

Pharaoh tried bribing the Hebrew midwives to kill the male children at their birth but they fooled Pharaoh claiming the Israelite women were so "vigorous" they gave birth before the midwives arrived. Pharaoh then ordered that all Israelite male children were to be thrown into the Nile, i.e., drowned.

One enterprising woman from the tribe of Levi gave birth to a son, kept him hidden for three months and then placed him in a little boat made of reeds where it would float past Pharaoh's daughter while she was bathing in the Nile. The Levite woman's daughter was one of the princess's slaves.

The princess adopted the boy, named him Moses[19]. Moses' sister, following her mother's instructions, asked the princess if she needed an Israelite woman to take care of the baby. Thus, Moses' mother was paid by the princess to nurse and care for the baby. As he matured, the Princess ensured that Moses had the best education possible in Egypt. Egypt was highly advanced in the science and the arts at that time.

His genetic mother undoubtedly told Moses of his origin and of the oppression of their people. He came to know his people and one day killed an Egyptian overseer who was beating one of his kin. To escape the wrath of Pharaoh, Moses fled to Midian on the Sinai Peninsula.

While resting near a well after his flight, Moses rescued the daughters of a local priest from an attack by some shepherds who claimed the well. The daughters, who

---

[19] "Moses" means "drawn out of the water" *Holman Illustrated Bible Dictionary*

thought Moses to be an Egyptian, informed their father of the rescue. Moses was invited to stay with Reuel (whose official title was Jethro), a priest in that land, and married one of the daughters.

> 21 And Moses was content to dwell with the man: and he gave Moses Zipporah his daughter. 22 And she bare *him* a son, and he called his name Gershom: for he said, I have been a stranger in a strange land. 23 And it came to pass in process of time, that the king of Egypt died: and the children of Israel sighed by reason of the bondage, and they cried, and their cry came up unto God by reason of the bondage. 24 And God heard their groaning, and God remembered his covenant with Abraham, with Isaac, and with Jacob. 25 And God looked upon the children of Israel, and God had respect unto *them*. Exodus 2:21–25 (KJV 1900)

The Fiery Bush

Moses earned his keep by tending Jethro's flocks. One day Moses led the flock to a place near a mountain called Horeb[29]. There Moses saw a bush on fire with a fire that seemed to have no effect on the bush.

As Moses approached the bush, God spoke to him:

> 5 "Do not come any closer," God said. "Take off your sandals, for the place where you are standing is holy ground." 6 Then he said, "I am the God of your father, the God of Abraham, the God of Isaac and the God of Jacob." At this, Moses hid his face, because he was afraid to look at God. Exodus 3:5–6 (NIV84)

God explained that He was hearing the cries of the Israelites in captivity and told Moses he was to return to Egypt to free them from captivity. When Moses asked a name to tell the Israelites who had sent him, God gave his *Eternal Name.*[30]

> 14 God said to Moses, "I AM WHO I AM. This is what you are to say to the Israelites: 'I AM has sent me to you.' " 15 God also said to Moses, "Say to the Israelites, 'The LORD, the God of your fathers—the God of Abraham, the God of Isaac and the God of Jacob—has sent me to you.' This is my name forever, the name by which I am to be remembered from generation to generation. Exodus 3:14–15 (NIV84)

Moses worried that the Israelites would not believe him. God told Moses to throw his staff to the ground – it became a snake; he picked it up and it was a staff again. God had Moses put his hand inside his cloak – when he took it out again it was leprous; he put his hand in the cloak, took it out again and it was normal. God promised if those two "tricks" didn't convince them, Moses could pour water from the Nile on the ground and it would become blood. Moses angered God by further evasion; he begged God to send someone else.

[10] Moses said to the LORD, "O Lord, I have never been eloquent, neither in the past nor since you have spoken to your servant. I am slow of speech and tongue." Exodus 4:10 (NIV84)

Though God was displeased, He relented:

[14] Then the LORD's anger burned against Moses and he said, "What about your brother, Aaron the Levite? I know he can speak well. He is already on his way to meet you, and his heart will be glad when he sees you. Exodus 4:14 (NIV84)

So, Moses returned to Egypt accompanied by his brother Aaron and confronted Pharaoh who promptly doubled and tripled the work required of the Israelites. The Israelites correctly placed the blame on Moses and Aaron and bitterly accused them of making their slavery worse. Moses inquired of God and was answered with God giving His name[31]:

[2] And God spoke to Moses, and he said to him, "I am Yahweh. [3] And I appeared to Abraham, to Isaac, and to Jacob as God Shaddai, but by my name Yahweh I was not known to them. [4] And I not only established my covenant with them to give to them the land of Canaan, the land of their sojourning, in which they dwelt as aliens, [5] but also, I myself heard the groaning of the Israelites, whom the Egyptians are making to work, and I remembered my covenant. Exodus 6:1–5 (LEB)

The Plagues

As Pharaoh continued to be stubborn, God brought a series of 10 plagues upon Egypt, each more severe than the last.

Each of the first 6 plagues (See Figure 1) was lifted to show Pharaoh that Moses – by God's hand – controlled the plagues. It was only with the plague of hail that Pharaoh first promised to allow the Israelites to leave. He changed his mind when the hail stopped.

Figure 1
The Plagues of Egypt

1. The Plague of Blood
2. The Plague of Frogs

3. The Plague of Gnats
4. The Plague of Flies
5. The Plague on Livestock
6. The Plague of Boils
7. The Plague of Hail
8. The Plague of Locusts
9. The Plague of Darkness
10. The Plague on the Firstborn

The same scenario played out with the locusts and darkness. With each of these 9 plagues, the economy of Egypt was further devastated – which didn't bother Pharaoh personally but which killed a portion of the population and destroyed flocks, crops and even the trees in the land. At this point God "used" Pharaoh to demonstrate that the Israelites were His people.[32]

Finally, Pharaoh (and God) had enough:

> [27] But the LORD hardened Pharaoh's heart, and he was not willing to let them go. [28] Pharaoh said to Moses, "Get out of my sight! Make sure you do not appear before me again! The day you see my face you will die."
> [29] "Just as you say," Moses replied, "I will never appear before you again." Exodus 10:27–29 (NIV84)

The Passover

The scenario of the 10th plague formed the basis for one of the most holy celebrations of the Israelites down to the time of Jesus and even still today – *the Passover.*

God had Moses tell the Israelites to mark the doorposts and lintels of their dwellings with the blood of the lamb that was part of the Passover ritual that included bread without leaven. Unleavened bread could be stored and carried with them when they left hastily.

That night:

> [29] At midnight the LORD struck down all the firstborn in Egypt, from the firstborn of Pharaoh, who sat on the throne, to the firstborn of the prisoner, who was in the dungeon, and the firstborn of all the livestock as well. [30] Pharaoh and all his officials and all the Egyptians got up during the night, and there was loud wailing in Egypt, for there was not a house without someone dead. Exodus 12:29–30 (NIV84)

The Exodus

That same night, Pharaoh summoned Moses and Aaron shortly after the death of his son and told them to go. They did but they followed Moses instructions as they were leaving:

> 35 The Israelites did as Moses instructed and asked the Egyptians for articles of silver and gold and for clothing. 36 The LORD had made the Egyptians favorably disposed toward the people, and they gave them what they asked for; so they plundered the Egyptians. Exodus 12:35–36 (NIV84)

They came into Egypt as 70 people with few possessions and left 430 years later – in 1445 BC[33] – well over a million souls loaded with wealth from Egypt.

Instead of heading directly east-northeast for Canaan by crossing an area controlled by the Philistines – where they might have been attacked and forced to return to Egypt[20] – God led them southeast to an area along the western edge of the Gulf of Suez. As they crossed the desert[21] God appeared to lead them in a "pillar of cloud" by day and a "pillar of fire" by night. Thus, they could travel without stopping until they camped on the shores of the Gulf at its narrowest point.[34]

Upon getting the report that the Israelites had left the country, Pharaoh and his officials realized that most of their work force had just walked away while at the same time many of their Egyptian servants had been killed in the plagues.

Pharaoh decided to recapture the Israelites.[22]

Crossing the Red Sea

Pharaoh in his personal chariot led the army of his best fighting men along with most of the chariots of Egypt filled with his best officers as they set out to capture the Israelites. When they neared the Israelites camp, the people railed against Moses:

> 11 Then they said to Moses, "Because *there were* no graves in Egypt, have you taken us away to die in the wilderness? Why have you so dealt with us, to bring us up out of Egypt? 12 *Is* this not the word that we told you in Egypt, saying, 'Let us alone that we may serve the Egyptians'? For *it would have*

---

[20] Exodus 13:17–18
[21] A desert has few obstacles to hinder even 1 million people on foot with their animals
[22] Exodus 4:5

been better for us to serve the Egyptians than that we should die in the wilderness." Exodus 14:11–12 (NKJV)

God intervened once again to save Israel and by so doing brought His final judgment of Egypt.

Before the Egyptians could attack God moved the "pillar of cloud" toward the Egyptians and the "pillar of fire" to Israel's side. Through the night, the dark cloud blinded the Egyptians and the fire gave the Israelites light to begin crossing the sea. God's power piled the waters on either side of the path leaving dry ground for the Israelites to cross.

As the sun began to rise that morning, the last of the Israelites reached the other shore and came up out of the sea bed. The Egyptians saw a dry pathway to pursue the Israelites. As the Egyptians set out across the dry path God slowed the Egyptians – the wheels of their chariots jammed mid-way across the bottom of the sea and they panicked:

> [25] He jammed the wheels of their chariots so that they had difficulty driving. And the Egyptians said, "Let's get away from the Israelites! The LORD is fighting for them against Egypt." Exodus 14:25 (NIV)

God told Moses to hold his staff over the sea and as he did the waters closed over the Egyptians – and the military power of the Egyptians was decimated. As the Israelites began moving on, they could see the bodies of the Egyptians floating in the waters or washed up on the shore.

This was the final judgment of Pharaoh and Egypt.[35]

Grumbling and Manna

For the next three days, the Israelites traveled through the desert of Shur without finding water and they began grumbling against Moses. They finally found water at Marah but it was too bitter until God showed Moses some wood to toss in that made it drinkable. They camped at the Oasis of Elim for a few days and set out again. [See Map 1 for probable locations.]

On the 15th day of the 2nd month after leaving Egypt they entered the Wilderness of Sin. The people again complained to Moses and Aaron:

> [3] And the children of Israel said to them, "Oh, that we had died by the hand of the LORD in the land of Egypt, when we sat by the pots of meat *and*

when we ate bread to the full! For you have brought us out into this wilderness to kill this whole assembly with hunger." Exodus 16:3 (NKJV)

To feed them, God caused "manna" to appear in the morning when the dew evaporated.

> [31] The people of Israel called the bread manna. It was white like coriander seed and tasted like wafers made with honey. Exodus 16:31 (NIV84)

God told the people that the manna would appear for 6 days but it only lasted during daylight. Any kept overnight rotted and smelled. However, on the 6th day they were to gather enough to eat the next day – a day of rest or Sabbath[36] – since the manna would keep on the Sabbath and be good throughout that day.

The Israelites continued complaining to Moses and Aaron over every discomfort. Even after Moses struck a rock in the middle of the desert which poured out enough water for all to drink, they groused. Even after the Israelites miraculously defeated the powerful army of the Amalekites, they whined and moaned.

This continued until Moses' father-in-law Jethro[37] suggested a new method of dealing with the people. He persuaded Moses to appoint tribal and clan leaders – officials over thousands, hundreds, fifties and tens – to act as judges for the people on all the minor complaints and problems. They still brought the more difficult problems to Moses but this process relieved some of the pressure on Moses and Aaron while at the same time pacifying at least some of the people.

Mt. Sinai and the Ten Commandments

At the end of the third month after the Israelites left Egypt, they came to the desert of Sinai and camped at the base of Mount Horeb – the area where Moses had seen the "burning bush".

God told Moses to remind the children of Israel of His Covenant with their ancestors. After hearing that Covenant restated, the Israelites replied with a promise they would keep the Covenant God had made with their ancestors – Abraham, Isaac and Jacob:

> [3] Then Moses went up to God, and the LORD called to him from the mountain and said, "This is what you are to say to the house of Jacob and what you are to tell the people of Israel: [4] 'You yourselves have seen what I did to Egypt, and how I carried you on eagles' wings and brought you to

myself. ⁵ <u>Now if you obey me fully and keep my covenant</u>, then out of all nations you will be my treasured possession. Although the whole earth is mine, ⁶ you will be for me a kingdom of priests and a holy nation.' These are the words you are to speak to the Israelites."

⁷ So Moses went back and summoned the elders of the people and set before them all the words the LORD had commanded him to speak. ⁸ <u>The people all responded together, "We will do everything the LORD has said."</u> So Moses brought their answer back to the LORD. Exodus 19:3–8 (NIV84)

On the third day, God spoke directly to the children of Israel giving them the 10 Commandments.

Figure 2
The Ten Commandments

¹ And God spoke all these words, saying: ² "I *am* the LORD your God, who brought you out of the land of Egypt, out of the house of bondage.

(1) ³ "You shall have no other gods before Me.

(2) ⁴ "You shall not make for yourself a carved image—any likeness *of anything* that *is* in heaven above, or that *is* in the earth beneath, or that *is* in the water under the earth; ⁵ you shall not bow down to them nor serve them. For I, the LORD your God, *am* a jealous God, visiting the iniquity of the fathers upon the children to the third and fourth *generations* of those who hate Me, ⁶ but showing mercy to thousands, to those who love Me and keep My commandments.

(3) ⁷ "You shall not take the name of the LORD your God in vain, for the LORD will not hold *him* guiltless who takes His name in vain.

(4) ⁸ "Remember the Sabbath day, to keep it holy. ⁹ Six days you shall labor and do all your work, ¹⁰ but the seventh day *is* the Sabbath of the LORD your God. *In it* you shall do no work: you, nor your son, nor your daughter, nor your male servant, nor your female servant, nor your cattle, nor your stranger who *is* within your gates. ¹¹ For *in* six days the LORD made the heavens and the earth, the sea, and all that *is* in them, and rested the seventh day. Therefore the LORD blessed the Sabbath day and hallowed it.

(5) ¹² "Honor your father and your mother, that your days may be long upon the land which the LORD your God is giving you.

(6) ¹³ "You shall not murder.

(7) ¹⁴ "You shall not commit adultery.

(8) ¹⁵ "You shall not steal.

(9) ¹⁶ "You shall not bear false witness against your neighbor.

(10) ¹⁷ "You shall not covet your neighbor's house; you shall not covet your neighbor's wife, nor his male servant, nor his female servant, nor his ox, nor his donkey, nor anything that *is* your neighbor's." Exodus 20:1–17 (NKJV)

In reiterating the Commandments in Deuteronomy Moses wrote that when God finished with the 10ᵗʰ Commandment, *He added nothing more and wrote those Commandments in stone.*

²² These are the commandments the LORD proclaimed in a loud voice to your whole assembly there on the mountain from out of the fire, the cloud and the deep darkness; and he added nothing more. Then he wrote them on two stone tablets and gave them to me. Deuteronomy 5:22 (NIV84)

Thus, the laws that were obeyed by Abraham²³, Isaac and Jacob as part of the Covenant were codified and written in stone for the Israelites. The stone tablets were kept in the Ark of the Covenant that was designed specifically to hold the tablets.

The people were so frightened by the earthquakes, the thunder and lightning and even more by the very voice of God, they begged Moses to intercede – "Let God to speak to Moses and let Moses tell us what God has said."²⁴

With God speaking only through Moses, He gave them the civic, domestic and religious laws for their nation. He promised to protect them and lead them to the land promised to Abraham, Isaac and Jacob. The children of Israel vowed to obey those laws and sealed that Covenant with blood.

The "law of Moses" (the law given by God *through* Moses) was treated differently from the 10 Commandments – placed in the "side of the Ark" rather than within the Ark – as verified by Moses and the writer of Hebrews³⁸.

Moses, Joshua and 70 elders (tribal leaders etc.) went up Mt. Sinai to meet with God but only Moses was allowed to come close to His presence. They stayed on the mountain for forty days and nights and received specific instructions concerning the Aaronic priesthood, the Ark of the Covenant, the tabernacle and other accoutrements of the formal worship service decreed by God. At the end of their visit God gave Moses the stone tablets with the Ten Commandments inscribed by God's own finger.

The Golden Calf

When Moses returned to the Israelites' camp he found that his brother Aaron – the just-named high priest of Israel – had been coerced into re-creating one of the gods of Egypt – Apis (the bull) – as a golden calf and many of the Israelites were dancing and having an orgy before the idol as part of their worship of Apis proclaiming Apis was "the god who brought them out of Egypt".²⁵

---

²³ Genesis 26:5
²⁴ Exodus 20:18–19
²⁵ Exodus 32:1–4

God became so angry that the Israelites would immediately abandon their blood-sealed promises that He told Moses He would destroy them and make Moses into a great nation.

Moses's discussion with God reveals something startling. God's mind can be changed by human argument. The argument Moses made was his reminding God of His unconditional Covenant and that destroying Israel would fuel lies about God.

> [11] But Moses sought the favor of the LORD his God. "O LORD," he said, "why should your anger burn against your people, whom you brought out of Egypt with great power and a mighty hand? [12] Why should the Egyptians say, 'It was with evil intent that he brought them out, to kill them in the mountains and to wipe them off the face of the earth'? Turn from your fierce anger; relent and do not bring disaster on your people. [13] Remember your servants Abraham, Isaac and Israel, to whom you swore by your own self: 'I will make your descendants as numerous as the stars in the sky and I will give your descendants all this land I promised them, and it will be their inheritance forever.'" [14] Then the LORD relented and did not bring on his people the disaster he had threatened. Exodus 32:11–14 (NIV84)

Moses becomes a Prophet

When the children of Israel asked Moses to be their liaison with God for their fear of Him, Moses told them what God said:

> [17] **The LORD said to me: "What they say is good. [18] I will raise up for them a prophet like you from among their brothers; I will put my words in his mouth, and he will tell them everything I command him. [19] If anyone does not listen to my words that the prophet speaks in my name, I myself will call him to account. Deuteronomy 18:17–19 (NIV84)**

Bible scholars suggest God was speaking of Jesus but it is likely that it also applies to any age where God would raise up a prophet from among the children of Israel to carry His message to the people.

Moses had a unique relationship with God:

> [4] At once the LORD said to Moses, Aaron and Miriam, "Come out to the Tent of Meeting, all three of you." So the three of them came out. [5] Then the LORD came down in a pillar of cloud; he stood at the entrance to the Tent and summoned Aaron and Miriam. When both of them stepped forward, [6] he said, "Listen to my words: "When a prophet of the LORD is among you, I

reveal myself to him in visions, I speak to him in dreams. 7 But this is not true of my servant Moses; he is faithful in all my house. 8 With him I speak face to face, clearly and not in riddles; he sees the form of the LORD. Why then were you not afraid to speak against my servant Moses?" Numbers 12:4–8 (NIV84)

Moses wrote the stories that had been handed down orally: the story of creation, the fall of man, the great flood, the tower of Babel, the Patriarchs and God's Covenant with mankind. Moses wrote (or perhaps dictated) the Pentateuch – the Torah.

As his time to die drew near Moses spoke to the Israelites:

32 Ask now about the former days, long before your time, from the day God created man on the earth; ask from one end of the heavens to the other. Has anything so great as this ever happened, or has anything like it ever been heard of? 33 Has any other people heard the voice of God speaking out of fire, as you have, and lived? 34 Has any god ever tried to take for himself one nation out of another nation, by testings, by miraculous signs and wonders, by war, by a mighty hand and an outstretched arm, or by great and awesome deeds, like all the things the LORD your God did for you in Egypt before your very eyes? Deuteronomy 4:32–34 (NIV84)

Moses' final warning to the Israelites is chilling because apparently, he foresaw the cycle of the Israelites' breaking their Covenant with God, enduring punishment, repenting and then repeating the sins over and again. Moses way that when that cycle reached a certain point, God would allow their nation to be nearly destroyed with the remnant to be scattered among the nations.

But Moses also saw that in that future God would not forget His Covenant with Abraham:

25 After you have had children and grandchildren and have lived in the land a long time—if you then become corrupt and make any kind of idol, doing evil in the eyes of the LORD your God and provoking him to anger, 26 I call heaven and earth as witnesses against you this day that you will quickly perish from the land that you are crossing the Jordan to possess. You will not live there long but will certainly be destroyed.

27 The LORD will scatter you among the peoples, and only a few of you will survive among the nations to which the LORD will drive you. 28 There you will worship man-made gods of wood and stone, which cannot see or hear or eat or smell.

29 But if from there you seek the LORD your God, you will find him if you look for him with all your heart and with all your soul. 30 When you are in distress and all these things have happened to you, then in later days you will return to the LORD your God and obey him. 31 For the LORD your God is a merciful God; he will not abandon or destroy you or forget the covenant with your forefathers, which he confirmed to them by oath. Deuteronomy 4:25–31 (NIV84)

Moses knew that Abraham's Covenant was *unconditional* but He also knew that the punishment under the conditional covenant the Israelites made with God would become ever more catastrophic with each episode of Israel's turning away from God.

The Additional-Conditional Physical Covenant

The book of Leviticus is a detailed description of the national and religious laws given by God through Moses at Mount Sinai. The latter part of the book records God's conditional Covenant with Israel. This conditional Covenant carried consequences that were not only immediate but also reached millennia into Israel's future.

God made promises of physical wealth, prosperity and greatness for Israel *if* they kept the Mt. Sinai Covenant:

> 1 'You shall not make idols for yourselves; neither a carved image nor a *sacred* pillar shall you rear up for yourselves; nor shall you set up an engraved stone in your land, to bow down to it; for I *am* the LORD your God. 2 You shall keep My Sabbaths and reverence My sanctuary: I *am* the LORD.
> 3 'If you walk in My statutes and keep My commandments, and perform them, 4 then I will give you rain in its season, the land shall yield its produce, and the trees of the field shall yield their fruit. 5 Your threshing shall last till the time of vintage, and the vintage shall last till the time of sowing; you shall eat your bread to the full, and dwell in your land safely. 6 I will give peace in the land, and you shall lie down, and none will make *you* afraid; I will rid the land of evil beasts, and the sword will not go through your land. 7 You will chase your enemies, and they shall fall by the sword before you. 8 Five of you shall chase a hundred, and a hundred of you shall put ten thousand to flight; your enemies shall fall by the sword before you. 9 'For I will look on you favorably and make you fruitful, multiply you and confirm My covenant with you. 10 You shall eat the old harvest, and clear out the old because of the new.
> 11 I will set My tabernacle among you, and My soul shall not abhor you. 12 I will walk among you and be your God, and you shall be My people. 13 I *am*

the LORD your God, who brought you out of the land of Egypt, that *you* should not be their slaves; I have broken the bands of your yoke and made you walk upright. Leviticus 26:1–13 (NKJV)

Figure 3
Mt. Sinai Covenant
Rewards for Obedience

1. Bountiful agriculture and harvests
2. Plentiful food
3. Peace in the land
4. No war in the country
5. Enemies defeated on the battlefield
6. 5 will defeat 100, 100 will defeat 10,000
7. Descendants will be numerous
8. God will confirm the Covenant
9. God will walk with the people and be their God
10. No longer slaves but free men

God also described in great detail the punishment that Israel would derive if it failed to keep the terms agreed to on Mt. Sinai. If they did not obey God they could expect the destruction of their culture, their cities, the lives of many of the people and – more importantly – a delay in the delivery of important physical promises of the Covenant God made with Abraham.

14 'But if you do not obey Me, and do not observe all these commandments, 15 and if you despise My statutes, or if your soul abhors My judgments, so that you do not perform all My commandments, *but* break My covenant, 16 I also will do this to you: I will even appoint terror over you, wasting disease and fever which shall consume the eyes and cause sorrow of heart. And you shall sow your seed in vain, for your enemies shall eat it. 17 I will set My face against you, and you shall be defeated by your enemies. Those who hate you shall reign over you, and you shall flee when no one pursues you.

18 'And after all this, if you do not obey Me, then I will punish you seven times more for your sins.

19 I will break the pride of your power; I will make your heavens like iron and your earth like bronze. 20 And your strength shall be spent in vain; for your land shall not yield its produce, nor shall the trees of the land yield their fruit.

21 'Then, if you walk contrary to Me, and are not willing to obey Me, I will bring on you seven times more plagues, according to your sins.

22 I will also send wild beasts among you, which shall rob you of your children, destroy your livestock, and make you few in number; and your highways shall be desolate.

²³ 'And if by these things you are not reformed by Me, but walk contrary to Me, ²⁴ then I also will walk contrary to you, and I will punish you yet seven times for your sins.

²⁵ And I will bring a sword against you that will execute the vengeance of the covenant; when you are gathered together within your cities I will send pestilence among you; and you shall be delivered into the hand of the enemy. ²⁶ When I have cut off your supply of bread, ten women shall bake your bread in one oven, and they shall bring back your bread by weight, and you shall eat and not be satisfied.

²⁷ 'And after all this, if you do not obey Me, but walk contrary to Me, ²⁸ then I also will walk contrary to you in fury; and I, even I, will chastise you seven times for your sins.

²⁹ You shall eat the flesh of your sons, and you shall eat the flesh of your daughters. ³⁰ I will destroy your high places, cut down your incense altars, and cast your carcasses on the lifeless forms of your idols; and My soul shall abhor you. ³¹ I will lay your cities waste and bring your sanctuaries to desolation, and I will not smell the fragrance of your sweet aromas. ³² I will bring the land to desolation, and your enemies who dwell in it shall be astonished at it. ³³ I will scatter you among the nations and draw out a sword after you; your land shall be desolate and your cities waste. ³⁴ Then the land shall enjoy its sabbaths as long as it lies desolate and you *are* in your enemies' land; then the land shall rest and enjoy its sabbaths. ³⁵ As long as *it* lies desolate it shall rest— for the time it did not rest on your sabbaths when you dwelt in it. ³⁶ 'And as for those of you who are left, I will send faintness into their hearts in the lands of their enemies; the sound of a shaken leaf shall cause them to flee; they shall flee as though fleeing from a sword, and they shall fall when no one pursues. ³⁷ They shall stumble over one another, as it were before a sword, when no one pursues; and you shall have no *power* to stand before your enemies. ³⁸ You shall perish among the nations, and the land of your enemies shall eat you up. ³⁹ And those of you who are left shall waste away in their iniquity in your enemies' lands; also in their fathers' iniquities, which are with them, they shall waste away. Leviticus 26:14–39

Figure 4
Mt. Sinai Covenant
Punishment for Disobedience

1. Disease and famine
2. Defeated by enemies
3. Ruled by enemies
4. Paranoia
5. Lethal weather patterns
6. Destruction of families and livestock

7. War
8. Plagues
9. Scattered among the nations
10. Cities in ruins
11. Lands devoured by enemies
12. 7 times punishment **(repeated 4 times)**

Figure 5
The "Seven Times" Punishment

In the books of Daniel and Revelation there is an expression used – "time, times and half a time" [Daniel 7:25, 12:7; Revelation 12:14]. That this period is 3 ½ years or 42 months or 1,260 days can be seen by these scriptures [Revelation 11:2, 3; 12:6]. In prophecy a "time" is one year; a "year" is 360 days according to the calendars used during Biblical times.

"Seven times" is 2,520 days. Using the "day for a year" concept [E5] *one multiplies 7 X 360 = 2,520 years.*

The flexibility shown for disobedience demonstrates God's grace to the children of Israel; He told them plainly that He would allow mistakes to be made and though there would be punishment, they could obtain forgiveness and again enjoy God's favor.   The consequences for failure to repent would worsen for the succeeding punishments until they would be eventually punished *seven times*!

Even then, God built into the Sinai covenant the promise that *after* the 7 times punishment – after they were properly humbled – God would "remember" His Covenant with Abraham, Isaac and Jacob.

> [40] '*But* if they confess their iniquity and the iniquity of their fathers, with their unfaithfulness in which they were unfaithful to Me, and that they also have walked contrary to Me, [41] and *that* I also have walked contrary to them and have brought them into the land of their enemies; if their uncircumcised hearts are humbled, and they accept their guilt— [42] then I will remember My covenant with Jacob, and My covenant with Isaac and My covenant with Abraham I will remember; I will remember the land. [43] The land also shall be left empty by them, and will enjoy its sabbaths while it lies desolate without them; they will accept their guilt, because they despised My judgments and because their soul abhorred My statutes. [44] Yet for all that, when they are in the land of their enemies, I will not cast them away, nor shall I abhor them, to utterly destroy them and break My covenant with them; for I *am* the LORD their God. [45] But for their sake I will remember the covenant of their ancestors, whom I brought out of the land

of Egypt in the sight of the nations, that I might be their God: I *am* the LORD.' "

46 These *are* the statutes and judgments and laws which the LORD made between Himself and the children of Israel on Mount Sinai by the hand of Moses. Leviticus 26:14–46 (NKJV)

As the Israelites were getting ready to leave Mt. Sinai and head for the "promised land", God promised to clear the land of Canaan for the Israelites. He warned the Israelites of the danger of leaving the indigenous people in place[26].

31 "I will establish your borders from the Red Sea to the Sea of the Philistines **(the Mediterranean Sea)**, and from the desert to the River **(the Euphrates)**. I will hand over to you the people who live in the land and you will drive them out before you. 32 Do not make a covenant with them or with their gods. 33 Do not let them live in your land, or they will cause you to sin against me, because the worship of their gods will certainly be a snare to you." Exodus 23:31–33 (NIV84)

The Book of Numbers records the story of the Israelites initial "scouting" foray into Canaan. God had Moses send 12 leaders – one from each ancestral tribe[27] to surveil the land and report on the people, the soil, the water and the cities. He asked them to bring back some samples of fruit from the land.

Two of the scouts (Joshua from the tribe of Ephraim and Caleb from the tribe of Judah) gave this report as spoken by Caleb:

30 Then Caleb silenced the people before Moses and said, "We should go up and take possession of the land, for we can certainly do it." Numbers 13:30 (NIV84)

The other 10 gave this report:

31 But the men who had gone up with him said, "We can't attack those people; they are stronger than we are." 32 And they spread among the Israelites a bad report about the land they had explored. They said, "The land we explored devours those living in it. All the people we saw there are of great size. 33 We saw the Nephilim **(giants)** there (the descendants of Anak come from the Nephilim). We seemed like grasshoppers in our own eyes, and we looked the same to them." Numbers 13:31–33 (NIV84)

---

26 Exodus 23:20–33; Numbers 33:50–56; Deuteronomy 7:1–6

27 Ephraim and Manasseh were counted as tribes – Levi was not counted among the 12 as they received no inheritance.

The Israelites rebelled, threatening to stone Moses, Joshua, Aaron and Caleb, elect a new leader and return to Egypt.

God again considered destroying the children of Israel and starting over with Moses.[28] Once again, God listened to Moses' pleas for the Israelites and forgave them but still gave them a harsh punishment for their lack of faith.

Since the scouts had spent 40 days surveilling Canaan, God used the "day for a year" concept[39] as their punishment:

> [29] In this desert your bodies will fall—every one of you twenty years old or more who was counted in the census and who has grumbled against me. [30] Not one of you will enter the land I swore with uplifted hand to make your home, except Caleb son of Jephunneh and Joshua son of Nun.
> [34] For forty years—one year for each of the forty days you explored the land—you will suffer for your sins and know what it is like to have me against you.' [35] I, the LORD, have spoken, and I will surely do these things to this whole wicked community, which has banded together against me. They will meet their end in this desert; here they will die." Numbers 14:29-30; 34-35 (NIV84)

The rest of the book of Numbers gives details of the 40 years that the Israelites wandered before entering the land of Canaan that God had promised them. [See Map 1] Time and again, the Israelites rebelled against Moses and against God and time and again were punished; yet they never seemed to learn the danger of rebelling against God.

Joshua and the Promised Land

The tribes of Gad and Reuben and one-half of the tribe of Manasseh took their inheritance on the east side of the Jordan River but sent their fighting men with the rest of the Israelites to help clear the land for the other tribes between the Jordan and the Mediterranean Ocean.

The places where the children of Israel stopped for a time on their journey from Egypt to the plains of Moab, across the Jordan from the city of Jericho are all listed in Numbers although most of the places cannot be located today by the names given then. Detailed instructions for allocating the "promised land" (Canaan) to the Israelite tribes are also listed.

---

[28] Numbers 14:10–19

Near the end of this period God had Moses ordain Joshua to be leader of the Israelites as Moses was not allowed to enter the Promised Land because of his and Aaron's disobedience at Meribah Kadesh[29]. Aaron had already died[30].

The book of Joshua relates the story of the Israelites conquering the land of Canaan. After they crossed the Jordan River near Jericho at Gilgal, all the males were circumcised who had not been circumcised during the 40 years spent in the "wilderness". All the men who were over 20 years old when they came out of Egypt died in that 40-year period.

During the 40 years of wandering in the wilderness, the Israelites didn't have to replace their clothing – it didn't wear out – and they never had to worry about food and water because manna appeared with the morning dew 6 days each week and God provided water miraculously if a local source was not available. These miracles stopped when the Israelites entered the "promised land."

> [10] On the evening of the fourteenth day of the month, while camped at Gilgal on the plains of Jericho, the Israelites celebrated the Passover. [11] The day after the Passover, that very day, they ate some of the produce of the land: unleavened bread and roasted grain. [12] The manna stopped the day after they ate this food from the land; there was no longer any manna for the Israelites, but that year they ate of the produce of Canaan. Joshua 5:10–12 (NIV84)

The Israelites first conquest was the heavily walled city of Jericho. Jericho was five miles west of the Jordan River and seven miles northwest of the Dead Sea on the Jordan River plain. Before they crossed the river, Joshua sent two spies to scout the city. They stayed with a prostitute named Rahab who strongly believed in God, who protected them from the authorities, who saved her whole family and entered the Israelite lineage[40] from whom was born the Messiah, Jesus.

The spies informed Joshua the walls were impenetrable but God solved that problem by having the walls fall outward[31].

This conquest so frightened the residents of Canaan that Israel had little trouble in taking territory as they came to it.

---

[29] Numbers 20:1–13
[30] Numbers 20:22–29
[31] That the walls of ancient Jericho fell outward *at one time* is a fact proven by relatively recent secular archeology.

After conquering a city named Ai and establishing a firm foothold in Canaan, Joshua held a ceremony to remind the Israelites of the Covenant made with God at Mt. Sinai. He read to them the "law of Moses" (most likely the text from Deuteronomy) and the terms of that Covenant:

> [34] Afterward, Joshua read all the words of the law—the blessings and the curses—just as it is written in the Book of the Law. [35] There was not a word of all that Moses had commanded that Joshua did not read to the whole assembly of Israel, including the women and children, and the aliens who lived among them. Joshua 8:34–35 (NIV84)

The tribes of Judah, Ephraim and Manasseh were assigned territory described by God to Moses before the Israelites' crossing into Canaan. Ephraim's territory and one-half[32] of Manasseh's territory extended along the Jordan River northward and westward; Judah's territory extended along the Jordan southward all the way to Edom and westward to designated points.

The other tribes' territories were divided and assigned by "lot" from the remaining territory. Benjamin's "lot" placed that tribe *between* Judah's territory and Ephraim and Manasseh's territory.

Thus, Ephraim and Manasseh received the "double portion" inheritance due to the physical birthright passed from Jacob to Joseph (Ephraim and Manasseh's father). Judah received an even larger territory bequeathed by God and containing the location that would become the capital city of the nation of Israel, Jerusalem, which reflects the "sceptre blessing" bestowed on Judah by Jacob. [See Map 2]

There was peace in the land for many years after the territory was allocated. Joshua was of the tribe of Ephraim and when he died at age 110 he was buried in the hill country of Ephraim. Before he died he again reminded the Israelites that the Sinai covenant at was *conditional*:

> [14] "Now fear the LORD and serve him with all faithfulness. Throw away the gods your forefathers worshiped beyond the River and in Egypt and serve the LORD. [15] But if serving the LORD seems undesirable to you, then choose for yourselves this day whom you will serve, whether the gods your forefathers served beyond the River, or the gods of the Amorites, in whose land you are living. But as for me and my household, we will serve the LORD."
>
> [19] Joshua said to the people, "You are not able to serve the LORD. He is a holy God; he is a jealous God. He will not forgive your rebellion and your

---

[32] The other half was east of the Jordan River

sins. [20] If you forsake the LORD and serve foreign gods, he will turn and bring disaster on you and make an end of you, after he has been good to you." Joshua 24:14–15; 19–20 (NIV84)

The Judges

After Joshua died Israel was led by judges for more than 325 years – Gideon, Deborah, Samson and Samuel are among the 12 judges during this period. The judges were chosen by God, talked to Him and were led by God, the same relationship as Moses and Joshua.

These "judges" were not only involved in judicial matters but also were leaders appointed by God to relieve the oppression of the Israelites by other nations. These nations were often the descendants of Ishmael, Esau, Moab and Ammon (the children of Abraham's nephew Lot) and the children of Keturah, Abraham's wife after the death of Sarah. All these people were the disinherited descendants of Abraham. For instance, Judges were raised up by God to defeat Moab (Ehud), Midian (Gideon), and Ammon (Jephthah).

These nations continued to attack and occasionally subdue at least portions of Israel's territory – so much so that one entire Psalm bemoans their oppression of Israel. Here is a pertinent excerpt:

> [4] "Come," they say, "let us destroy them as a nation, that the name of Israel be remembered no more." [5] With one mind they plot together; they form an alliance against you— [6] the tents of Edom and the Ishmaelites, of Moab and the Hagrites, [7] Gebal, Ammon and Amalek, Philistia, with the people of Tyre. [8] Even Assyria has joined them to lend strength to the descendants of Lot. *Selah* Psalm 83:4–8 (NIV84)

Samuel, the last Judge

Israel's eventual division and destruction was set in motion during the time of Samuel.

Late in the period of the judges, a man of the tribe of Ephraim had two wives, one of whom was in the mold of Sarah, Rebekah and Rachel[33] in that Hannah was exceptionally beautiful but unable to bear children. The other wife had many children and ridiculed Hannah because she had none. Hannah prayed to God to give

---

[33] The wives of Abraham, Isaac and Jacob

her a son and promised that son would be dedicated to God and be a Nazarite[41]. God heard her prayer and she gave birth to Samuel and gave him to the priest Eli.

Samuel was chosen by God to replace Eli, who failed to train his two wicked sons who brought shame to all of Israel. They were killed by the invading Philistine army as they were capturing the Ark of the Covenant. Upon hearing of their deaths and the capture of the Ark, Eli was so distraught he fell off his chair and broke his neck and died. All this was prophesied by Samuel and the people of Israel accepted Samuel as a prophet.

When Samuel was an old man, his apparent heirs – sons Joel and Abijah – accepted bribes and perverted justice so the Israelites did not trust God to provide a leader. Because all the other nations around them had human kings, they came to Samuel and demanded that he anoint a human king to rule over them. God told Samuel that the Israelites were not rejecting him (Samuel) but rather were rejecting God as their King.

Samuel told them the evils that would come by rejecting God and desiring a human king. He enumerated a list of abuses kings would deliver to the Israelites just because they were kings and human.[34] There would be little that the common people could do to stop the wrongdoing of the kings. The worst part, in retrospect, was the last part of the message Samuel delivered to the Israelites:

> [18] When that day comes, you will cry out for relief from the king you have chosen, but the LORD will not answer you in that day." 1 Samuel 8:18 (NIV)

Samuel anointed a man from the tribe of Benjamin, Saul[35], who was quite handsome and said to be "a head taller" than any other Israelite. Saul did well for a time and the Israelites were pleased with their human king but it was not long before the human king was seduced by the power of *mammon*[42] – the gathering of wealth and power by amassing followers and then oppressing them.

Status of Covenants before entering the Age of Kings

As discussed in the first chapter, at the end of Jacob's life the birthright of the *unconditional* Covenant God made with Abraham was divided into two distinct parts:

(1.) The physical birthright (bequeathed to Ephraim and Manasseh) and

---

[34] 1 Samuel 8:4–18
[35] Saul began to reign over the 12 tribes of Israel in approximately 1050 BC.

(2.) The spiritual birthright (bequeathed to Judah) which included the line of Israelite royalty that eventually included Jesus.

Parts of the physical birthright were bestowed with the Israelites upon obtaining control of the "promised land", and with Abraham's almost innumerable descendants controlling all the land between the "river of Egypt" and the Euphrates River, promises 6, 12 and 13 were fulfilled. Numerous kings were the descendants of the patriarchs and of Sarah (to whom the promise was also made) so promises 15 and 17 were fulfilled. These and other promises fulfilled are shown in Table 2-1.

Unfulfilled promises include blessings for the whole world (5), an Israelite king from the tribe of Judah, "possessing the gates of their enemies", becoming a nation and a group of nations for Ephraim and Manasseh and "other nations bowing down" to Abraham, Isaac and Jacob's descendants (22).

At the end of the age of judges, the twelve tribes of Israel have been a single nation out of captivity for nearly 400 years. After the exodus, Moses' covenant was added to Abraham's covenants which became the Law of Israel. Moses also became the first prophet who was the person through whom God spoke to the nation Israel.

As we cover the Kingdom era of Israel, we will continue to trace the trail of the Covenants and their fulfillment. Though God is merciful and forgiving, He is also *just*; He keeps His promises. How many times would God punish Israel, get them to repent but return to their idol worship, forgetting God and their blood covenant promises. How far would God go before enforcing the 7 times punishment?

The Sinai Covenant will also be traced; as the age of kings unfolds Samuel's warning against human kings will prove ever more prophetic.

Table 2-1
Covenant Promises Bible Verses Sources (1050 BC)

Covenant Promises	Sources
1. God would make Abraham's name great	Gen 12:2
2. Abraham's descendants to become a great nation	Gen 12:2
3. God would bless Abraham	Gen 12:3; 13-15
4. God would protect Abraham	Gen 12:3; 28:13-15
5. All nations of the world blessed through Abraham	Gen 12:3; 22:15-18; 28:13-15
6. Abraham's descendants to	Gen 12:7; 13:14-15;

have the land of Canaan	17:8; 28:3−4; 13−15; 35:11−12; 48:3−4; 50:24−25; Ex 3:6−8; 16,17
7.Abraham would have innumerable descendants	**Gen 13:16; 15:5; 22:15−18**
8. Abraham's descendants spend 400 years in slavery	**Gen 15:13**
9. God to punish the nation that held them in slavery	**Gen 15:14; Ex 3:18−22**
10. Abraham's descendants to bring great wealth from slavery	**Gen 15:14; 50:24−25; Ex 3:6−8; 16,17, 18-22**
11. Abraham would die at "a good old age"	**Gen 15:15**
12. In the fourth generation Abraham's Covenant children would return to Canaan	**Gen 15:16; Ex 3:6−8, 16,17**
13 Abraham's descendants to possess all land from the Euphrates River to the "river of Egypt"	**Gen 15:18**
14. Abraham would be the father of many nations	**Gen 17:5−6**
15. Kings would come out of his descendants	**Gen 17:5−6**
16. God would be Abraham's and his descendants God	**Gen 17:7,8**
17. Nations and kings would come from Sarah	**Gen 17:16**
18. God would give Abraham a son by Sarah	**Gen 17:19; 18:10**
19. God named their son Isaac and confirmed he would be the Covenant son	**Gen 17:19, 21; 18:14**
20.God promised to bless Ishmael, making him into a great nation	**Gen 17:20; 21:12, 13; 25:12−18**
21.God made the Covenant unconditional	**Gen 22:15−18**
22. Their descendants to "possess the gates of their enemies"; become a "company of nations;" and nations to bow down	**Gen 22:15−18; 24:60; 27:27−29; 35:11−12; 48:3−4**

to them	
23 Ephraim and Manasseh would bear the name of Israel	**Gen 48:5,6, 15,16**
24 Manasseh would become a great nation	**Gen 48:17–20; 49:22–26**
25 Ephraim would be greater still and become a company of nations	**Gen 48:17–20; 49:22–26**
26. Judah was promised the scepter until Shiloh (Jesus) comes	**Gen 49:8–10**

Promises at least partially kept
Promises not yet kept

Maps

Map 1

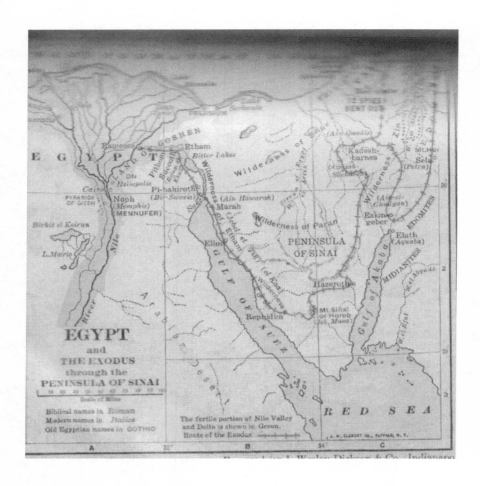

Map 2

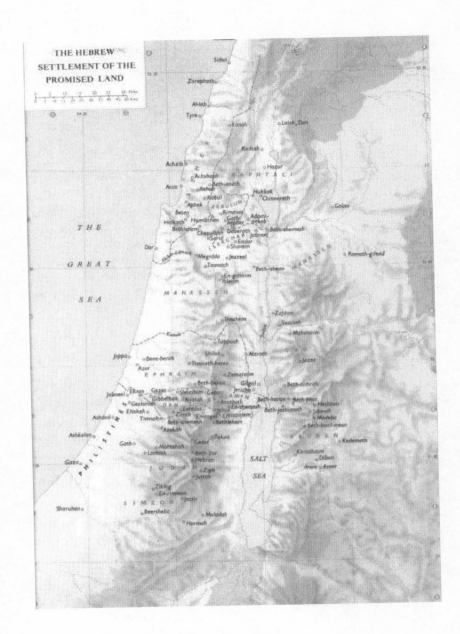

THE HEBREW
SETTLEMENT OF THE
PROMISED LAND

* * *

CHAPTER 3

The Kingdoms

The "Golden Age" of Israel was the reign of Solomon – the last 40 of the 160 years during which all Israel was ruled by a monarch (1090 – 970).   During its Golden Age, Israel had no truly competing nations around them.   Most of the neighboring nations paid tribute, allowing Israel to accumulate great wealth.   Israel controlled all the land God promised Abraham – "from the river of Egypt to the Euphrates".   Israel had significant military forces equipped with the best horses, chariots and weapons, but that military power was seldom used during Solomon's reign since there were no major conflicts.

Assyria, the first of several Empires to arise after Israel's decline, was a weak, feudal nation at that time; their weakness was partially due to tremendous losses of manpower during battles with King David – Solomon's father – who assembled a large military force during his reign.   The once powerful Egypt could scarcely mount an army much less threaten their neighbors; the Medes, Persians and Babylonians would not rise to their power for several centuries.   Additionally, Solomon married the daughter of Egypt's Pharaoh to insure a peaceful relationship; similar liaisons were made with other adjacent nations.

The Moabites, the Philistines, the Ammonites, the Edomites, the Ishmaelites, the Midianites and other surrounding nations[36] were soundly defeated by Israel's first two kings (Saul and David).   But the sins of the third king (Solomon) brought about the division of Israel.

The division of Israel at the end of Solomon's reign formally separated the promised physical and spiritual blessings from the Covenant God made with Abraham, Isaac and Jacob by placing those holding the spiritual birthright in one kingdom (Judah) and those holding the physical birthright into another kingdom (Ephraim and Manasseh held the name Israel[37]).

---

[36] See Ancient Israel Map after End Notes
[37] Genesis 48:14–16

This Kingdom of Israel lasted for just over 200 years while the Kingdom of Judah survived another 145 years after Israel fell. The people of the spiritual birthright retained their identity and – at least in part – never lost it. The holders of the physical birthright disappeared from the both the Bible and secular history with the demise of their kingdom.

With the great division of Israel, He who knows "the end from the beginning"[38] set the stage for ultimate delivery of the spiritual birthright in the First Century AD in the person of the Son of God, Jesus. The final delivery of the physical birthright promises would not be completed for some three thousand years. However, we'll show later in this book that the hand of God was preparing a mission for the physical birthright holders that would augment and assist the spread of the church Jesus would establish and the spiritual blessings therefrom.

The Kingdom United

The kings of the full kingdom of Israel were Saul, David and Solomon. We begin with Israel's first king, Saul.

After the Israelites rejected God as their king and insisted on a human king, Samuel – with God's direction – anointed Saul as the first king of Israel. Before passing his authority to Saul, Samuel said goodbye to the Israelites with this warning:

> 13 Now here is the king you have chosen, the one you asked for; see, the LORD has set a king over you. 14 If you fear the LORD and serve and obey him and do not rebel against his commands, and if both you and the king who reigns over you follow the LORD your God—good! 15 But if you do not obey the LORD, and if you rebel against his commands, his hand will be against you, as it was against your fathers. 1 Samuel 12:13–15 (NIV84)

Saul

Saul was a big, handsome man from the tribe of Benjamin[43] whose appearance pleased and reassured the Israelites. His initial success at raising an army and beginning to drive the Philistines out of the hill country and back to their own land bolstered their confidence. However, he quickly exhibited the rashness of judgment, lack of self-confidence – and more importantly – a lack of faith in God which eventually caused his downfall.

---

[38] Isaiah 46:9–10

Preparing for an important battle, the newly-formed army was frightened because of the large Philistine force arrayed against them. As Saul's soldiers saw the mass of foot soldiers and some 3,000 chariots, they began hiding in caves and thickets, among the rocks, and in pits and cisterns and some crossed the Jordan River to get out of the battle area.

Samuel promised to join them, offer a sacrifice and ask God's blessings on the battle.

Saul waited the time set by Samuel – seven days – but when the high priest did not arrive early on the seventh day, Saul became impatient and fearful and offered the sacrifice himself – just before the high priest arrived. Samuel condemned Saul for his impetuousness which resulted in his disobedience of God's instructions. Consequently, Samuel told Saul that his lineage would not inherit the throne.

However, Saul's son Jonathan was a man of faith. In spite of Samuel's condemnation of his father, Jonathan decided to attack the Philistines himself with just his armor bearer.

> 6 Then Jonathan said to the young man who bore his armor, "Come, let us go over to the garrison of these uncircumcised; it may be that the LORD will work for us. For nothing restrains the LORD from saving by many or by few." 1 Samuel 14:6 (NKJV)

Jonathan attacked an outpost, slew 20 or more soldiers and when God added an earthquake to the sudden attack, the Philistines panicked and began killing each other in their fear. Saul mustered his army, the deserters returned and Israel's army defeated the Philistines at the Bozez – Seneh pass after which the Philistines retreated to their own country. Over the next few years the Moabites, the Ammonites, the Edomites were defeated as well[39].

Although he was guilty of insubordination to God by making the sacrifice himself, Saul was given another chance. Samuel ordered Saul to completely destroy the Amalekites including their herds. It was the Amalekites who had launched a sneak attack on the Israelites as they were leaving Egypt and extremely vulnerable. God had promised their treachery would be severely punished[40].

Saul was given many chances to repent of his sins and his reckless behavior but he could never sustain repentance. Saul destroyed the Amalekites but not completely as God ordered[41]; he kept the king alive along with the best of the herds. When

---

39 1 Samuel 13:16–14:48
40 Exodus 17:14–16

confronted, Saul claimed he intended the herds to be sacrificed to God. After this transgression God rejected Saul as king with finality.

Saul was troubled by an evil spirit after God withdrew His spirit from Saul[42]. Nowhere was this more apparent than with Saul's attitude toward David. On the one hand he admired David and could feel kindly toward him. Frequently, David was called to play the harp (David was a maestro) for King Saul to ease his mind. But mostly Saul was jealous of David. In fact, once he realized David was to be his successor rather than his son, He tried on numerous occasions to kill David.

One major factor piquing Saul was David's popularity with the people of Israel. The fact that David was more successful at commanding the armies of Israel and much loved by the Israelites made Saul extremely jealous and envious of David.

> 6 Now it had happened as they were coming *home*, when David was returning from the slaughter of the Philistine, that the women had come out of all the cities of Israel, singing and dancing, to meet King Saul, with tambourines, with joy, and with musical instruments. 7 So the women sang as they danced, and said: "Saul has slain his thousands, And David his ten thousands." 1 Samuel 18:6−7 (NKJV)

After God rejected Saul, Samuel mourned for him. It grieved God that He had made Saul king only to have Saul refuse His guidance. He instructed Samuel to anoint a new king.

> 34 Then Samuel left for Ramah, but Saul went up to his home in Gibeah of Saul. 35 Until the day Samuel died, he did not go to see Saul again, though Samuel mourned for him. And the LORD was grieved that he had made Saul king over Israel.
>
> 1 The LORD said to Samuel, "How long will you mourn for Saul, since I have rejected him as king over Israel? Fill your horn with oil and be on your way; I am sending you to Jesse of Bethlehem. I have chosen one of his sons to be king." 1 Samuel 15:34−16:1 (NIV84)

After Samuel's death, Saul's madness drove him to consult a necromancer − the witch of Endor. The witch called forth an apparition, which Saul took to be the dead Samuel so Saul asked the apparition of his fate. Although the spirit was not Samuel − Samuel was dead[44] − the spirit accurately predicted Saul and his sons would be killed by the approaching Philistine army and that the army of Israel would be defeated as well[43].

---

[41] 1 Samuel 15:1−3
[42] 1 Samuel 16:14, 23
[43] 1 Samuel 31:1−13

David

With the exceptions of Abraham and Moses, David is the most important character of the Old Testament. David was a man of action, a man of passion, and his zeal occasionally brought him into conflict with God.

Yet in the many songs[44] he wrote in praise of God and God's laws we see a humble man zealous for righteousness. In the Biblical anecdotes of his life he shows his unmitigated courage in the face of danger and absolute faith that God would deliver him. We also see him committing grievous sins – adultery, murder – and yet penitent and humbly willing to pay the price of his sins. David is the only character in the Bible who was said to be "a man after God's own heart"[45]. For many, David is the greatest human king in all of history.[45]

Selecting David

God sent Samuel to Bethlehem to pick as the next king one of the sons of Jesse, a man from the tribe of Judah. The new king would move the royal line to the tribe of Judah as Jacob had prophesied[46].

Upon arriving, Samuel invited Jesse and his sons to join him in offering a sacrifice. Seven of Jesse's sons were brought before Samuel and each one looked like a king to Samuel. But God rejected each of them telling Samuel,

> 7 "Do not consider his appearance or his height, for I have rejected him. The LORD does not look at the things man looks at. Man looks at the outward appearance, but the LORD looks at the heart." 1 Samuel 16:7 (NIV84)

Samuel found that Jesse had an eighth son, David[46] who was tending sheep so Samuel sent for him. God approved and Samuel anointed David as the chosen one of God.

> 12 So he sent and had him brought in. He was ruddy, with a fine appearance and handsome features. Then the LORD said, "Rise and anoint him; he is the one." 13 So Samuel took the horn of oil and anointed him in the presence of his brothers, and from that day on the Spirit of the LORD came upon David in power. Samuel then went to Ramah. 1 Samuel 16:12–13 (NIV84)

---

44 Psalms
45 1 Samuel 13:14; Acts 13:22
46 Genesis 49:8–10

David's Psalms

David was an accomplished musician with the harp, and unmatched as a song writer with a number of Psalms to his name.

Psalm 8 reflects his faith, humility and depth of thought; it is a thing of beauty even in translation[47]:

> 3 When I consider your heavens, the work of your fingers, the moon and the stars, which you have set in place, 4 what is man that you are mindful of him, the son of man that you care for him?
>
> 5 You made him a little lower than the heavenly beings and crowned him with glory and honour. 6 You made him ruler over the works of your hands; you put everything under his feet: 7 all flocks and herds, and the beasts of the field, 8 the birds of the air, and the fish of the sea, all that swim the paths of the seas.
>
> 9 O Lord, our Lord, how majestic is your name in all the earth!
>
> Psalm 8:3–9 (NIV84)

Psalm 110[47] shows his prophetic skills in David foretelling the advent of Jesus and His priesthood. Jesus quoted David and stunned the religious leaders of His day into silence by asking them whose son was the Messiah. He said David was speaking "by the spirit".[48]

> 41 While the Pharisees were gathered together, Jesus asked them, 42 "What do you think about the Christ? Whose son is he?" "The son of David," they replied. 43 He said to them, "How is it then that David, speaking by the Spirit, calls him 'Lord'? For he says, 44 "'The Lord said to my Lord: "Sit at my right hand until I put your enemies under your feet."' 45 If then David calls him 'Lord,' how can he be his son?"

---

47 Quoted in Hebrews 2:5–8
48 Matthew 22:44; Mark 12:36, Luke 20:42, Acts 2:34

[46] No one could say a word in reply, and from that day on no one dared to ask him any more questions. Matthew 22:41–46 (NIV84)

Few are they who have not heard this song of David:

> 1 The LORD *is* my shepherd; I shall not want. 2 He makes me to lie down in green pastures; He leads me beside the still waters. 3 He restores my soul; He leads me in the paths of righteousness For His name's sake. 4 Yea, though I walk through the valley of the shadow of death, I will fear no evil; For You *are* with me; Your rod and Your staff, they comfort me. 5 You prepare a table before me in the presence of my enemies; You anoint my head with oil; My cup runs over. 6 Surely goodness and mercy shall follow me All the days of my life; And I will dwell in the house of the LORD Forever. Psalm 23:1–6 (NKJV)

David and Goliath

As the youngest brother David was the keeper of his father's sheep even after Samuel's anointing. Diligent in protecting the flock, David killed both a bear and a lion using his sling. That weapon proved to be equally lethal when slaying the giant Goliath.

After the Philistine rout at the Bozez – Seneh pass[49], several years passed with no conflict. But while David was in service to Saul – providing harp music and song to calm the troubled king – the Philistines once again came against Israel. This time they had their own not-so-secret weapon – Goliath.

The average height of an Israeli at that time was likely less than five feet four inches.

Goliath was from the Philistine city of Gath; he was over 9 feet tall and was most likely a descendant of the Anakim – descendants of Anak from the Nephilim[50]. With

---

[49] 1 Samuel 14:4–5
[50] Numbers 13:33

his bronze coat of mail, bronze greaves, bronze javelin, spear with an iron spearhead, and huge sword, he must have presented an invincible image to the Israelis.

For forty days, Goliath came before the Israelites and challenged them to send their champion to battle him. If Goliath won, the Israelites would serve the Philistines; if their champion won, the Philistines would serve Israel.

While serving in Saul's court David also continued to watch over Jesse's sheep. Jesse's other sons were encamped against the Philistines with Saul's army. One day Jesse called David in to take grain, bread and cheese to his sons and his sons' commanders at the encampment.

While bringing food to them, David heard Goliath's challenge.

> 22 David left his things with the keeper of supplies, ran to the battle lines and greeted his brothers. 23 As he was talking with them, Goliath, the Philistine champion from Gath, stepped out from his lines and shouted his usual defiance, and David heard it. 24 When the Israelites saw the man, they all ran from him in great fear. 1 Samuel 17:22–24 (NIV84)

David was unafraid.

> 26 David asked the men standing near him, "What will be done for the man who kills this Philistine and removes this disgrace from Israel? Who is this uncircumcised Philistine that he should defy the armies of the living God?" 1 Samuel 17:26 (NIV84)

Saul had promised the hand of his daughter and great wealth to anyone who could kill Goliath. David's brothers taunted him as being conceited since Samuel's private anointing. However, other soldiers told Saul about David. Saul brought David before him and offered him armor, a helmet and a sword but David put those things aside.

> 34 But David said to Saul, "Your servant has been keeping his father's sheep. When a lion or a bear came and carried off a sheep from the flock, 35 I went after it, struck it and rescued the sheep from its mouth. When it turned on me, I seized it by its hair, struck it and killed it. 36 Your servant has killed both the lion and the bear; this uncircumcised Philistine will be like one of them, because he has defied the armies of the living God. 37 The LORD who delivered me from the paw of the lion and the paw of the bear will deliver me from the hand of this Philistine." Saul said to David, "Go, and the LORD be with you." 1 Samuel 17:34–37 (NIV84)

Goliath was enraged that the Israelites would send out this "little boy" to face him.

> [42] He looked David over and saw that he was only a boy, ruddy and handsome, and he despised him. [43] He said to David, "Am I a dog, that you come at me with sticks?" And the Philistine cursed David by his gods. [44] "Come here," he said, "and I'll give your flesh to the birds of the air and the beasts of the field!" [45] David said to the Philistine, "You come against me with sword and spear and javelin, but I come against you in the name of the LORD Almighty, the God of the armies of Israel, whom you have defied.
>
> [46] This day the LORD will hand you over to me, and I'll strike you down and cut off your head. Today I will give the carcasses of the Philistine army to the birds of the air and the beasts of the earth, and the whole world will know that there is a God in Israel. 1 Samuel 17:42–46 (NIV84)

David slung a stone and it sank in Goliath's forehead where his helmet was open and the giant fell. David cut off the giant's head with Goliath's own sword and the Philistines ran from the scene in fear. The army of Israel pursued and slew a large part of the Philistine army.

Saul's son Jonathan loved David and many times helped thwart Saul's plots to kill David. After David killed Goliath, Jonathan gave David his own royal robe, armor and sword. Jonathan and David remained good friends all of Jonathan's life.

King David

After Saul's death, David was first selected only as king of Judah with Saul's son Ishbosheth as king over Israel. But Ishbosheth was assassinated[51] and shortly thereafter David was named king over all Israel.

One of David's first acts was to capture the city of Jebus, also called Jerusalem, and established it as the capital city of the nation of Israel. It came to share the name "the city of David" with Bethlehem where David was born and reared.[48] Jebus was located on the northern border of the tribe of Judah's territory and bordered the territories of the tribes of Benjamin and Ephraim – more or less in the middle of the country – and it pleased most of the Israelites that David was king over all Israel.

Within a few years David had defeated most of the nations around Israel and established the borders of the Promised Land proclaimed by God to Abraham,[52] from

---

[51] Not on David's orders
[52] Genesis 15:18-21

the Mediterranean to the Euphrates; from northern Syria to the borders of the Arabian Peninsula.

David's reign was tumultuous – many of the troubles brought on by his foray into polygamy even before his throne was established. He first married Michal, the daughter of Saul who eventually came to despise him and bore him no children. Abigail, the wisest of his wives gave him a son. His most famous wife – Bathsheba – gave him Solomon and other children. David had many wives and concubines but only eight wives are named in the Bible[53].

Although David was said to be "a man after God's own heart", he was not without many flaws.

A major flaw was exposed when he committed adultery with Bathsheba. She was the wife of Uriah, the Hittite. While Uriah was away fighting with Israel's army, David stayed in Jerusalem. Unable to sleep one evening while walking on the roof of his palace he saw Bathsheba naked (she was bathing) and decided he had to have her. She became pregnant.

Shortly after, when Uriah returned he refused to sleep with his wife. He was a man of honor and was mindful of his fellow warriors still on the battlefield. David plied him with alcohol but even when drunk, Uriah's devotion to his duty as a soldier prevented him from having sex with his wife thus thwarting David's subterfuge. He was hoping to claim his child was the offspring of Uriah. David then compounded his sin by giving orders to place Uriah at the front of the battle, in the most dangerous position. Uriah was killed.

David's punishment was severe. The prophet Nathan confronted David with his sin; the baby he fathered with Bathsheba died and Nathan told David "the sword will never depart from your house". The story of the rest of David's reign is filled with pathos and betrayal by his sons and some he thought were his close friends. God also denied David the right to build a temple for Him in Jerusalem and left that to his and Bathsheba's son Solomon.

David hated the violence of his reign. He was determined that his successor would not have to rule over such chaos and mayhem. Many of his Psalms reflect that determination.

It is an interesting point that many of the people and events of the Bible can only be found in the Bible. That has led some historians – even Bible historians – to doubt the existence of leading characters. A case in point is King David himself.

---

[53] 1 Chronicles 3:1–9

Until 1993, there was no mention of David found in ancient contemporary writing. But archeology continues to add credibility to Bible stories. In the case of David, the following shows support from a recent archeological artifact.

> An Aramaic inscription including the words "house [dynasty] of David" was found in 1993 in the ruins of the city of Dan. It dates to the 9th century B.C. and is the only known mention of David in ancient contemporary writings outside the Old Testament itself. [49]

David died after a long illness when he was 71. He is remembered for his musical and poetic talent and by his many Psalms. He was held as the standard for a "good" king throughout both Judah and Israel's kingdoms.

Though he made many mistakes, he always admitted his sins publicly and to God and asked for forgiveness. His faith in God remained strong. He solidified Israel as a nation setting the stage for the golden years of Solomon's reign – the height of economic and political power ever reached for the nation of Israel.

God loved David with all his faults and made a personal Covenant with him.

> "'The LORD declares to you that the LORD himself will establish a house for you: [12] When your days are over and you rest with your fathers, I will raise up your offspring to succeed you, who will come from your own body, and I will establish his kingdom. [13] He is the one who will build a house for my Name, and I will establish the throne of his kingdom forever. [14] I will be his father, and he will be my son. When he does wrong, I will punish him with the rod of men, with floggings inflicted by men. [15] But my love will never be taken away from him, as I took it away from Saul, whom I removed from before you. [16] Your house and your kingdom will endure forever before me; your throne will be established forever.'" 2 Samuel 7:8–16 (NIV84)

Jesus was referred to as the Son of David multiple times in the New Testament; Jesus was born in Bethlehem – also referred to as the "city of David" because it was David's birthplace and boyhood home.

Solomon

The years of King Solomon's reign *were* the "Golden Age" of Israel.

Solomon, son of David and Bathsheba, was David's youngest son. His reign represents the greatest power and prestige, the greatest economic and political hegemony in the history of the nation of Israel. The kingdom he inherited from David was one essentially at peace with all its neighbors and quite wealthy.

Solomon was an exceedingly handsome man, "bright and ruddy" like his father, with dark locks with a golden glow and his appearance was considered "the fairest of ten thousand"[54]. He was wise even as a young man – in his late teens or early 20's when he took the throne – wise enough to ask God for wisdom to rule[50].

Solomon's Wisdom

Solomon's philosophy, wit and wisdom, are known by many people who have never read the Bible. A song using these words was a musical *anthem* of the 1960's:

> [1] To everything *there is* a season, A time for every purpose under heaven: [2] A time to be born, And a time to die; A time to plant, And a time to pluck *what is* planted; [3] A time to kill, And a time to heal; A time to break down, And a time to build up; [4] A time to weep, And a time to laugh; A time to mourn, And a time to dance; [5] A time to cast away stones, And a time to gather stones; A time to embrace, And a time to refrain from embracing; [6] A time to gain, And a time to lose; A time to keep, And a time to throw away; [7] A time to tear, And a time to sew; A time to keep silence, And a time to speak; [8] A time to love, And a time to hate; A time of war, And a time of peace. Ecclesiastes 3:1–8 (NKJV)

Solomon taught that there is little difference between man and animals without God:

> [18] I said in my heart, "Concerning the condition of the sons of men, God tests them, that they may see that they themselves are *like* animals." [19] For what happens to the sons of men also happens to animals; one thing befalls them: as one dies, so dies the other. Surely, they all have one breath; man has no advantage over animals, for all *is* vanity. [20] All go to one place: all are from the dust, and all return to dust. [21] Who knows the spirit of the sons of men, which goes upward, and the spirit of the animal, which goes down to the earth? [22] So I perceived that nothing *is* better than that a man should rejoice in his own works, for that *is* his heritage. For who can bring him to see what will happen after him? Ecclesiastes 3:18–22 (NKJV)

And who has not heard at least one of these proverbs of Solomon?

> [6] Go to the ant, you sluggard! Consider her ways and be wise, Proverbs 6:6 (NKJV)

---

[54] Song of Solomon 5:10–16

¹⁰ "The fear of the LORD *is* the beginning of wisdom, And the knowledge of the Holy One *is* understanding. Proverbs 9:10 (NKJV)

²⁴ He who spares his rod hates his son, But he who loves him disciplines him promptly. Proverbs 13:24 (NKJV)

¹ A soft answer turns away wrath, But a harsh word stirs up anger. Proverbs 15:1 (NKJV)

¹⁸ Pride *goes* before destruction, And a haughty spirit before a fall. Proverbs 16:18 (NKJV)

¹ A *good* name is to be chosen rather than great riches, Loving favor rather than silver and gold. Proverbs 22:1 (NKJV)

⁶ Train up a child in the way he should go, And when he is old he will not depart from it. Proverbs 22:6 (NKJV)

Solomon's wisdom has virtually no parallel among men even to this day[51].

Inordinate Wealth

God not only granted Solomon great wisdom but also gave him great wealth and honor[52].

David was not allowed by God to build a temple in Jerusalem but he did gather the materials and accumulated much of the wealth that Solomon used in the temple's construction[55].

Solomon built the temple – possibly the most ornate structure ever built by man. Three entire chapters[56] are devoted to the description of the preparation for construction, the furnishings, the design of all the interior and exterior features and the intricate carved and molded gold and bronze pieces made to the specifications God gave to David. It must have been almost unbelievable, especially in those days and that culture.

When the temple was finished, the Ark of the Covenant was placed within the "most holy place". There was nothing in the Ark at that time but the two stone tablets on which God had written the 10 Commandments with His own finger.[57]

The description of Solomon's throne reveals a throne unequaled for opulent extravagance.

---

[55] 1 Chronicles 28:1–29:9
[56] I Kings 5:1 – 7:51
[57] 1 Kings 8:9

[18] Moreover the king made a great throne of ivory and overlaid it with pure gold. [19] The throne had six steps, and the top of the throne *was* round at the back; *there were* armrests on either side of the place of the seat, and two lions stood beside the armrests. [20] Twelve lions stood there, one on each side of the six steps; nothing like *this* had been made for any *other* kingdom. 1 Kings 10:18−20 (NKJV)

The Queen of Sheba

The kingdom of Sheba covered the greater part of what today is called Yemen. It bordered on the Red Sea and contained one of the more fertile parts of all Arabia. It was founded by Sheba, a son of Jokshan[58], one of Abraham's sons by his second wife Keturah. That very wealthy country controlled many of the trade routes from the Persian Gulf and the Indian Ocean across the Arabian Peninsula to all the kingdoms and nations around the Mediterranean. The journeys were made by camel "trains".

The Queen of Sheba made that arduous journey because even thousands of miles from Jerusalem, Solomon's name and wisdom were well known. She brought gifts of many rare spices and 120 talents[59] of gold and perhaps had an affair with Solomon. Some who read the book called Song of Solomon interpret some of the sensuous passages of that scripture to be referring to the "Queen of the South[60]". She was astounded with Solomon's ability to answer any question she asked and by the wealth she saw that was extraordinary even to this queen of a wealthy and powerful nation.

Solomon's fall from grace

Solomon inherited his father's proclivity for polygamy and amplified that trait amassing 700 wives and 300 concubines. Israel paid a high price for Solomon's catering to his many wives. It was these wives who convinced Solomon to bring idol worship into Jerusalem and even into the temple itself[61].

This man whom God had the prophet Nathan name Jedidiah (darling of the Lord)[62] listened to his wives and built "competing" temples to Molech, Chemosh and Ashtaroth and installed the "high places" for worship of Astarte and Baal[63].

---

[58] Genesis 25:3
[59] About 4 metric tons according to the Bible footnote
[60] Luke 11:31
[61] I Kings 11:1-13
[62] 2 Samuel 12:24-25
[63] 1 Kings 11:1−8

Because of this and his many other sins, God took the kingdom away but not while Solomon lived.

> [11] So the LORD said to Solomon, "Since this is your attitude and you have not kept my covenant and my decrees, which I commanded you, I will most certainly tear the kingdom away from you and give it to one of your subordinates. [12] Nevertheless, for the sake of David your father, I will not do it during your lifetime. I will tear it out of the hand of your son. [13] Yet I will not tear the whole kingdom from him but will give him one tribe for the sake of David my servant and for the sake of Jerusalem, which I have chosen." 1 Kings 11:11–13 (NIV84)

Though Solomon's age cannot be firmly established, extrapolating from the scriptures the best estimate of his age at death is 60 or 61 years of age.

Solomon's death marked the beginning of the end of Israel's prosperity and hegemony and the start of a decline that would see 10 of the 12 tribes slaughtered or captured and deported to the cities of the Medes. These Medean cities lay in the far north of the Assyrian empire – which had subjugated the Medes. The Assyrians destroyed the kingdom of Israel in about 723 BC leaving only the kingdom of Judah extant at that time. About two hundred years later, the kingdom of Judah would also be destroyed.

The Kingdom Divided

Rehoboam, eldest son of Solomon, became king of Israel upon Solomon's death.

Rehoboam was a brash and arrogant young man without the wisdom of his father Solomon. Solomon had taxed the Israelites heavily with the construction of the magnificent temple, his equally opulent palace and other such construction but the Israelites supported that effort for their love of David and Solomon.

With Solomon's death, the Israelites wanted relief from the burden of heavy taxes and the conscription of labor and materials used in the constructions projects of Solomon. They approached Rehoboam and demanded he lighten their yoke. Rehoboam asked for three days before giving them an answer.

He consulted the wise men who had counseled Solomon who advised him to do what the people asked to insure his throne. Not liking their advice, he turned to the young men who had grown up with him and who now served in his government for their advice – which he followed.

¹⁰ Then the youngsters who had grown up with him spoke to him, saying, "Thus you shall say to this people who spoke to you: 'Your father made our yoke heavy, but you lighten *it* for us,' you shall say to them, 'My little finger is thicker than my father's loins.⁵³ ¹¹ So then, my father loaded a heavy yoke on all of you, but I will add to your yoke; my father disciplined you with whips, but I will discipline you with scorpions!'" 1 Kings 12:10–11 (LEB)

At this outrageous answer from Rehoboam, the Israelites, the 10 tribes led by Jeroboam – an Ephraimite who once served in Solomon's court who had already rebelled once against Solomon – immediately declared their independence. When Rehoboam marshalled the armies of Judah and Benjamin – 180,000 strong – to bring the Israelites in line, the prophet Shemaiah brought the word of God.

²⁴ 'This is what the LORD says: Do not go up to fight against your brothers, the Israelites. Go home, every one of you, for this is my doing.'" So they obeyed the word of the LORD and went home again, as the LORD had ordered. 1 Kings 12:24 (NIV84)

The Kingdom of Israel

Jeroboam was named king of Israel – ten tribes – leaving Judah, Benjamin and most of Levi as the kingdom of Judah – and he set about to insure his throne would last. He surmised that if the Israelites went back to Jerusalem and visited the temple for annual festivals they would eventually reject Jeroboam and return to Rehoboam and Judah.

Jeroboam set the pattern for all the kings of Israel from his day until the kingdom's destruction: he set up golden calves in Bethel and Dan and proclaimed that these were the "gods who brought them out of Egypt"; he established his own festival dates to replace those given in the Law of Moses; he banished the Levites who were scattered throughout the kingdom and named the "lowest" people to take the Levites' place as priests as well.

In the Biblical account of the 20+ kings of Israel, not one of them abandoned this idolatry and each king is summarized in statements like this of king Baasha:

³⁴ He did evil in the eyes of the LORD, walking in the ways of Jeroboam and in his sin, which he had caused Israel to commit. 1 Kings 15:34 (NIV84)

In making the northern kingdom's priests the creatures of the king and evicting the Levites, the kingdom of Israel lost its best spiritual leaders, teachers and advocates for keeping the Mt. Sinai Covenant[64]. Israel killed some of their local prophets and some of the prophets that came from Judah.

They ignored the prophets they didn't kill – among them Ahijah, Jehu, Elijah, Elisha, Jonah, Amos, Hosea, Micah and Isaiah, seven of whom have an Old Testament book attributed to them.

Elijah

Elijah, the Tishbite from Gilead has been called "the grandest and most romantic character that Israel has ever produced"[65]. His normal dress was a girdle of skins about his loins and (on occasion) a mantle of sheepskin across his shoulders. His hair was long and thick hanging down his back.

The story of the prophet Elijah is inextricably tied to one of the most evil kings of the Kingdom of Israel – Ahab, the son of Omri who was the 7th king of Israel after Jeroboam. He reigned from 874 to 853 BC – about 56 years after the nation of Israel split into the Kingdoms of Judah and Israel.

Elijah's story is also tied to Ahab's wife, Jezebel, the daughter of the king of Sidon, one of the Phoenician cities God told the children of Israel to destroy. If those cities and the Canaanite nations weren't destroyed, they would be constant trouble for Israel[66].

The Sidonians worshipped both Baal and Astarte and their sexual proclivities were entwined with their worship – their temple prostitutes lured many of the Israelites into sexual sin and idolatry over the years. Their practices were still extant during the time of the Greek and Roman Empires and touched some in the early churches[67] during New Testament times.

Jezebel, like her husband, was one of the most evil persons described in the Old Testament.

> [29] In the thirty-eighth year of Asa king of Judah, Ahab son of Omri became king of Israel, and he reigned in Samaria over Israel twenty-two years. [30] Ahab son of Omri did more evil in the eyes of the LORD than any of those before him. [31] He not only considered it trivial to commit the sins of Jeroboam son of Nebat, but he also married Jezebel daughter of Ethbaal king

---

[64] 2 Chronicles 11:13–17
[65] Smith's Bible Dictionary
[66] Numbers 33:55-56
[67] Revelation 2:14–15

of the Sidonians and began to serve Baal and worship him. 32 He set up an altar for Baal in the temple of Baal that he built in Samaria. 33 Ahab also made an Asherah pole and did more to provoke the LORD, the God of Israel, to anger than did all the kings of Israel before him. 34 In Ahab's time, Hiel of Bethel rebuilt Jericho. He laid its foundations at the cost of his firstborn son Abiram, and he set up its gates at the cost of his youngest son Segub, in accordance with the word of the LORD spoken by Joshua son of Nun. 1 Kings 16:29–34 (NIV84) [68]

Elijah's first appearance in the Bible was before King Ahab where Elijah said:

> 1 "As the LORD, the God of Israel, lives, whom I serve, there will be neither dew nor rain in the next few years except at my word." 1 Kings 17:1 (NIV84)

There was no rain for three years. Ahab and Jezebel put a price on Elijah's head and sent their army after him. God fed Elijah for a time by having ravens bring him food to his hideout east across the Jordan River from Ahab's territory in a ravine that also had a small brook for his water supply. When that creek dried up from no rain, Elijah roomed for a time with a widow in Sidon (Jezebel's home) whose handful of flour and a little jug of oil provided the basis for Elijah's and the widow and her son's food for about two years.

When Elijah first met the widow, she was searching for some sticks to make a fire to cook the small amount of flour and oil she had left for one last meal before she and her boy died of starvation because of the drought. Samuel told her to make a meal for all three of them; she did and there was no less oil and flour. Still, she questioned why the flour and oil did not run out. Shortly after Elijah moved in, the boy became ill and died. Elijah asked and God granted the boy's revival and the widow asked no more questions but kept cooking the oil and flour to feed her, Elijah and her son.

The Contest at Mount Carmel

After two years with the widow, Elijah discovered Jezebel was killing all of God's prophets she could locate. Obadiah, a prophet like Elijah, was responsible for hiding a hundred of those prophets and when Elijah approached, he told the story of Jezebel's pogrom.

---

[68] Joshua 6:26 Joshua pronounced a curse on anyone rebuilding Jericho

Elijah sent Obadiah to invite Ahab to bring his 450 prophets of Baal and Jezebel's 400 prophets of Asherah (Astarte/Ishtar) for a contest on Mount Carmel between God and Baal/Astarte. Ahab invited all the people around to watch the spectacle.

The prophets of Baal prepared their offering but Elijah told them not to light the fire but rather have Baal send fire to burn the offering to show he accepted it. The prophets prayed all morning, dancing around the altar, and indulged in their usual practice of flagellation and called on their god. He didn't answer.

Elijah began to mock them in the afternoon:

> [27] At noon Elijah began to taunt them. "Shout louder!" he said. "Surely he is a god! Perhaps he is deep in thought, or busy, or traveling. Maybe he is sleeping and must be awakened." 1 Kings 18:27 (NIV84)

Near sunset Elijah called all the people to gather around. He rebuilt the altar, using 12 stones symbolizing the tribes of Israel and prepared the sacrifice on that altar with a ditch dug all the way around it. He then had them drench the altar and the sacrifice three times so much so that the trench was filled with water. He then asked God to burn the altar and all that was on it:

> [38] Then the fire of the LORD fell and burned up the sacrifice, the wood, the stones and the soil, and also licked up the water in the trench. 1 Kings 18:38 (NIV84)

In their repentance – recognizing they had been worshipping a false god – the Israelites seized the prophets of Baal and Astarte and killed them all. Shortly thereafter, the rain returned to the kingdom of Israel but the peoples' hearts quickly returned to their former state.

Jezebel was furious that her prophets had been slain and sent this word to Elijah:

> [2] "May the gods deal with me, be it ever so severely, if by this time tomorrow I do not make your life like that of one of them." 1 Kings 19:2 (NIV84)

Elijah literally ran for his life, to the south all the way to Mount Horeb, the "mountain of God" – where God spoke the 10 Commandments to the Israelites – where he hid in a cave. This "man of God" who at times seemed fearless, was alone and afraid.

The Cave

God appeared to Elijah in the cave and asked him what he was doing there.

> [14] He replied, "I have been very zealous for the LORD God Almighty. The Israelites have rejected your covenant, broken down your altars, and put your prophets to death with the sword. I am the only one left, and now they are trying to kill me too." 1 Kings 19:14 (NIV84)

God had Elijah come out of the cave and stand on the mountain to experience "the presence of the Lord". First a wind so powerful that it broke stone passed but God was not in the wind; an earthquake shook the whole mountain but God was not in the earthquake:

> [12] And after the earthquake a fire; *but* the LORD *was* not in the fire: and after the fire a still small voice. 1 Kings 19:12 (KJV 1900)

In that "still, small voice" (as the KJV so poetically translates the Hebrew) God spoke to Elijah explaining that He still had "7,000 in Israel" who were not following Baal but still following Him. He then gave Elijah instructions on how to complete his mission and appoint his successor.

Elijah returned to Jezreel where Jezebel had arranged the murder of Naboth (a man who would not sell a vineyard Ahab wanted) and confronted Ahab about this great sin. He prophesied the end of Ahab and the end of Jezebel:

> [19] Say to him, 'This is what the LORD says: Have you not murdered a man and seized his property?' Then say to him, 'This is what the LORD says: In the place where dogs licked up Naboth's blood, dogs will lick up your blood—yes, yours!'"
> [23] "And also concerning Jezebel the LORD says: 'Dogs will devour Jezebel by the wall of Jezreel.' 1 Kings 21:19, 23 (NIV84)

Both prophecies came to pass.

For well over a decade, Elijah was under a death warrant issued by Jezebel and pursued wherever he went. When his work was done, during the reign of Ahab's son Ahaziah, God removed Elijah from that territory. Ahab died in 853 BC; Ahaziah died in 851 BC. It was shortly after the death of Ahaziah that God *sent the whirlwind and "flaming chariot" that picked up Elijah*[69] leaving his successor Elisha as God's spokesman to the kingdom of Israel.

---

[69] 2 Kings 2:1–18

¹¹ Then it happened, as they continued on and talked, that suddenly a chariot of fire *appeared* with horses of fire and separated the two of them; and Elijah went up by a whirlwind into heaven. 2 Kings 2:11 (NKJV)[54]

Prophecy depicted Elijah playing a part in the advent of Jesus on this earth:

⁵ Behold, I will send you Elijah the prophet Before the coming of the great and dreadful day of the LORD: ⁶ And he shall turn the heart of the fathers to the children, And the heart of the children to their fathers, Lest I come and smite the earth with a curse. Malachi 4:5–6 (KJV 1900)

Jonah and Ninevah

"Jonah and the Whale" (the story of the prophet) is often taught in Bible classes and some of the story has made its way into our common culture and language. What is not well known is the reason Jonah ran away when God told him to preach to the city of Ninevah, the capital of the Assyrian Empire. Jonah was to warn of the city's destruction unless they repented of their sins.

God had Jonah instruct the evil king Jeroboam II on how to restore the boundaries of the northern kingdom[70] showing His mercy even though the people were worshipping idols. Though Jonah and other prophets told Jeroboam and the leaders of Israel of their coming fate, they would not "hear".

Jonah had seen how evil the kingdom of Israel had become and was familiar with the prophecies of its demise. He knew that the kingdom of Israel would eventually fall to the Assyrians.

Jonah was highly offended that God was sending him to tell the Assyrian capital city to repent. This was the Empire that would kill many of his kinfolk and descendants and deport others to lands far away. He knew that repentance leads to God's forgiveness. If Ninevah would repent God would spare the city from the destruction Jonah was to proclaim and Jonah *wanted* God to destroy Ninevah.

Instead, Ninevah repented[71] making Jonah furious[72].

Though Assyria stopped assaulting the kingdom of Israel for nearly 100 years, they reverted to their warring ways eventually destroying Israel. We see Jonah's story has implications far beyond this simple tale[55].

---

[70] 2 Kings 14:23–27

[71] Jonah 3:1–10

[72] Jonah 4:1–11

The Kings of Israel

For a little more than 200 years and through 20+ kings, shown in table 3-1 the kingdom of Israel knew no peace; knew almost no time without blatant idolatry. One of these kings – Ahaz – sacrificed his own son to Baal or Molech. Almost every king of Israel was assassinated and most of them had their families slaughtered as well – removing any threat to the assassin's claim on the throne.

Still, God sent them warning after warning; through Isaiah, through Hosea, through Amos[56]. The kingdom of Israel would not listen and so their prophesied 7 – times punishment finally came. Two of the most poignant of those prophecies:

> 4 Then the LORD said to Hosea, "Call him Jezreel, because I will soon punish the house of Jehu for the massacre at Jezreel, and I will put an end to the kingdom of Israel. 5 In that day I will break Israel's bow in the Valley of Jezreel." Hosea 1:4–5 (NIV84)
>
> 9 "For I will give the command, and I will shake the house of Israel among all the nations as grain is shaken in a sieve, and not a pebble will reach the ground. Amos 9:9 (NIV84)

The Kingdom of Judah

Rehoboam was the first king of Judah, ruling for 17 years before his son Abijah became king. Shown in Table 3-1 the kingdom of Judah also had some 20 kings over the nearly 350 years of its history. In many ways the Jews were like their brothers in the kingdom of Israel. Theirs were mostly bad kings who returned to idolatry again and again from the time of Solomon to their destruction in 586 BC.

The main difference is that 7 kings out of the 20 made at least some effort to return to Mt. Sinai Covenant status with God. One king, Josiah who reigned for 40 years, ordered repairs to the temple and the "book of the law"[73] – probably what we call the book of Deuteronomy – was found hidden in the walls of the temple. When the priest read the book to Josiah, he immediately re-instigated all of the laws and rituals from that book including the Passover, which had not been celebrated for several hundred years.

In general, however, the kingdom of Judah had some despicably bad kings who set up worship of Baal and Astarte in the temple itself, sacrificed their own children in the fires to Molech and slaughtered thousands of innocents in the streets of Jerusalem. Their kings were fickle; they allied with the kingdom of Israel, with

---

[73] Deuteronomy 31:24-26

Aram, with Egypt, with Moab, with Assyria and with Babylon at various times and went to war with all of them and many other nations surrounding them.

Judah was also given its warning of destruction by God through the prophets – Zephaniah, Micah, the prophetess Huldah, Jeremiah, Habakkuk, Nahum, Ezekiel. Isaiah, after warning the kingdom of Israel of its doom spent some time prophesying to Judah of its coming destruction because of those kings and the sins of the people of Judah.

Babylon had invaded Judah in 609 BC as allies with the Medes while conquering the remnants of the Assyrian Empire. They made Judah a vassal kingdom, carried off a few captives including one king and much treasure and placed their puppet Jewish king under their direct authority. Zedekiah agreed to this but soon rebelled against Babylon whereupon Nebuchadnezzar brought the full force of his siege engines and vast army against Jerusalem.

In 586 BC, Babylon razed Jerusalem and the temple to the ground, killed more than half the inhabitants, took all of the "ruling class" people and much of the rest of the population back to Babylon. Among those "nobles" who were spared and brought up in Nebuchadnezzar's court were Daniel and 3 of his peers who are known in the book bearing Daniel's name by their Babylonian names: Shadrach, Meshach and Abednego.

Jeremiah had prophesied that the Jews' exile in captivity would last 70 years and that proved a true prophecy. Jeremiah himself was spared and given letters of safety by Nebuchadnezzar who knew of Jeremiah's prophecies. Jeremiah and his scribe, Baruch, and at least two of King Zedekiah's daughters escaped the carnage and were headed for Egypt in the last account of them given in the scriptures.

Two Distinct Future Paths for the Unconditional Covenants

We can follow Judah all the way to Christ but the same cannot be said of Israel.

The books of Daniel, Ezra, Nehemiah, Haggai and Zechariah cover some portions of the inter-testament period; some apocryphal books cover the period from the destruction of Jerusalem and the temple to the time of Jesus of Nazareth. Nowhere in any of those books is there mention of the citizens of Israel who were deported by Assyria in 721 BC.

The name Ephraim is mentioned once in the New Testament – the name of a village [John 11:54]; Manasseh is mentioned once [Revelation 7:6] (the name in Matthew 1:10 is of a Jew); there is a prophetess from the tribe of Asher mentioned once [Luke 2:36]. 10 of Jacob's sons are mentioned in Revelation 7:5-8 along with Manasseh but instead of Ephraim the name Joseph appears and for some reason, Dan is omitted altogether.

Those deportees included the physical birthright holders – the tribes of Ephraim and Manasseh. They disappeared from the Bible and from secular history as well except for one brief mention in the writings of the Jewish historian Flavius Josephus writing under the auspices of the Roman government.

In Josephus' <u>Antiquities of the Jews Book XI, Chapter V</u>, he relates the Jewish leader Ezra's reading of a letter from Xerxes, the ruler of Persia, at a time when the Jews were about to be released from captivity and allowed to return to Jerusalem.

> So, he read the epistle at Babylon to those Jews that were there; but he kept the epistle itself and sent a copy of it to all those of his own nation that were in Media. And when these Jews had understood what piety the king had towards God, and what kindness he had for Esdras [this is Josephus' name for Ezra, to whom one of the books of the Old Testament is attributed], they were all greatly pleased; nay, many of them took their effects with them, and came to Babylon, as very desirous of going down to Jerusalem; but then the entire body of the people of Israel remained in that country; wherefore there are but two tribes in Asia and Europe subject to the Romans, while the ten tribes are beyond Euphrates till now, and are an immense multitude, and not to be estimated by numbers.

Josephus says it was the *"Jews"* in Medea who were "greatly pleased" and many of whom "took their effects with them, and came to Babylon, as very desirous of going down to Jerusalem". The distinction between the "Jews" and the "Israelites of the 10 tribes" explains why in Jesus' day, the only member of one of the ten tribes mentioned in all of the Gospels and the book of Acts is one "prophetess" from the tribe of Asher[74].

Saying that the "ten tribes" of Israelites were "beyond the Euphrates till now" indicates that in the last decades of the 1st Century AD when Josephus was writing, the Israelites were still identifiable in the Parthian Empire and not subject to the Roman Empire.

Though God had blessed the Israelites, brought them out of Egyptian captivity, had given them the 10 Commandments and the Law of Moses, had fed and protected them for 40 years in the deserts, had given them the Promised Land and brought them to the height of their power and wealth during the reign of Solomon, the

---

[74] Luke 2:36

physical birthright promises had not all been delivered. The promises *not delivered* are listed with their Biblical sources in the table below.

Covenant Promises	Sources
22.Their descendants to "possess the gates of their enemies"; become a "company of nations;" and nations would bow down to them	Gen 22:15–18; 24:60; 27:27–29; 35:11–12; 48:3–4
23 Ephraim and Manasseh would bear the name of Israel	Gen 48:5,6, 15,16
24 Manasseh would become a great nation	Gen 48:17–20; 49:22–26
25 Ephraim would be greater still and become a company of nations	Gen 48:17–20; 49:22–26

Judah remained captive for 70 years and many of the Jews returned to Palestine. The circumstances of that return clearly demonstrate the hand of God at work and the reason why the Jews were not dispersed among the nations at that time as were the people of Israel.

The prophecies of Daniel and other prophets offer some insight as to God's plans for the future of *all* the Israelites but the physical birthright holders have disappeared. How could God deliver on His *unconditional* promises if the recipients have disappeared? What plans did God have for the Israelites?

We have reached a significant point in our investigation of Israel's covenants with God. Moses' *conditional* covenant was continually broken over several centuries by both kingdoms. God's punishments finally culminated in the disappearance of the Israel tribes and captivity of the people of Judah.

We are at the crossroads where the Judah line still identifiable as a people and is headed in a direction where it will fulfill the spiritual promise. But the physical promise reserved for the birthright holders in the 10 Tribes seems untraceable since they are now unidentifiable as Israelites. How, we ask, is it possible to trace any fulfillment of the physical covenant promises to them?

To answer that question, we must go to the prophets and non-Biblical historical sources. Table 3.1 below gives a rough timetable relating prophets to the reign of Israel's and Judah's kings. This may be helpful as we cover some of the prophets in more depth in terms of their prophecies for the 10 tribes. Beginning in chapter 5 we must revert to secular history to look for clues.

Date	Judah	Israel	Prophet	Comment - Cite
930	Rehoboam	Jeroboam	Shemaiah Ahijah	Forbad Judah war with Israel Prophesied Jeroboam's destruction
909		Nadab		
908		Baasha	Jehu	Prophesied Baasha's destruction
913	Abijah			
910	Asa			
886		Elah		
885		Zimri/ Omri		
874		Ahab	Elijah	Elijah warned Ahab and Jezebel of their destruction
872	Jehoshaphat			
853	Jehoram	Ahaziah		Elijah predicted Ahaziah's destruction
852		Joram	Elisha	Elisha helped Joram defeat Moab
841	Ahaziah	Jehu		
841	Queen Athaliah			
835	Joash		Jonah	Joash repaired the temple and mostly did what was right in God's eyes
814		Jehoahaz		Israel was being oppressed by Aram and God let Jehoahaz defeat Aram
798		Jehoash		
796	Amaziah (Uzziah)			
793		Jeroboam II	Amos Hosea	Although maintaining idolatry,

				Jeroboam II restored the borders of the Kingdom of Israel
752		Zechariah/ Shallum Menahem		Assyria first attacked Israel during the reign of Menahem but was bribed and withdrew.
750	Jotham		Isaiah Micah	
742		Pekahiah/ Pekah		Pekah assassinated Pekahiah
735	Ahaz			Ahaz sacrificed his son to Baal and allied with Assyria against Israel and Aram
732		Hoshea		Hoshea allied with Egypt against Assyria. Assyria conquered Israel and deported many to the land of the Medes
723		Assyria		2 Kings 17:7–41
715	Hezekiah			Isaiah kept Hezekiah from surrendering to Assyria and promised deliverance. In one night, 185,000 Assyrians were killed in their sleep and the Assyrian Empire began to fall from that moment on – eventually being conquered by Babylon. Isaiah prophesied the eventual Babylon captivity.
696	Manasseh			Manasseh sacrificed his own son to Baal and slaughtered

				thousands of innocents. More prophecies of Babylonian captivity
642	Amon		Zephaniah	Amon was assassinated
640	Josiah		Huldah a prophetess who helped Josiah	Josiah found the book of the law during temple repairs and instigated reforms
612			Nahum	
609	Jehoahaz		Jeremiah	Judah became a vassal of Egypt
609	Jehoiakim		Habakkuk	Babylon invaded Israel, defeated Egypt and made Judah a vassal.
598	Jehoiachin			
597	Zedekiah			Zedekiah was a vassal to Nebuchadnezz ar but rebelled bringing on the final attack
593			Ezekiel	Those who were not killed in the Babylonian attack fled to Egypt
586	Babylon		Daniel	Included in those who fled to Egypt were Jeremiah and the daughters of Zedekiah

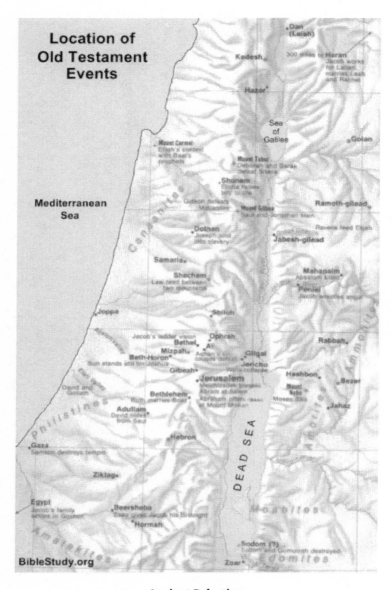

Ancient Palestine

* * *

CHAPTER 4

The Prophets

Moses was the first prophet recorded in the Bible. The Biblical prophets that are best known are those whose prophecies were collected into separate books bearing their names. By tradition, they are grouped together without regard to chronological order. Those whose writings were lengthy are called "major" prophets – a designation based solely on the length of their books – Isaiah, Jeremiah, Ezekiel and Daniel. The other prophets' books are much shorter and are called "minor" prophets. Other significant prophets can be found in the Biblical historical books but either they wrote nothing or their prophecies were not collected.

The great "age of the prophets" lasted less than two centuries – from the 8th Century to the Exile of the Jews to Babylon – and was dominated by Isaiah and Jeremiah. Warnings against idolatry and forgetting God's Covenants with Israel are found in Amos, Hosea, Nahum, Zephaniah and Habakkuk while Ezekiel's concern involved primarily the Exile and the "last days".

For our purpose, the most important prophet for tracing the Israel kingdom after dispersion is Daniel.

Prophets of Israel and Judah

The prophets who were active during the rule of the kings of Israel and Judah are identified in Table 3.1. Following the span of the reigns of the various kings is the only Biblical way to track the time elapsed and identifying the prophet who was active during the reign of a specific king helps put their prophecies in better perspective.

Israel had two highly significant prophets who did not have Bible books attributed to them. These are Elijah and Elisha, who are major historical characters covering 60 years in the 9th Century BC in the reigns of four Israel kings, Ahab, Ahaziah, Joram, and Jehu.

Though Elijah called the people of the ten tribes to repentance on Mount Carmel, reminded them of their Covenant with God, and helped rid them of the prophets of Baal and Astarte, it was only a temporary reprieve. Neither he nor Elisha provided significant prophecies regarding the covenant promises. However, two minor prophets, Amos and Hosea with Bible books bearing their names, are very significant in following the Lost Tribes' trail.

Israel Disappears into Assyria and is "sifted" into other Nations

By 720 BC, the Kingdom of Israel was no more; in 721 BC the holders of the physical birthright promised to Abraham, Isaac, Jacob and Joseph (Ephraim and Manasseh) were deported and dispersed among other nations. Assyria – their captor – brought people from other lands to inhabit the territory of the Kingdom of Israel.[57] In these scriptures, the kingdom is referred to as Samaria[58], its capitol.

> [5] Now the king of Assyria went throughout all the land and went up to Samaria and besieged it for three years. [6] In the ninth year of Hoshea, the king of Assyria took Samaria and carried Israel away to Assyria, and placed them in Halah and by the Habor, the River of Gozan, and in the cities of the Medes. 2 Kings 17:5–6 (NKJV)
>
> [24] Then the king of Assyria brought *people* from Babylon, Cuthah, Ava, Hamath, and from Sepharvaim, and placed *them* in the cities of Samaria instead of the children of Israel; and they took possession of Samaria and dwelt in its cities. 2 Kings 17:24 (NKJV)

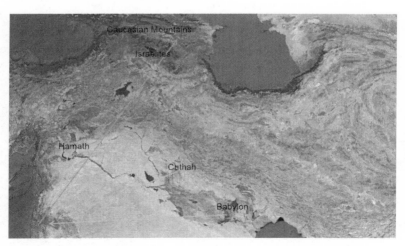

The cities of the Medes were located in today's Azerbaijan, eastern Turkey, Georgia, northern Iraq and Iran. In 94 AD, when Josephus said the Israelites were "beyond the Euphrates" in Medea[59], this is the area to which he referred. The last

88

250 miles along the orange line in the inset map were cities of Medea where the Israelites were relocated. The native people of that area were Indo-European peoples known as Aryans; the Israelites scattered among them just as God predicted.

> 16 So they left all the commandments of the LORD their God, made for themselves a molded image *and* two calves, made a wooden image and worshiped all the host of heaven, and served Baal. 17 And they caused their sons and daughters to pass through the fire, practiced witchcraft and soothsaying, and sold themselves to do evil in the sight of the LORD, to provoke Him to anger. 18 Therefore the LORD was very angry with Israel and removed them from His sight; there was none left but the tribe of Judah alone. 2 Kings 17:16–18 (NKJV)

Amos and Hosea were prophets during the reign of Jeroboam II at the beginning of the 8th Century BC. Amos stated how the people of the 10 tribes were literally to be sifted among the people of other nations.

> 8 "Behold, the eyes of the Lord GOD *are* on the sinful kingdom, And I will destroy it from the face of the earth; Yet I will not utterly destroy the house of Jacob," Says the LORD. 9 "For surely I will command, And will sift the house of Israel among all nations, As *grain* is sifted in a sieve; Yet not the smallest grain shall fall to the ground. Amos 9:8–9 (NKJV)

Hosea predicted the destruction of Israel.

> 13 But you have planted wickedness, you have reaped evil, you have eaten the fruit of deception. Because you have depended on your own strength and on your many warriors, 14 the roar of battle will rise against your people, so that all your fortresses will be devastated— as Shalman devastated Beth Arbel on the day of battle, when mothers were dashed to the ground with their children. 15 Thus will it happen to you, O Bethel[75], because your wickedness is great. When that day dawns, the king of Israel will be completely destroyed. Hosea 10:13–15 (NIV84)

Jeremiah's prophecy in the latter part of the 7th Century BC explained God's divorce from the "harlot," the Kingdom of Israel, and noted Judah's similar behavior:

> 6 The LORD said also to me in the days of Josiah the king: "Have you seen what backsliding Israel has done? She has gone up on every high mountain

---

[75] Bethel and Dan were the locations of the two golden calf gods set up by Jeroboam and retained by every king of Israel.

and under every green tree, and there played the harlot. 7 And I said, after she had done all these *things,* 'Return to Me.' But she did not return. And her treacherous sister Judah saw it. 8 Then I saw that for all the causes for which backsliding Israel had committed adultery, I had put her away and given her a certificate of divorce; yet her treacherous sister Judah did not fear, but went and played the harlot also. Jeremiah 3:6–8 (NKJV)

Although Hosea prophesied the destruction of the Kingdom of Israel by Assyria, and their long period away from God, He also offered hope for their future:

4 "I will heal their backsliding, I will love them freely, For My anger has turned away from him. 5 I will be like the dew to Israel; He shall grow like the lily, And lengthen his roots like Lebanon. 6 His branches shall spread; His beauty shall be like an olive tree, And his fragrance like Lebanon. 7 Those who dwell under his shadow shall return; They shall be revived *like* grain, And grow like a vine. Their scent *shall be* like the wine of Lebanon. 8 "Ephraim *shall say,* 'What have I to do anymore with idols?' I have heard and observed him. I *am* like a green cypress tree; Your fruit is found in Me." Hosea 14:4–8 (NKJV)

Jeremiah prophesied of Israel's eventual return to God; he also predicted the reunion of Judah and Israel at some glorious time in the future:

7 For thus says the LORD: "Sing with gladness for Jacob, And shout among the chief of the nations; Proclaim, give praise, and say, 'O LORD, save Your people, The remnant of Israel!' 8 Behold, I will bring them from the north country, And gather them from the ends of the earth, *Among* them the blind and the lame, The woman with child And the one who labors with child, together; A great throng shall return there. 9 They shall come with weeping, And with supplications I will lead them. I will cause them to walk by the rivers of waters, In a straight way in which they shall not stumble; For I am a Father to Israel, And Ephraim *is* My firstborn. Jeremiah 31:7–9 (NKJV)

27 "The days are coming," declares the LORD, "when I will plant the house of Israel and the house of Judah with the offspring of men and of animals. 28 Just as I watched over them to uproot and tear down, and to overthrow, destroy and bring disaster, so I will watch over them to build and to plant," declares the LORD. 29 "In those days people will no longer say, 'The fathers have eaten sour grapes, and the children's teeth are set on edge.' 30 Instead, everyone will die for his own sin; whoever eats sour grapes—his own teeth will be set on edge.

31 "The time is coming," declares the LORD, "when I will make a new covenant with the house of Israel and with the house of Judah. 32 It will not

be like the covenant I made with their forefathers when I took them by the hand to lead them out of Egypt, because they broke my covenant, though I was a husband to them," declares the LORD. 33 "This is the covenant I will make with the house of Israel after that time," declares the LORD. "I will put my law in their minds and write it on their hearts. I will be their God, and they will be my people. 34 No longer will a man teach his neighbor, or a man his brother, saying, 'Know the LORD,' because they will all know me, from the least of them to the greatest," declares the LORD. "For I will forgive their wickedness and will remember their sins no more." Jeremiah 31:27–34 (NIV84)

And finally, the prophet Zechariah called out the holders of the physical birthright to the fulfillment of their promise. Ephraim, who with Manasseh held the physical birthright, was promised that their descendants would be gathered together, redeemed and return to God.

> 7 *Those of* Ephraim shall be like a mighty man, And their heart shall rejoice as if with wine. Yes, their children shall see *it* and be glad; Their heart shall rejoice in the LORD. 8 I will whistle for them and gather them, For I will redeem them; And they shall increase as they once increased. 9 "I will sow them among the peoples, And they shall remember Me in far countries; They shall live, together with their children, And they shall return. Zechariah 10:7–9 (NKJV)

Although the 10-tribes of the Kingdom of Israel cannot be found in secular history and are virtually unmentioned in the New Testament scriptures, Old Testament prophecies make it clear that they are yet identifiable to God.

Later in this book we'll describe an unexpected finding that these Israelites were tasked with spreading the Gospel of Jesus – the always amazing hand of God at work.

The Kingdom of Judah

In Table 3.1, we see Judah had the Major Prophets Isaiah, Jeremiah, Ezekiel and Daniel and the Minor Prophets Jonah, Zephaniah, Nahum, Micah and Habakkuk. Shemaiah, Ahijah, and Jehu were prophets early in the Judah kingdom but did not make any significant prophecies bearing on our thesis.

In 586 BC, the Kingdom of Judah was no more.

> 19 Also Judah did not keep the commandments of the LORD their God, but walked in the statutes of Israel which they made. 20 And the LORD rejected all the descendants of Israel, afflicted them, and delivered them into the hand

of plunderers, until He had cast them from His sight. 2 Kings 17:19–20 (NKJV)

Almost all the inheritors of the spiritual birthright promised to Abraham, Isaac, Jacob and Judah were either killed or captured and exiled to Babylon:

> [15] And the LORD God of their fathers sent *warnings* to them by His messengers, rising up early and sending *them*, because He had compassion on His people and on His dwelling place. [16] But they mocked the messengers of God, despised His words, and scoffed at His prophets, until the wrath of the LORD arose against His people, till *there was* no remedy.
>
> [17] Therefore He brought against them the king of the Chaldeans, who killed their young men with the sword in the house of their sanctuary, and had no compassion on young man or virgin, on the aged or the weak; He gave *them* all into his hand. [18] And all the articles from the house of God, great and small, the treasures of the house of the LORD, and the treasures of the king and of his leaders, all *these* he took to Babylon. [19] Then they burned the house of God, broke down the wall of Jerusalem, burned all its palaces with fire, and destroyed all its precious possessions. [20] And those who escaped from the sword he carried away to Babylon, where they became servants to him and his sons until the rule of the kingdom of Persia, [21] to fulfill the word of the LORD by the mouth of Jeremiah, until the land had enjoyed her Sabbaths. As long as she lay desolate she kept Sabbath, to fulfill seventy years. 2 Chronicles 36:15–21 (NKJV)

Unlike their Israelite brothers from the 10 tribes, the Jews were not "sifted" among the nations[76]; they did not forget who they were; they did not forget the Covenant God made with Abraham, Isaac and Jacob; they did not forget the Covenant God made with the 12 tribes at Mt. Sinai. Instead they repented:

> [39] Why should any living man complain when punished for his sins? [40] Let us examine our ways and test them, and let us return to the LORD. [41] Let us lift up our hearts and our hands to God in heaven, and say: [42] "We have sinned and rebelled and you have not forgiven. Lamentations 3:39–42 (NIV84)

They longed to return to Jerusalem and the Promised Land; they gathered the scrolls that contained the stories of the patriarchs and the writings of Moses. They found scribes among the Levites who could copy and maintain those stories and the stories of Joshua, the Judges, Samuel, Ruth and the Psalms of David and others, the proverbs of Solomon and the wisdom of Ecclesiastes and Job as well as the stories and prophecies of God's prophets. The elders and priests helped them compose the

---

[76] Amos 9:8–9

books of I & II Samuel, I & II Kings, I & II Chronicles. For good measure they began to commit to writing the *oral history* of Israel which eventually became the Talmud[60].

They were devastated – they could not believe God would punish them so severely yet they had seen it with their own eyes and were forced to recognize that their lot had been of their own making. Eventually they came to *know* they deserved what had happened to them. They begged God for forgiveness and to allow them to return to their homeland.

God heard them but his prophets had warned them of their coming captivity over and again and even foretold how long that punishment would last – 70 years.

> [11] This whole country will become a desolate wasteland, and these nations will serve the king of Babylon seventy years. Jeremiah 25:11 (NIV84)

The Jews would remain a people and culture intact through the fall of three Empires and the rise of a fourth Empire around them[77]. It can be clearly shown that the hand of God was facilitating the *final* delivery of the spiritual birthright promise to Abraham, Isaac, Jacob and Judah. That birthright was personified in the Son of God, Jesus.

God expedited their return after the 70 years with their culture restored to near Mt. Sinai levels. Their future would encompass their return, their rebuilding Jerusalem and the temple and their repopulating the land of Canaan.

That future would provide the culture and the people appropriate for the arrival of the Messiah. The genetic bloodlines God put in place beginning with Abraham and Sarah would produce Miriam (Mary) at the perfect time to be the virgin mother of the Messiah.

The rise of the Roman Empire would provide an international infrastructure more sophisticated than any before in the history of the world – that infrastructure would expedite the exponential growth of the church the Messiah would found.

But at this time, the Jews were a broken people in exile and captivity on the banks of the Euphrates River not far from where Abraham was born.

> [1] By the rivers of Babylon we sat and wept when we remembered Zion. Psalm 137:1 (NIV84)

---

[77] Babylon, Medo-Persian and Greek/Macedonian Empires fell; the Roman Empire arose

Up to now any prophecies about future identification of the lost tribes are very general. They state that God shall have them return to Him, but do not provide any clues to the path the physical birthright inheritors have taken the past 2000 years. We find our most significant clue up to this point with the prophet Daniel.

We first learn of Daniel as a young prince, a captive of the army of Babylon, who was sent to King Nebuchadnezzar's court for training.

Daniel

In 609 BC, Jehoiakim became king of Judah. In 606 BC, King Nebuchadnezzar raided Judah and made it a vassal state to Babylon. Judah had been warned by the prophet Habakkuk and others that Babylon was going to attack but, as usual, they ignored the warning.

> 5 "Look at the nations and watch— and be utterly amazed. For I am going to do something in your days that you would not believe, even if you were told. 6 I am raising up the Babylonians, that ruthless and impetuous people, who sweep across the whole earth to seize dwelling places not their own. 7 They are a feared and dreaded people; they are a law to themselves and promote their own honor. Habakkuk 1:5–7 (NIV84)

Nebuchadnezzar looted some of the treasures in the temple and ordered one of his officials to select some of the royal family and some of the nobles to bring back to Babylon to be trained to be in service to his court. Among that nobility were young Daniel and three of his peers.

> 3 Then the king instructed Ashpenaz, the master of his eunuchs, to bring some of the children of Israel and some of the king's descendants and some of the nobles, 4 young men in whom *there was* no blemish, but good-looking, gifted in all wisdom, possessing knowledge and quick to understand, who *had* ability to serve in the king's palace, and whom they might teach the language and literature of the Chaldeans. 5 And the king appointed for them a daily provision of the king's delicacies and of the wine which he drank, and three years of training for them, so that at the end of *that time* they might serve before the king. 6 Now from among those of the sons of Judah were Daniel, Hananiah, Mishael, and Azariah. 7 To them the chief of the eunuchs gave names: he gave Daniel *the name* Belteshazzar; to Hananiah, Shadrach; to Mishael, Meshach; and to Azariah, Abed-Nego. Daniel 1:3–7 (NKJV)

They were given Chaldean names to further isolate them from their own culture and were treated to food from the king's own table. These very young men – boys actually – brought their culture with them; they refused to consume the food and drink that had been sacrificed or dedicated to idols and convinced their keeper of the efficacy of that diet by being the healthiest of all the young men around them. God blessed all four by helping them absorb the literature and language of Babylon during their three years training.

When the young men were questioned by Nebuchadnezzar, he was quite impressed:

> [18] At the end of the time set by the king to bring them in, the chief official presented them to Nebuchadnezzar. [19] The king talked with them, and he found none equal to Daniel, Hananiah, Mishael and Azariah; so they entered the king's service. Daniel 1:18–19 (NIV84)

In the second year of Daniel's service to Nebuchadnezzar's court, he interpreted a dream for the king that contained a prophecy that is vital for understanding the future of the people of the "lost ten tribes" of Israel. That prophecy – describing a giant statue made of 4 sections – lays the foundation for explaining the transition of the Israelites who were "sifted" among the people of the cities of Medea to their being among the people of Central and Western Europe who destroyed the Roman Empire. That transition will be covered in depth in later chapters of this book as the correlation of Daniel's prophecy to secular history and the future of the people of Israel is explored.

Nebuchadnezzar's dream, Daniel's interpretation of that dream and the ramifications of that dream are explored at length later in this chapter.

The interpretation of that dream led Nebuchadnezzar to place Daniel and his three friends in high positions in his government. They were so good at their jobs that they maintained their high station when Babylon fell and a new Empire arose to power. But even then, these upright Jewish young men were despised by the Babylonians who constantly sought their destruction. One such incident is the most well-known of the stories about Daniel.

In the lions' den

Those familiar with the Bible know at least some of the story of "Daniel in the Lions' Den". That story occurred after the Babylonian Empire had fallen to the forces of the Medo-Persian Empire. From the time they entered service to Babylon, Daniel and his three friends were resented by the native petty politicians, the mystic set – magicians, astrologers, seers – and the "wise men" who gathered at the seat of power.   That resentment entrapped them especially when they practiced their religion.

The Medean king Darius, appointed by the Persian Cyrus the Great to administer the Babylon province, was persuaded by these sycophants to issue a strict religious prohibition against praying to anyone other than Darius.   The penalty for anyone violating that order was to be thrown into a den of lions.

Daniel did not try to hide his religion.

> ¹⁰ Now when Daniel knew that the writing was signed, he went home. And in his upper room, with his windows open toward Jerusalem, he knelt down on his knees three times that day, and prayed and gave thanks before his God, as was his custom since early days. Daniel 6:10 (NKJV)

He was brought before Darius who realized he had been manipulated and tried to postpone the execution.   However, he was reminded by Daniel's accusers that by Medo-Persian law, decrees issued by a king could not be changed[61].

> ¹⁶ So the king gave the command, and they brought Daniel and cast *him* into the den of lions. *But* the king spoke, saying to Daniel, "Your God, whom you serve continually, He will deliver you." Daniel 6:16 (NKJV)

God did deliver Daniel and the next morning when Darius saw that Daniel was untouched through the night, he repaid Daniel's accusers for their treachery.

> ²⁴ And the king gave the command, and they brought those men who had accused Daniel, and they cast *them* into the den of lions—them, their children, and their wives; and the lions overpowered them, and broke all their bones in pieces before they ever came to the bottom of the den. Daniel 6:24 (NKJV)

Never again did anyone attempt to bring harm to Daniel as he helped rule the province[78].

Shadrach, Meshach and Abednego

When Nebuchadnezzar appointed Daniel and his three friends to high positions in his government, the "wise men" looked for a way to attack Daniel; they had to settle for entrapping his young friends.   The king had attempted to create the statue of the dream Daniel interpreted and declared that all must bow and worship that statue

---

[78] Daniel 6:28

with the punishment for failing to do so being "tossed in a fiery furnace". The wise men informed the king that the three Jews who were administrators over the home province refused to bow.

When they were brought before Nebuchadnezzar, when threatened with the sure death of the fiery furnace, these three young men gave one of the most powerful statements of faith recorded in the Bible:

> [16] Shadrach, Meshach and Abednego replied to the king, "O Nebuchadnezzar, we do not need to defend ourselves before you in this matter. [17] If we are thrown into the blazing furnace, the God we serve is able to save us from it, and he will rescue us from your hand, O king. [18] But even if he does not, we want you to know, O king, that we will not serve your gods or worship the image of gold you have set up." Daniel 3:16–18 (NIV84)

They were tied up and thrown into a furnace that was so hot it killed the soldiers who threw Shadrach, Meshach and Abednego into the flames. As he watched the supposed execution, Nebuchadnezzar then saw something that shocked him to his core.

> [24] Then King Nebuchadnezzar leaped to his feet in amazement and asked his advisers, "Weren't there three men that we tied up and threw into the fire?" They replied, "Certainly, O king." [25] He said, "Look! I see four men walking around in the fire, unbound and unharmed, and the fourth looks like a son of the gods." Daniel 3:24–25 (NIV84)

The king called to them and the three came out of the fire with no sign of having been burned at all – their hair was not singed; their garments were intact and there was even no smell of anything burned.

> [28] Then Nebuchadnezzar said, "Praise be to the God of Shadrach, Meshach and Abednego, who has sent his angel and rescued his servants! They trusted in him and defied the king's command and were willing to give up their lives rather than serve or worship any god except their own God. [29] Therefore I decree that the people of any nation or language who say anything against the God of Shadrach, Meshach and Abednego be cut into pieces and their houses be turned into piles of rubble, for no other god can save in this way." [30] Then the king promoted Shadrach, Meshach and Abednego in the province of Babylon. Daniel 3:28–30 (NIV84)

To trace Daniel's prophecies related to the future of the descendants of the physical birthright inheritors – the kingdom of Israel – Nebuchadnezzar's first dream interpreted by Daniel must be closely examined.

Nebuchadnezzar's Dream

In the second year of Daniels service to Nebuchadnezzar, the king had a dream that troubled him. He called his "wise men" and "seers" and asked them to interpret his dream. Nebuchadnezzar was obviously savvy and realized that if he told these charlatans the details of the dream they could "wing it" and offer various interpretations. Not only that – Nebuchadnezzar *could not remember the dream* but he knew it was important and troubling.

He insisted that they first tell him what he had dreamed and that way – by their knowing what he had dreamed – he could be sure that their explanation was accurate. When none of the "wise men" and "seers" of his court could describe the dream to him, he ordered them all executed – including Daniel and his friends.

When the executioner approached him, Daniel went before Nebuchadnezzar and asked for time so that he, Daniel, could interpret the dream. Daniel and his three friends prayed all that night asking God for help. During the night in a vision, God gave Daniel the dream and its interpretation. He then went before the king giving all the credit to God:

> The king asked Daniel (also called Belteshazzar), "Are you able to tell me what I saw in my dream and interpret it?"
>
> Daniel replied, "No wise man, enchanter, magician or diviner can explain to the king the mystery he has asked about, but there is a God in heaven who reveals mysteries. He has shown King Nebuchadnezzar what will happen in days to come. Your dream and the visions that passed through your mind as you lay on your bed are these:
>
> "As you were lying there, O king, your mind turned to things to come, and the revealer of mysteries showed you what is going to happen. As for me, this mystery has been revealed to me, not because I have greater wisdom than other living men, but so that you, O king, may know the interpretation and that you may understand what went through your mind.
>
> "You looked, O king, and there before you stood a large statue--an enormous, dazzling statue, awesome in appearance. The head of the statue was made of pure gold, its chest and arms of silver, its belly and thighs of bronze, its legs of iron, its feet partly of iron and partly of baked clay. While you were watching, a rock was cut out, but not by human hands. It struck the statue on its feet of iron and clay and smashed them. Then the iron, the clay, the bronze, the silver and the gold were broken to pieces at the same time and became like chaff on a threshing floor in the summer. The wind

swept them away without leaving a trace. But the rock that struck the statue became a huge mountain and filled the whole earth. NIV Daniel 2:26-35

Daniel's Interpretation

Daniel then gave Nebuchadnezzar God's explanation of the dream:

"This was the dream, and now we will interpret it to the king. You, O king, are the king of kings. The God of heaven has given you dominion and power and might and glory; in your hands he has placed mankind and the beasts of the field and the birds of the air. Wherever they live, he has made you ruler over them all. You are that head of gold.

"After you, another kingdom will rise, inferior to yours. Next, a third kingdom, one of bronze, will rule over the whole earth. Finally, there will be a fourth kingdom, strong as iron--for iron breaks and smashes everything--and as iron breaks things to pieces, so it will crush and break all the others. Just as you saw that the feet and toes were partly of baked clay and partly of iron, so this will be a divided kingdom; yet it will have some of the strength of iron in it, even as you saw iron mixed with clay. As the toes were partly iron and partly clay, so this kingdom will be partly strong and partly brittle. And just as you saw the iron mixed with baked clay, so the people will be a mixture and will not remain united, any more than iron mixes with clay.

"In the time of those kings, the God of heaven will set up a kingdom that will never be destroyed, nor will it be left to another people. It will crush all those kingdoms and bring them to an end, but it will itself endure forever. This is the meaning of the vision of the rock cut out of a mountain, but not by human hands--a rock that broke the iron, the bronze, the clay, the silver and the gold to pieces.

"The great God has shown the king what will take place in the future. The dream is true and the interpretation is trustworthy." NIV Daniel 2:36-45

Daniel told Nebuchadnezzar that he (Babylon) was the "head of gold". Who are the other three kingdoms represented in that statue? History shows that the Medo-Persian Empire conquered Babylon and the Persian Empire was in turn conquered by Alexander the Great and the Macedonian/Greek Empire, which was also, in turn, conquered by the Roman Empire[62].

The statue of Nebuchadnezzar's dream had a chest and two arms of silver that correspond well with the combined Empire of the Medes and Persians.

The Macedonian/Greek Empire of Alexander the Great is represented by the "belly and thighs"[63].

The rest of the body, the two legs and two feet and even the 10 toes[64], fits better metaphorically with the Roman Empire that split into two parts[65].

We conclude therefore: the four human kingdoms of Nebuchadnezzar's dream are Babylon, Medo-Persia, Greece and Rome.

But what can we say with any certainty about the enigmatic "stone" that destroyed the statue?

The Stone Kingdom

> [34] You watched while a stone was cut out without hands, which struck the image on its feet of iron and clay, and broke them in pieces. [35] Then the iron, the clay, the bronze, the silver, and the gold were crushed together, and became like chaff from the summer threshing floors; the wind carried them away so that no trace of them was found. And the stone that struck the image became a great mountain and filled the whole earth. Daniel 2:34–35 (NKJV)

From the 35th verse we understand that the fifth kingdom destroyed Rome, and that any trace of it and the three prior historical kingdoms is like "chaff" that "the wind carried away." Further the stone kingdom became so great that it filled the entire earth. We can also surmise that the stone kingdom arises around the 14th century A.D. before or a little after the complete destruction of Rome.

Where does that take us?

First, some questions need answered to set the scope of further investigation

- When was Rome completely destroyed and by whom?
- Is the stone kingdom physical also?
- What kingdom has become so great that it has filled the entire earth?
- What are important time line dates achieved from Daniels predictions?

Daniel described the "rock cut out of a mountain, but not by human hands" as being an empire that God would cause to be established that would "fill the whole world". Furthermore, it would destroy the Roman Empire and the remains of the previous empires and would appear – begin to grow – at the time of the last 10 kings of the Roman Empire.

44 And in the days of these kings the God of heaven will set up a kingdom which shall never be destroyed; and the kingdom shall not be left to other people; it shall break in pieces and consume all these kingdoms, and it shall stand forever. 45 Inasmuch as you saw that the stone was cut out of the mountain without hands, and that it broke in pieces the iron, the bronze, the clay, the silver, and the gold—the great God has made known to the king what will come to pass after this. The dream is certain, and its interpretation is sure." Daniel 2:44–45 (NKJV)

Some, such as Matthew Henry[66], have interpreted this fifth kingdom to be the church Jesus initiated through his disciples after his resurrection throughout the Acts Period. We can consider the church well established in the third and fourth decade of the First Century and began growing rapidly.

But if they mean more specifically the Roman Catholic Church there are serious problems with it fitting Daniel's prophecy. Certainly, the Roman Catholic Church has to some extent "filled the whole world," especially when one includes its Protestant daughters and all the other Christian churches who owe no allegiance to Rome. The church Jesus established is still standing, and arguably Jesus rules over its members. But that is as much as can be fitted to the conditions predicted.

For example, the Roman Empire was extant for more than 1,200 years after the time of Jesus, yet at no time did the Roman Catholic Church contain more than a small percentage of the world population. Besides, though Jesus rules in the hearts of Christians, and the Catholic Church has held some measure of political power, no one would claim the Catholic Church had anything to do with the overthrow of the Roman Empire. Moreover, the Bible clearly states that the Kingdom of God will not be fully established on this earth until the return of Jesus[79].

William MacDonald[67] suggests that Jesus, Himself is the stone cut out of the mountain and to the extent that Jesus holds all authority in heaven and earth that is true but this does not represent the reality of the destruction of the Roman Empire by human forces that showed little sign of being under the control of heavenly forces. Some of those human forces disintegrated within a few decades.

Still others, such as Hindson & Kroll[68] suggest that the kingdom established is the "spiritual Kingdom of God" and had no physical reality.

Jesus' statement that "all authority in heaven and in earth has been given to me"[80], is a statement that God, the Father had restored Him to His previous station[81] and

---

[79] Revelation 19:11–20:6; 1 Thessalonians 4:13–18
[80] Matthew 28:18

was no indication that Jesus had begun directly ruling over the physical kingdoms of this earth. The scope of history for the last 2,000 years does not indicate that Jesus has been or is presently ruling over any governments throughout that time.

The first four kingdoms were formed by the political machinations of men. The Stone Kingdom was "cut out of a mountain" by God.[69]

Just because the "stone was cut out of a mountain, but not by human hands" does not mean it must be a spiritual kingdom. God can establish things physical as well as spiritual.

All four of the earlier empires – Babylon, Medo-Persian, Greek and Roman – were physical empires. Is there any reason we should not think the fifth kingdom – the "Stone Kingdom" – is also a physical kingdom?

There are many instances in Bible prophecy where the term "mountain" is used to represent a nation or a people[82]. Since the Stone Kingdom was formed by God and "not by human hands", this simply means it is a kingdom unlike any planned and executed by men. If the stone kingdom is the recipient of Israel's physical covenants, then that is all the more reason this fifth kingdom must be physical, not spiritual.

The Stone Kingdom was to be set up "in the time of those kings" and the stone "struck the statue on its feet of iron and clay and smashed them". "Those kings" must refer to the last kings of the fourth kingdom – the Roman Empire – who ruled until the 1400's AD.

Figure 4.1

[81] John1:1, 2, 14
[82] Jeremiah 51:25; Ezekiel 17:22,23; Amos 4:1,6:1; Zechariah 4:7 et al

By the time of the last kings of Rome, the Stone Kingdom was to be established and eventually grow until it filled the entire earth. The Roman metaphor – the "iron" kingdom – is completed in the "ten toes". Daniel says the Stone Kingdom "struck the statue on its feet of iron and clay and smashed them."[83]

While there were many political subdivisions that changed from time to time, the Roman Empire was composed primarily of 10 major political divisions, each with its own "king"[70]. The Roman Empire map (Fig 4.1) illustrates this.

Over the years from the height of the Roman Empire until its final destruction in the 1400's, various "barbarian" armies continually attacked the Empire. These barbarians were known under various names as recorded by Roman and Greek historians. Huns, Ostrogoths and others eventually destroyed the Byzantine (Eastern Roman Empire) while the Arabic people decimated the Empire's holdings in Palestine and throughout North Africa eventually giving way the Ottoman Turk Empire.

Among those who attacked the Western Empire (Rome) out of Europe were the Scythians[84], Teutons[85], Cimbri[86], Saxons[87], Celts[88], various Germanic tribes, the

---

[83] **Daniel 2:34**

[84] Colossians 3:11

[85] A member of an ancient probably Germanic or Celtic people – *Merriam-Webster's Collegiate Dictionary*

Goths, the Ostrogoths and others, all of whose ancestry can be traced in some way to the Indo-Europeans who originated from the Caucasian Mountain area described as the land of Medea – today's Azerbaijan, Armenia, Georgia, northwestern Iran, northern Iraq and eastern Turkey.

There are numerous historians[89] who trace the origins of these people to the very areas north of Mesopotamia where the captured Israelites of the Kingdom of Israel and a few from the Kingdom of Judah were relocated by the Assyrian Empire in 721 B.C. This is the area called "beyond the Euphrates" by Josephus late in the first Century AD.

These people were a major part of the forces that destroyed the Roman Empire including the "ten toes" that were the last kings of that Empire. The time span of those four empires prophesied in the second chapter of Daniel lasts until the 1400's A.D. [71]

> While you were watching, a rock was cut out, but not by human hands. It struck the statue on its feet of iron and clay and smashed them. Then the iron, the clay, the bronze, the silver and the gold were broken to pieces at the same time and became like chaff on a threshing floor in the summer. The wind swept them away without leaving a trace. But the rock that struck the statue became a huge mountain and filled the whole earth. NIV Daniel 2:34-35

Another prophecy – from the New Testament – supports this suggested time frame.

The apostle John writing from the Isle of Patmos included an enigmatic[72] prophecy in the 12th chapter of the New Testament book of Revelation promising the children of Israel a "place of safety" over the next 1,260 years:

> [1] A great and wondrous sign appeared in heaven: a woman clothed with the sun, with the moon under her feet and a crown of twelve stars on her head. [2] She was pregnant and cried out in pain as she was about to give birth. [3] Then another sign appeared in heaven: an enormous red dragon with

---

[86] Gomer – The eldest son of Japheth, Gen. 10:2, 3, the progenitor of the early Cimmerians, of the later Cimbri and the other branches of the Celtic family, and of the modern Gael and Cymri. *Smith's Bible Dictionary*

[87] A member of a Germanic people that entered and conquered England with the Angles and Jutes in the fifth century A.D. and merged with them to form the Anglo-Saxon people – *Merriam-Webster's Collegiate Dictionary*

[88] A member of a division of the early Indo-European peoples distributed from the British Isles and Spain to Asia Minor – *Merriam-Webster's Collegiate Dictionary*

[89] To be cited at length in Chapter 5

seven heads and ten horns and seven crowns on his heads. 4 His tail swept a third of the stars out of the sky and flung them to the earth. The dragon stood in front of the woman who was about to give birth, so that he might devour her child the moment it was born. 5 She gave birth to a son, a male child, who will rule all the nations with an iron scepter. And her child was snatched up to God and to his throne. 6 The woman fled into the desert to a place prepared for her by God, where she might be taken care of for 1,260 days. Revelation 12:1–6 (NIV84)

The woman is Israel; the son is Jesus; the dragon is Satan.[90] After a war in heaven, Satan was cast out taking one-third of the angels with him. This was good news because the "accuser of the brethren"[91] had been cast down. This was bad news for the earth because Satan and those angels were cast down to the earth and Satan was angry and looking for revenge.[92]

13 When the dragon saw that he had been hurled to the earth, he pursued the woman who had given birth to the male child. 14 The woman was given the two wings of a great eagle, so that she might fly to the place prepared for her in the desert, where she would be taken care of for a time, times and half a time, out of the serpent's reach. 15 Then from his mouth the serpent spewed water like a river, to overtake the woman and sweep her away with the torrent. 16 But the earth helped the woman by opening its mouth and swallowing the river that the dragon had spewed out of his mouth. 17 Then the dragon was enraged at the woman and went off to make war against the rest of her offspring—those who obey God's commandments and hold to the testimony of Jesus. Revelation 12:13–17 (NIV84)

Though only a small portion of the Jews accepted Jesus, they escaped to neighboring countries avoiding their destruction in Jerusalem[73]. They spread all over central and western Europe so that all the European countries had (and still have) a sizable contingent of Jews. In Western Europe and the British Isles, the Jewish and Gentile Christians were freed from the persecution of the Roman Empire. Their "invisible"[93] brothers and sisters – now sifted among the nations – shared that protection and we'll show later that those Israelites were the real impetus for the exponential growth of the church in the first three centuries AD.

In 94 AD Josephus wrote that large numbers of Israelites from the Kingdom of Israel were "beyond the Euphrates" and were not under the control of the Roman

---

[90] Who made use of King Herod in the attempt to kill Jesus [Matthew 2:1–12]

[91] Job 1:11; 2:5; Zechariah 3:1; Luke 22:31

[92] Revelation 12:7–12

[93] Amos 9:8–9

Empire. The scriptures say those Israelites deported from their homeland were "placed in the cities of the Medes". [94]

The woman from Revelation 12 represents the descendants of the 12 tribes – not just the Jews – Israelites who were brought out of Egyptian slavery "on the wings of an eagle"[74]. Rather than being pursued by the Egyptian Army, the Jewish and Gentile followers of Christ and the Israelites were avoiding the army of the Roman Empire. We'll learn later that for many years the people of the 10 tribes were sheltered in the Parthian Empire – beyond the Euphrates.

The "woman" of Revelation was to be safe and nourished for 1,260[75] years.

The Israelites and Jews and their Christian brethren were given the "wings of a great eagle" to fly to a place of safety prepared by God in the desert or wilderness. Where would they would be safe from the Roman Army for 1,260 years[95]?

The eagle's wings were given to God's people who "obey God's commandments and hold to the testimony of Jesus." The Christian Jews qualify of course but so do all the "Gentiles" who converted to Christianity since Paul refers to them as "spiritual Israel"[96]. The Israelites in the Parthian Empire made new converts as they spread over northern and Western Europe. There they were in "uncivilized" territory (wilderness) but safe from the Roman Army.[76]

So up to this point we can confidently determine who the four kingdoms in Daniels prophecy were, that the last one was the Roman Empire and that it was finally destroyed in 1453 AD. We cannot have the same confidence that the "Stone Kingdom" is physical rather than spiritual, but at the same time cannot find any evidence of a "spiritual kingdom" "filling the entire world" or having anything to do with the destruction of the Roman Empire up to and around 1400 AD.

At this point Daniel is one of "four witnesses" who bring us to the 1400 – 1800 AD period
God's unconditional prophecy of political and economic hegemony for Ephraim and Manasseh's descendants that was not delivered prior to this time
The "7 – times" punishment of 2,520 years prophesied in Leviticus chapter 26 resulting in the destruction of the kingdom of Israel in 721 BC with a delay of 2,520 years for the delivery of that economic and political hegemony no sooner than ~1800 AD
Daniel's chapter2 prophecy of the rise of the Stone Kingdom after the destruction of the Roman Empire which occurred no later than May 1453
John's prophecy of a place of safety for the Israelites and Christians was to last 1,260 years from sometime in the 1st Century. That would be no later than 1350 (assuming John wrote the book of

---

[94] 2 Kings 17:5–6
[95] Revelation 12:6; 12:14
[96] Galatians 3:26–29

Revelation in 90 AD) by which time the Roman Empire was in the last stages of destruction and the fledgling Stone Kingdom was able to defend itself.

Can we also conclude anything about a possible physical kingdom that began growing in 1400 AD that has become so great it has filled the entire earth?

Locating the Stone Kingdom

The 14th Century AD is considered the beginning of the rise of Western Civilization.

> Europe experienced the Renaissance from the 14th to the 17th century, heralding an age of technological and artistic advance and ushering in the "Age of Discovery" which saw the rise of such global European Empires as those of Spain, Portugal and Britain. The Industrial Revolution began in Britain in the 18th century. Under the influence of the Enlightenment, the Age of Revolution emerged from the United States and France as part of the transformation of the West into its industrialized, democratized modern form. The lands of North and South America, South Africa, Australia and New Zealand became first part of European Empires and then home to new Western nations, while Africa and Asia were largely carved up between Western powers[77].

The people who destroyed the Roman Empire, among whom were many people whose ancestors came from the area called Medea in the Bible, are the people who helped form the nations of Western Europe: Norway, Sweden, Denmark, Germany, Netherlands, Belgium, Switzerland, France, Spain and Portugal.

One must include England, Ireland, Scotland and Wales among those nations that we call today Western Civilization. Several other nations – Spain, Italy, Holland, France – formed "empires" but Great Britain was the progenitor of the most powerful nations in Western Civilization worldwide – the United States of course and the "commonwealth" nations of Canada, Australia and New Zealand. The British Empire included South Africa and India for many years and the British influence remains to be seen in those nations today.

If the "ten lost tribes" were "sifted" among those nations, perhaps the delivery of the Covenant physical birthright to those who held the birthright – Ephraim and Manasseh – has been made. If so we need to identify the people who received that birthright blessing.

4,000 years ago, God promised unconditionally "all the world would be blessed" because of the Covenant He made with Abraham. The spiritual part of that promise was completed with the birth, life, death and resurrection of Jesus of Nazareth, His establishing His church and installing a New Covenant that included not only Israel but every nation, every race and every individual human on this earth. However, many parts of the world received no blessing at all from the teaching of Jesus because He was not known to them.

It was not until the rise of the British Empire and the United States that missionaries spreading the gospel of Jesus reached most of the "common people" of this planet. The Catholic Church through Spain and Italy did spread the gospel in their brief stints as world powers but their efforts were more focused on the government level rather than the approach of the English-speaking missionaries in reaching the common people.

The physical Covenant blessings were delayed 2,520 years because Israel broke the conditional covenant made with God at Mt. Sinai and warranted the "7-times" punishment described in Leviticus chapter 26. From the destruction of Israel in 720 BC to 1800 AD is 2,520 years. This concept – "a day for a year" – was discussed at length in chapter two. This same concept appears in John's prophecy recorded in Revelation chapter 12 as described above – time, times and half-a-time = 360 days per year multiplied by 3 plus 180 days = 1260 years.

These parts of the physical Covenant promises were never delivered in Biblical times:

Covenant Promises	Sources
22. Their descendants to "possess the gates of their enemies"; become a "company of nations;" and nations would bow down to them	Gen 22:15–18; 24:60; 27:27–29; 35:11–12; 48:3–4
23 Ephraim and Manasseh would bear the name of Israel	Gen 48:5,6, 15,16
24 Manasseh would become a great nation	Gen 48:17–20; 49:22–26
25 Ephraim would be greater still and become a company of nations	Gen 48:17–20; 49:22–26

How would we know if the physical covenant promises have finally been delivered?

The political and economic hegemony promises are spectacular: "possessing the gates of their enemies" coupled with "nations bowing down to them" implies political and economic control without the necessity of warfare and conquering and perhaps includes the provision of benevolent benefits to the people of those nations; Ephraim's promise of becoming a "company of nations" suggests several countries sharing political and cultural ethos and goals and a common, mutually agreed upon form of government; the kinship of brothers Ephraim and Manasseh implies the commonwealth of Ephraim and the "great nation" of Manasseh sharing at least some common ethos and culture but perhaps maintaining different forms of government.

When these similar political and economic characteristics are added to the enormous wealth and power promised in the Covenant God made with the patriarchs that were part of the physical birthright, the beneficiaries of these blessings may well be obvious when one observes world history from the 7th Century BC to the present specifically looking for their delivery.

Factors

1. Daniel's prophecy covers the succession of empires through the Roman Empire to the 1400's
2. The secular trail – Babylon, Medo-Persian, Greek and Roman empires – ends in the 1400's
3. Western Civilization began to be formed in 1400; Great Britain, the British Commonwealth and the United States rose to power and prominence 400 years later
4. DNA studies would not be definitive for Israelites "sifted" among many nations but if the promised blessings for the Israelites are delivered, their presence in the most blessed countries would be indicated
5. Blessings of enormous wealth, economic and political power should be obvious
6. The Bible shows God's "default" position on human government is one of relative freedom for citizens thereof – look for at least partially democratic governments
7. The blessings promised were to be a blessing to the whole world
8. If the blessings can be identified by nations and countries, those holding the physical Covenant birthright will be found "sifted" among the citizens of those countries

3-4-6-7-8

Since the 1500's, from where have almost all the great advances in the things that make life better for the "average man" come? From where have the great advances in agriculture, medicine, transportation, clothing, housing, and the other every day needs of the "common man" come?

How is it that the average lifespan of all of humanity has more than doubled in the past 400 years? From where came the knowledge and techniques to eradicate or at least treat most of the diseases that were a sure death sentence in the 1500's?

Which was the first country to eliminate and outlaw slavery? Which nation and "company of nations" spread the "common law" of Western Civilization (based on Bible principles) throughout the world? Which nation has become the greatest exporter of Christian "missionaries" to the world?

Which nation and "company of nations" set up the principles of private property coupled with a banking system that allows free trade throughout the world and placed the accumulation of personal wealth within reach of the "common man"?

Which nation and "company of nations" defeated the Axis powers in World War II thereby stopping the extermination of not only the Jews but also dozens of other peoples considered "inferior races" by the Axis powers?

Which powerful nations are the first on the scene with aid wherever natural disasters strike throughout the world, thereby forestalling the many diseases that usually follow in the aftermath of those disasters?

Which nation and "company of nations" have literally taught millions throughout the world to improve their agricultural techniques and supplied food for starving populations during drought and other famine conditions? Which nation and "company of nations" advocate freedom for the "common man" throughout the world?

All the people of the world have been greatly blessed by the advances of Western Civilization and especially the benevolent hegemony of that nation and "company of nations" beginning with the British Empire and continuing currently with the world's only "superpower" – the United States.

3-5-8

The "company of nations" – the British Commonwealth nations – beginning in the 18th Century – became the most geographically extensive empire in world history and were for a time the foremost global power, superseded only by the United States after World War II with the nation and "company of nations" remaining the closest of allies.

The British Empire literally controlled the "gates of their enemies" – the British dominated the sea-lanes of the world and no one could travel far without passing through one of the land or sea "gates" controlled by the British[78]. Even today, no country and few people are long without some influence of Western Civilization, dominated by Britain and the United States.

Along with the other promises, the final four promises made by God to Abraham arguably have been fulfilled by Great Britain, the United States and Western Civilization.

We can therefore say without reservation that *to this date and time*, only the US, the Commonwealth of Great Britain and – to a lesser extent the other nations of Western Civilization – have reaped benefits very much like those promised to Abraham's descendants. Because those benefits have been shared with every nation across this globe, *all the people of the world have been truly blessed just as God promised.*

4-5-6-8

This is all that can be gleaned from prophecy and for that matter scripture, itself, in tracing the lost tribes. We have strong evidence for tracking the Israelites to Medea and for picking them up again in Western Europe around 1500 AD. We then see the bulk of the Covenant promises completed by the 1800s. Tracing the Israelites from Medea to Western Europe, the Commonwealth of Great Britain and the United States will rely solely on secular history. We will take that up in the next Chapter.

* * *

PART II
ISRAEL'S SECULAR
TRAIL

CHAPTER 5

The First Scattering

Assyria to the end of the Parthian Empire (721 BC – 271 AD)

In His Covenant with Abraham, God promised Abraham's descendants would become a nation and a "company of nations" with political and economic hegemony – "possessing the gates of their enemies" and having "nations bow down to them". The promise was inherited by Abraham's son Isaac and Isaac's son Jacob – whose name was changed to Israel. The promise was bequeathed by Jacob specifically to his son Joseph's two sons – his "adopted" grandsons Ephraim and Manasseh making them 2 of the 12 tribes of Israel[97].

The promise was not delivered by the time Israel was destroyed in 721 BC. In chapter two, we cited the prophecy and explained the timeline of the 7-times punishment – the 2,520 years before delivering the Covenant blessings. That timeline began in 721 BC with the Israelites exported to the cities of the Medes.

In that destruction and deportation, Ephraim and Manasseh's descendants disappeared from the Bible and from clear identification in secular history. To locate and follow the trail requires special methodology.

Criteria for Detecting Israel's Secular Trail

We have developed criteria useful in tracing the secular trail of the 10 tribes. The criteria consist of 5 factors which when documented offer strong evidence of Israel's presence and influence.

> **1 The G Factor**
> Specific **G**eographical points where either historical documentation indicates Israel's presence or clear analysis provides high likelihood of

---

[97] There was no tribe of Joseph; Levi, the tribe of priests, had no inheritance and were not counted among the 12

Israel's presence in the area. People (like Medes) are inherent in the geographical location (like Medea).

> **2 The P Factor**
>
>   Critical **P**ersons who had a special effect on Israelites environment by bringing in some semblance of Israel's God centered culture and morality.

> **3 The A Factor**
>
>   Specific **A**rcheological or written documents that give some evidence of Israel's presence at specific geographical points within certain time periods.

> **4. The M Factor**
>
>   The **M**igration pressures caused by wars and conquests resulting in the movement of the Israelites and at least some blending of bloodlines and ancestry into the resultant peoples of specific geographical areas

> **5. The T Factor**
>
>   **T**echnology, government and/or cultural advances that correspond in time with the likely presence of Israel suggesting the advances being influenced by Israel.

In addition to the 5 secular factors, the factor of Old Testament Prophecy is utilized, particularly in helping establish time periods for special events.

These Trail Detecting Criteria can now be applied to the locations where we suspect Israel passed through and had a noticeable influence on nations, kingdoms, and Empires. This chapter begins the trail in Assyria in the 8th century BC and completes the first major leg of their long path to Central Europe at the end of the 6th century AD.

Two points in the trail have strong documented evidence of the 10 tribes' presence both geographically and historically. The first, of course, is Assyria in 721 BC while the second is 7½ centuries later in Medea and surrounding areas.

Assyria and Medea

We will tie down these two geographical points first with the strongest evidence available then back them up with the secondary evidence found. The secondary evidence will also help fill in critical historical and geographical points between 721 BC and 94 AD.

Primary Evidence

The starting point (G1) for the secular path of Israel is 721 BC in Assyria.

The destruction of the Kingdom of Israel and the deportation of its residents by the Assyrian Empire in 721 BC is described in some detail in the Bible. Israel's destruction and the deportation have also been confirmed by archeologists[79] who deciphered the stone tablets in the great library found in the ruins of Nineveh (A1), capital of the Assyrian Empire.[80]

This was not the first Assyrian deportation experienced by the Israelites. In 740 – 730, Assyria attacked outer provinces of the Kingdom during the reign of King Pekah and took many captives including the entire tribe of Naphtali and deported them.

> [29] In the time of Pekah king of Israel, Tiglath-Pileser king of Assyria came and took Ijon, Abel Beth Maacah, Janoah, Kedesh and Hazor. He took Gilead and Galilee, including all the land of Naphtali, and deported the people to Assyria. 2 Kings 15:29 (NIV84)

One successor to king Tiglath-Pileser[81] claims to have deported over 27,290 captives from the siege in 721 BC. Another successor – Sennacherib – claims that their total forays which included those outlying sections of Israel produced more than 200,000 captive Israelites.[82]

Whatever the exact numbers of the deportees, many thousands of Israelites were settled in the cities of Medea in the years following 721 BC[83]. (M1)

The other *trusted* geographical/historical point for the 10 tribes is in Medea and surrounding areas in 94 AD. It comes from Josephus' _Antiquities of the Jews_.[98] Josephus relates the content of a letter from Xerxes – ruler of Persia and son of Darius – given to the Jewish leader Ezra which he sent to the Israelites in Medea.

The Persian king Cyrus had issued a decree that the Jews should be allowed to return to Jerusalem and rebuild the city and the temple. The letter was lost for some time – both Cyrus and Darius had died – but found by Xerxes in the Persian library at Ecbatana, the capital of Medea. By Medean and Persian law, Xerxes was bound to carry out the decrees of previous kings. This letter resulted in the Jews' release from captivity and their being encouraged to return to Jerusalem with the Persian Empire supplying money and protection.

> So, he read the epistle at Babylon to those Jews that were there; but he kept the epistle itself, and sent a copy of it to all **those of his own nation that**

---

[98] _Book XI, Chapter V, 131 – 133_

were in Media. And when these **Jews** had understood what piety the king had towards God, and what kindness he had for Esdras[99] they were all greatly pleased; nay, many of them took their effects with them, and came to Babylon, as very desirous of going down to Jerusalem; *but then the entire body of the people of Israel remained in that country; wherefore there are but two tribes in Asia and Europe subject to the Romans, while the ten tribes are beyond Euphrates till now, and are an immense multitude, and not to be estimated by numbers.* (G2)

The phrase "ten tribes are beyond Euphrates" gives the critical location of the 10 tribes; "till now" would mean the time Josephus was writing *Antiquities* – approximately 94 AD.[100]

Beyond the Euphrates would have included the modern regions of Azerbaijan, Armenia, Georgia, Kurdistan, Iran, Iraq and Eastern Turkey – all controlled in the 1st Century AD by the Parthian Empire. When the Jews of Medea left for Babylon to join the Jewish exiles returning to Palestine, the Israelites of the 10 tribes remained in that area which was not subject to Roman rule.

Josephus gives us three pieces of information that are important in following Israel's trail. First, the 10 tribes were still recognizable; they had not been fully integrated with the Medes and Persians. Second, they were clustered in one large area "beyond the Euphrates". And third, their numbers were immense, so immense that their numbers could not be estimated.

Since Josephus was a first-rate historian we can rely on his statement the 10 tribes were clustered in one general area, were still distinguishable in 94 AD, and were immense in size. It is certainly anyone's guess to how large Israel was in the first century AD, but an estimate of more than 500,000 "beyond the Euphrates" would not be unreasonable.

The Israelites' presence in such large numbers must have had considerable effect on the Medeans, the Babylonians, the Persians and the other peoples who inhabited the great expanse of lands "beyond the Euphrates". There were there half-a-million Israelites in Medea and environs and perhaps other hundreds of thousands were likely spread over the vast territory of the Parthian Empire.

If it seems strange that there is no extant documentation of the Israelites in the secular history of the Medes, Babylonians or Persians of that time, that can be

---

[99] This is Josephus' name for Ezra, to whom one of the books of the Old Testament is attributed

[100] https://en.wikipedia.org/wiki/Josephus

attributed to the bias of the Greek and Roman historians from that era. They were focused on the Roman Empire and Greek culture so the origin and ancestry of the "barbarians" east of the Empire were of little importance except when they affected the Roman Empire.

Secondary Evidence

Returning to the Assyrian period, we can start to fill in the missing years of Israel with other clues for identifying their presence.

It was a common practice of the Assyrians to deport captives far away from their homeland in other countries and to bring captives from other conquered areas to replace them. At the time of their deportation, Assyria controlled the territory of Medea. The Kingdom of Israel homeland was in ruins and a large portion of their population slaughtered. Those taken captive were deported to the cities of Medea.

Assyria itself was soon to decline and fall.[84] However, over several decades the Medes' conflict with Assyria had decimated their population. This was all the more reason for Assyria to relocate the Israelites among the cities of Media – it helped restore the population.

> Tiglath-Pileser III, in his campaigns, which extended from Ararat (Urartu) to the mountains south of the Caspian Sea, subdued the Medes. Annexing Media to Assyria, he deported 65,000 of its population, whom he replaced with inhabitants of other countries.[101]

With the approval of Babylon's king Nabopolassar, the Medes (perhaps with Israelites in the ranks of the Medean Army seeking revenge) under king Cyaxares, besieged Nineveh, turned the city to rubble and secured the end of the Assyrian Empire in 625 B.C.[85]

Babylon and Medea then divided the Assyrian provinces among themselves, with the Medeans taking over a large part of the countries including those we call Georgia, Azerbaijan, Iran, Syria, and Armenia. Nabopolassar's son, Nebuchadnezzar, married Cyaxares' daughter, securing the bond between the two countries. During the era of Babylonian king Nebuchadnezzar and the time of Jeremiah the prophet (about 605–552 B.C.), the Medean kingdom reached its peak of domination.

Medea (625 – 552 BC)

---

[101] http://www.jewishvirtuallibrary.org/medes-and-media

Medea (G3) is the second key reference point in the path taken by Israel after being conquered by Assyria. It was to the "cities of the Medes" to which the 10 tribes of the kingdom of Israel were deported.

> [5] The king of Assyria invaded the entire land, marched against Samaria and laid siege to it for three years. [6] In the ninth year of Hoshea, the king of Assyria captured Samaria and deported the Israelites to Assyria. He settled them in Halah, in Gozan on the Habor River and in the towns of the Medes. 2 Kings 17:5–6 (NIV84)[86]

The first historical mention of Media is recorded in the texts of the Assyrian king Shalmaneser III (858–824 BC). In those texts, the people are known as those of the land of "Mada". The inhabitants were the Medes.[87]

Deioces

> [8] "Surely the eyes of the Sovereign LORD are on the sinful kingdom. I will destroy it from the face of the earth— yet I will not totally destroy the house of Jacob," declares the LORD. [9] "For I will give the command, and I will shake the house of Israel among all the nations as grain is shaken in a sieve, and not a pebble will reach the ground. Amos 9:8–9 (NIV84)

The Lord declared, "I will not totally destroy the house of Jacob" and "not a pebble will reach the ground"[102]. In chapter two, we cited the prophecy and explained the prophesied 7-times punishment of Israel – the 2,520 years before the physical Covenant blessings would be delivered. That timeline began in 721 BC with the Israelites exported to the cities of the Medes.

However, the Lord declared, "I will not totally destroy the house of Jacob" and "not a pebble will reach the ground". One of those "pebbles" *may* have been essential in uniting the Medes.

The "pebble's" name was Deioces.

According to Eusebius[103], Herodotus[104] and Ctesias[105], the people of Medea were united under strange circumstances by **Deioces** (P1), son of Phraortes[88]. Of no

---

[102] Amos 9:8–9
[103] Bishop of Caesarea (in Palestine) about 313 AD
[104] Greek historian 484 - 420 BC

military fame and without any unusual physical strength or appearance, Deioces rose to power on the strength of his character.

Based on Herodotus's writings, Deioces was the first Median king to have gained independence from the Assyrians. He contemplated the project and plan of forming a single Median government; and in an anarchistic era in the Medes, he tried to enforce justice in his own village and earned a credibility and fame as a neutral judge Thus, the territory of his activity was expanded and the peoples of other villages also resorted to him.

However, he eventually announced that the judgments were too troublesome for him and he was not willing to continue working. Following this resignation, theft and chaos increased and the Medians gathered and chose him as the king this time.[106]

There is some archeological data that suggests Deioces may have been an Israelite:

The cuneiform library of Ninevah mentions a "local Zagros king"[89] as one of the captives deported to Medea by Sargon II. That king is called Dāiukku in the cuneiform text. Deioces' name has been mentioned in various forms in different sources.

Herodotus stated his name as Dēiokēs Δηιόκης; in Assyrian texts, he was mentioned as Da-a-a-uk-ku and in Elamite ones, as Da-a-hi-ú-uk-ka and Da-a-ya-uk-ka. Deioces' name is derived from the Iranian word, Dahyu-ka, and is the junior noun of the word dahyu, meaning "the land". [107]

The historians relate that his fame spread to all Medea and soon Deioces was elected king of Medea. His followers built a most imposing capital for him called Ecbatana (modern Hamadan). After he became king he began ruling by issuing written declarations rather than meeting face to face those who came to him for judgments. This tradition developed under Deioces lasted for many generations – all the way through the rise and fall of the Medo-Persian Empire.[90]

Deioces held a ceremony for the first time; Herodotus states that Deioces stayed in his palace and his connection was by sending to and receiving messages from the outside. No one was able to contact the king directly and the petitions and messages were performed only by the messengers. This limitation was intended to arouse a

---

[105] Greek physician and historian circa 415 – 380 BC. In the court of Artaxerxes II Mnemon who wrote history of Persia & Medea

[106] https://www.turkaramamotoru.com/en/deioces-707451.html

[107] https://www.turkaramamotoru.com/en/deioces-707451.html (Encyclopædia Iranica)

sense of fear and respect among the people. It was forbidden to laugh or expectorate in the king's presence.

One of his other actions was creating a group called "The King's Eyes and Ears", which consisted of people assigned to spy for the king himself. This type of organization was maintained through the Achaemenid era[108] and used often in the later Parthian Empire.

All of the most important decisions affecting important people or the whole kingdom or a large portion of their kingdom were made by written edict. These were considered to be sacred by their government and were relatively rare. One reason was that once an edict was issued by the king it could *never* be rescinded even by the king who issued the edict.[91]

Even if it were his grandson who truly united Medea, it is Deioces who is credited with setting up the government system that became the standard for the Medes (T1).

When the Persians conquered Medea, they made the Medes "junior" partners but definitely treated them with respect. Their strong presence in the government of the Persian Empire is indicated in that, throughout its tenure, the empire was known as the "Medo-Persian" Empire. Among those standards were the rules for "decrees" issued by Medo-Persian kings – decrees issued by the king could *never* be rescinded[92], not even by the king himself.

7th century writing discovery

No Medean written documents of any kind had ever been found. Most archeologists and linguists believed that writing did not appear in Medea until the 5th Century AD.

That is, until 2015 when a major discovery was found in the Republic of Georgia.

The territory of the Republic of Georgia today was included in the kingdom of Medea in the 7th Century BC along with Azerbaijan, Armenia, Kurdistan, Northern Iran, Northern Iraq and Eastern Turkey. Medea was the land south of the Caucasian Mountains – the territory between the Black Seas and the Caspian Sea extending southward.

There were scholars, scribes, priests and other educated Israelites among the thousands of Israelite captives deported to the cities of the Medes in 721 BC. As they associated with the Medes, these former captive Israelites must have put that

---

[108] *Ibid*

education and training to use to earn their living and become productive members of the Medean nation.

In 2015, some unpaid college students from Tbilisi State University (Tbilisi is the capital of today's republic of Georgia) excavated a site discovered in 2007 during work to widen the Tbilisi-Senaki-Leselidze highway and made a startling discovery.

National Geographic in September 2015[109] published an article called *Ancient Script Spurs Rethinking of Historic 'Backwater'*, subtitled "At a temple site in the Republic of Georgia, letters carved in stone could change the way we see the development of writing."

This photograph from *National Geographic* (picture credited to Shalva Lejava) shows the source of archeologists' and linguists' excitement – the lettering etched on the side of a collapsed stone altar at the ancient temple site of Grakliani. (G4) (A2)

The question as to who did this writing is what spurred the excitement and what brought *National Geographic* to publish this article.

Figure 5-1

In the *National Geographic* article, Vakhtang Licheli stated that this was the oldest example of a native alphabet in the Caucasus area. "There is no doubt that the carvings are part of an alphabet rather than a decorative pattern." He also stated that it's reasonable to assume "that **the writing dates to the seventh century B.C.,** when the temple is believed to have been built." Shards of pottery found at the site

109   https://news.nationalgeographic.com/2015/09/150916-caucasus-writing-republic-of-georgia-grakliani-iron-age/

are emblematic of that period. Their color, material, and design, Licheli says, resemble those from similar sites in Georgia, leaving little doubt as to their age.

The *National Geographic* article continued,

> "These few letters in stone upend traditional historical narratives about the native population of the region the Greeks and Romans called Iberia (not to be confused with the modern-day Iberian Peninsula – Spain, Portugal et al), which bordered the Georgian coast of the Black Sea."

What has this to do with the captive, deported Israelites living among the "cities of the Medes"? Again, quoting from the National Geographic article:

> Another question that intrigues Licheli is why three letters carved on one corner of a stone altar in the temple, also newly discovered, seem to bear no relation to the letter on the stone slab.
>
> "Maybe there were two languages in one temple," he conjectures—two ethnically related Iberian groups, each with its own script, living side by side. "This is very unusual, not just for Georgians but in the whole world. The script as a whole bears no relation to any other alphabet, although Licheli detects similarities to letters in ancient Greek and *Aramaic*".[93]

Figure 5.2

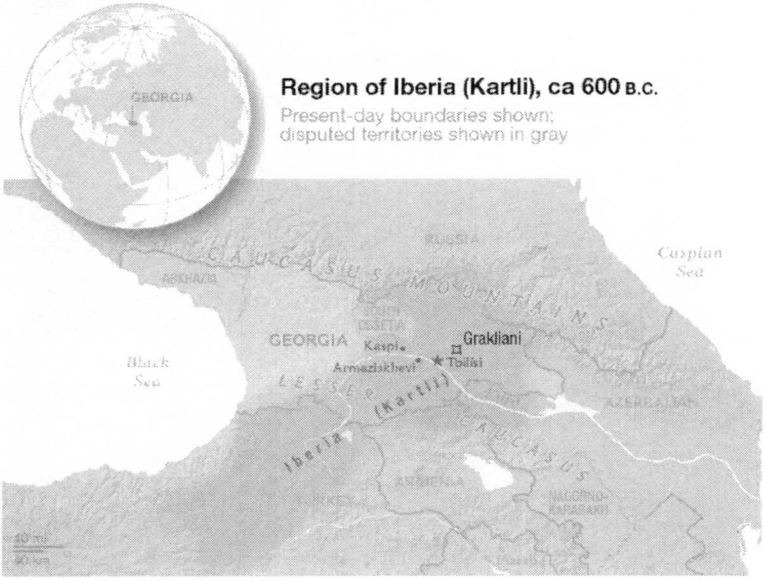

Region of Iberia (Kartli), ca 600 B.C.
Present-day boundaries shown;
disputed territories shown in gray

Writing of this same archeological find, the official Republic of Georgia archeological website adds:

> Everything we have unearthed at Grakliani Hill testifies to existence of a very highly developed society. Here lived tremendously advanced people, both culturally and economically, who had a very active relationship with all nearby hotbeds of civilization such as Mesopotamia, Urartu and Achaemenid Iran. It is apparent that locals had adapted all technological innovations and useful cultural elements that existed at that time as well.[110]

The educated Israelites who had been scattered among the Medean people would have recalled their ties to the various nations of Mesopotamia *et al* when Israel was a viable nation. It was likely the Israelites among them who were advanced and had a relationship with nearby civilizations and adapted those "technological innovations and useful cultural elements". (T2)

Related to the letters on the collapsed altar: in chapter one, we noted that Abraham's family clan remained in Haran when Abraham received his call from God and moved on to Palestine. Later, Abraham's son Isaac and Isaac's son Jacob returned to Haran to find their wives among their relatives still living there. The village and the later the city and eventually the nation called the Arameans[94] – named after Abraham's nephew Aram[95] who was the leader of the clan. This was the origin of the Aramaic language and Aramaic (their language almost interchangeable with Hebrew) was most likely the language of Abraham, Isaac and Jacob.

Until the 2015 discovery, linguists and archeologists thought there was no written language in the Medean territory. There were certainly educated people among those captives who could have created the script that so excited the archeological and linguistic professionals.

The artist who carved the Aramaic (Hebrew) letters into the base of that idol in the 7th Century BC was most likely an Israelite.

Considering that Deioces was likely an Israelite and the individual who carved that Aramaic (Hebrew) writing on the altar in the republic of Georgia was likely an Israelite, the governing style of the founder of the Medean Empire and his subsequent dealing with his subjects takes on a different meaning.

It shows that although God had punished the Israelites and let them be removed from the "promised land", they were still under His guidance. Deioces changed the

---

[110]   https://www.georgianjournal.ge/discover-georgia/30010-discoveries-at-grakliani-hill-will-change-history.html

way the Middle-Eastern kings treated their people and how they ran their governments – to the benefit of all humanity as well as to the Israelites. The pattern continued, with Deioces' descendants like Cyrus the Great setting ruling standards copied for the next 1500 years and possibly affecting the political structures found in Western Civilization.

Cyrus the Great (525 – 404 BC)

Cyrus the Great (P2), who established the Medo-Persian Empire (G5) that conquered Babylon, adhered to principles and morals like those established in Medea by Deioces.

It is quite likely that Cyrus was a descendant of Deioces. In establishing his rule over the whole area, he may have conquered the Medean Kingdom ruled by his *grandfather*. This would explain why the secondary rulers were always Medes.[96]

The Medo-Persian Empire is called the Achaemenid Empire in most secular histories as they suggest his descent from Achaimenes[111], a 7th century BC Persian king, who founded a dynasty that could have led to Cyrus.

Cyrus the Great became one of the most respected monarchs in all of history[97] in no small part because he institutionalized the principles and morals like those of Deioces.

> The Achaemenid Empire left a lasting impression on the heritage and the cultural identity of Asia, Europe, and the Middle East, as well as influencing the development and structure of future empires. In fact, the Greeks and later on the Romans copied the best features of the Persian method of governing the empire, and vicariously adopted them.[112] (T3)

Georg W. F. Hegel in *The Philosophy of History* introduces the Persian Empire as the "first empire that passed away" and its people as the "first historical people" in history. According to his account:

> The Persian Empire is an empire in the modern sense – like that which existed in Germany, and the great imperial realm under the sway of Napoleon; for we find it consisting of a number of states, which are indeed dependent, but which have retained their own individuality, their manners, and laws. The general enactments, binding upon all, did not infringe upon

---

[111] Merriam-Webster, I. (2003). Merriam-Webster's collegiate dictionary. (Eleventh ed.). Springfield, MA: Merriam-Webster

[112] https://en.wikipedia.org/wiki/Achaemenid_Empire#Legacy

their political and social idiosyncrasies, but even protected and maintained them; so that each of the nations that constitute the whole, had its own form of constitution. As light illuminates everything – imparting to each object a peculiar vitality – so the Persian Empire extends over a multitude of nations, and leaves to each one its particular character. Some have even kings of their own; each one its distinct language, arms, way of life and customs. All this diversity coexists harmoniously under the impartial dominion of Light … a combination of peoples – leaving each of them free. Thereby, a stop is put to that barbarism and ferocity with which the nations had been wont to carry on their destructive feuds.[113]

The Bible refers to Cyrus in laudatory terms: as "God's shepherd, God's anointed, Cyrus – the one whose right hand was held by God, the one summoned by God by name though he (Cyrus) did not acknowledge God". Cyrus was the one who would send the Jews home from exile to rebuild Jerusalem.[114]

> [13] I will raise up Cyrus in my righteousness: I will make all his ways straight. He will rebuild my city and set my exiles free, but not for a price or reward, says the LORD Almighty." Isaiah 45:13 (NIV84)

Deioces' governing style led Cyrus to carry out God's plan for the Medo-Persian Empire to "rebuild His city and set His exiles free". Not only did Cyrus' decree allow the return of the Jews from Babylon but paid their expenses for travel and the materials for rebuilding Jerusalem and the temple from the Empire's treasury.

The Greek-Macedonian Empire

Alexander the Great conquered Persia and Medea in 330 BC but died shortly afterward at the age of 33 in Babylon. Greek culture spread throughout the known world but its military power waned with the death of Alexander. The Macedonian Empire split into 4 sections with two strongest generals establishing their bases in Egypt (Ptolemy) and Syria (Seleucus I Nicator). Mesopotamia was somewhat ignored as these generals warred with each other until about 152 BC when the Parthian king, Mithradates I, conquered the Greeks in that area on the way to consolidating the Parthian Empire.

The Parthian Empire (247 BC – 224 AD)

---

[113] *The Philosophy of History* Georg Wilhelm Friedrich Hegel © Batoche Books 52 Eby Street South Kitchener, Ontario N2G 3L1 Canada

[114] Isaiah 44:28–45:3

The Parthian Empire is the most intriguing of all the powers in Europe and Asia for the 500 years surrounding the turn of the millennium.

Who were the Parthians? There is no mention of them in the Old Testament or in the archives of the Assyrian libraries at Ninevah. They are not mentioned in Asia until the 6th Century BC.

> The first certain occurrence of the name is as Parthava in the Bīsitūn inscription (c. 520 BC) of the Achaemenian king Darius I, but Parthava may be only a dialectal variation of the name Parsa (Persian).[115]

Figure 5.3

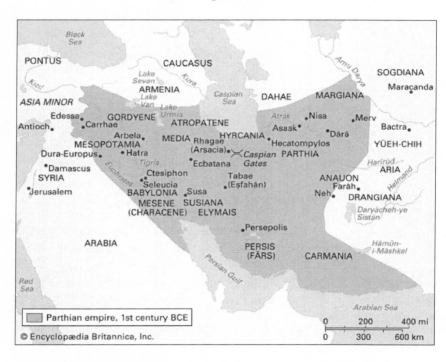

A group of three nomadic tribes made up the Dahae (see Figure 5.3) from which it is believed the Parthians came. The Parni (Aparni) and two tribes of Scythian Sakis comprised the Dahae who were known to be violently opposed to the Greek Empire. They had joined the Persian Army in repulsing the Greeks from further inroads into Asia. These people ranged from the southern shores of the Caspian Sea, adjacent to

---

[115] https://www.britannica.com/place/Parthia#ref225961

the land of Medea and from the eastern shores of the Caspian Sea to the Amu Darya River[116] – where Alexander was stopped.

This is a great swathe of verdant, agricultural land about 200 miles across that runs from the western shore of the Caspian Sea curving around that body of water and stretching to the Amu Darya River. It closely resembles the Sixteen Lands – the legendary homeland of the Aryans as described in the Vendidad.[98] It was a magnificent homeland for those who knew how to farm and raise herds of livestock.

George Rawlinson[117] wrote that several Greek historians claimed "Scythians"[99] had revolted against the Medes and Persians and migrated east of the Caspian Sea – it was sparsely populated in the 7th and 6th Centuries BC. This fits perfectly the scenario that these "Scythians" were Israelites finding a home for their swelling populations. They would have little trouble settling among the sparse population of the Aryans who resided there. (M2)

According to Rawlinson, Diodorus Siculus, a Greek historian of the 1st Century BC, said that the Parthians had "passed from the dominion of the Assyrians to that of the Medes...to a similar position under the Persians". Israelites became Medes; became Persians; became Scythians; became Dahae *and then became Parthians.*

At the death of Alexander in 323 BC and as the Greek Empire lost its control over the area, many of these Dahae nomads migrated to Parthia and adopted the speech of the Parthians and became part of the settled population. (M3)

Parthia and Hyrcania (Figure 5.3) were one province from 320 – 250 BC under the Greek/Seleucid rule after the fall of the Medo–Persian Empire. A revolt and the death of the Seleucid ruler at the hands of the Dahae solidified them as the first district of the Parthian Empire.

Arsaces

According to tradition, Arsaces I (P3) (c. 247 BC– c. 211 BC) was the first ruler of the Parthians and founder of the Parthian empire. Some historians say Arsaces was a governor under Diodotus, king of the Bactrian Greeks when he revolted and fled westward to establish his own rule. Others say he was a Parni king among the Dahae. In either case, the ruling family in Parthia became known as the Arsacid dynasty, and Parthian kings were always called Arsacid.

---

[116] Much of this information comes from https://www.britannica.com/place/Parthia
[117] 19th Century historian (1812-1902)

Arsaces I is also referred to as a Scythian; he launched his struggle against the Seleucids from 247 BC, the year from which the Parthians dated their history.

By 200 BC, Arsaces' successors were firmly established along the southern shore of the Caspian Sea. Later, through the conquests of Mithradates I (reigned 171–138 BC) and Artabanus II (reigned 128–124 BC), all of the Iranian Plateau and the Tigris-Euphrates valley came under Parthian control.

A most intriguing practice of the Parthians is that their kings were all from the Arsacid line but they were placed on their thrones by a vote among what *Britannica* and other histories call "the central Asian tribe of the Sacaraucae."[100] (P4) That tribe was from the Dahae and are referred to as Scythians by some ancient historians.

The Parthians controlled most of the trade routes between Asia and the Greco-Roman world, and this control brought them great wealth, which they used on their extensive building activities. The Parthian state held similar power and territory and emulated the Achaemenian dynasty for nearly half a millennium – some Parthian kings claimed genetic descent from Cyrus. The Parthian Empire's arrival coincided with the expansion of Rome and played a significant role in the destinies of the world during the last three centuries BC and the first two centuries AD.

Parthians – Israelites?

We *know* that a large population of Israelites were in the area; therefore, it is not unreasonable to assume that at least *some* of the nomads – especially the Sakae Scythians – and *some* of the Parthians were the descendants of the deported Israelis.

Rawlinson quotes the classical historians Strabo, Justin and Arrian in stating: "The manners of the Parthians had, they tell us, much that was Scythic in them. Their language was half Scythic, half Median. They armed themselves in the Scythic fashion. They were, in fact, Scyths in descent, in habits, in character." [101] (A3)

Though the history of the Arsacids is sketchy it is also likely that the line of kings who came from Arsaces were from those same people. It is not unreasonable to speculate that the Parthian Empire was ruled by Israelites who were *elected* by other Israelites – the Sacaraucae.

Britannica reports that more than 2,000 Parthian ostraca [102] (A4) were discovered in 1949-58 at the Parthian Arsacid capital Nisa (G6) – located in today's Turkmenistan – and states, *"The Parthian script was derived from the Aramaic (Hebrew) alphabet."*

Steven M. Collins[103] in his book on the "lost 10 tribes" offers some interesting data on the Parthians, relying heavily upon Rawlinson and Rawlinson's translations and interpretations of Greek and Roman historians.

> The Parthian monarchs, whose faces are shown on their coins, clearly exhibit facial features of the white race, supporting a Semitic origin for the Parthian nation. Whether we look at their language, their names or their faces, all hard evidence indicates a Semitic origin for the Parthians. (A5)

Figure 5.4

Coin of Mithridates II of Parthia. (Image from Wikipedia)

Jesus' Apostles Brought Christianity to the Parthians

Josephus did not consider the ten tribes to be "lost" at all, but rather living in known geographical locations. It is significant that the Apostle Peter wrote the book of I Peter from the city of Babylon (I Peter 5:13). Since Babylon was a city of the Parthian Empire at that time, it indicates that Peter had heeded Jesus Christ's instructions to Apostles to go to "the lost sheep of the House of Israel" by traveling to territory ruled by the ten tribes.

> Historical accounts also assert that the Apostle Thomas traveled within Parthia. Indeed, the early church historian Eusebius identified Thomas as the apostle sent to the Parthians. There are historical records which link the Apostle Thomas to the Parthian king Gondophares (mentioned earlier), who reigned in ancient India. The presence of the apostles of Jesus Christ in Parthian territory shows their recognition that the Parthians were Israelites.

> It is also significant that there were Parthian believers in the God of Israel who made pilgrimages to Jerusalem for the annual Holy Days of God. Acts 2:11 states that Parthians were present at the Pentecost Day when the Holy Spirit was poured out to the Apostles. The Medes, Elamites and "dwellers in Mesopotamia" mentioned in Acts 2:9 had all come from Parthian provinces. Since part of the ten tribes had been settled in Media (II Kings 17:6), it is

likely that the "Medes" who made a religious pilgrimage to Jerusalem were Israelites from the ten tribes.[118]

William Steuart McBirnie[119] published perhaps the most thorough study ever done of the acts of the *other* original apostles – other than Peter, James, and John – who have little or no mention chronologically after the 1st chapter of Acts. McBirnie spent nearly 20 years tracking down the historical traces of the other apostles as well as investigating legends and myths associated with them. In his chapter on Thomas, McBirnie spends most of his discussion covering the historical evidence of Thomas in India. There are at least two rather large Christian sects there who claim their spiritual heritage from Thomas.

Of special interest for our thesis is Thomas' passage through Mesopotamia and the Parthian Empire.

> It is evident that Thomas visited Babylon. The Holy Apostolic and Catholic Church of the East officially records that their church in Babylon was started by Thomas and Peter. One congregation that still exists today *(1973)* and claims to have been found by Thomas is in Resaieh (today called Rezaiyeh, the capital of West Azerbaijan province in NW Iran, near Lake Urmia). Still others claim to have been visited by Thaddeus or other apostles in the first Century AD.

> Thomas came to this country and instructed thousands upon thousands of people in the true faith of our Lord. He set up churches for their worship, ordained the necessary clergy to care for those churches. He endured some persecution and eventually was martyred in India.[120] (G7)

McBirnie considered the legends of the Syrian-Indian Church regarding Thomas confirmed. Thomas spent years in Parthia but also spent considerable time in India. The legends of Thomas in India are even more abundant than in the Muslim countries that occupy Mesopotamia today.

Secular history also confirms the spread of Christianity. *Britannica* offers, "In the first two centuries of the Common era, Christianity and various baptismal sects also began to expand into Mesopotamia."[121]

---

[118] *The "Lost" Ten Tribes of Israel...Found!* Copyright 1992 Steven M. Collins CPA Books Boring, Oregon 97009

[119] William Steuart McBirnie, PhD *The Search For the 12 Apostles* ©1973 Tyndale House Publishers, Carol Stream, IL 60188

[120] *Ibid Chapter 9, pgs. 115 -128*

[121] https://www.britannica.com/place/Parthia#ref225961

McBirnie spends an entire chapter providing evidence of the apostle Thaddeus' presence in Armenia, Arabia, Syria, Mesopotamia and Persia – all provinces of the Parthian Empire in the 1st Century.

McBirnie writes, "The association of the Armenian Church with the Apostles is one of the firmest facts in all post-Biblical Christian historical tradition", "Armenia became the first Christian nation in the world" and "King Tiridates, together with the nobility of his country, were baptized by St. Gregory the Illuminator." [122]

McBirnie says the generally accepted chronology gives a period of eight years to the mission of Thaddeus (35-43 AD) and sixteen years to Bartholomew (44-60 AD) in Armenia with both later moving on to other provinces of the Parthian Empire.

Thus, five apostles are feasibly associated with preaching the Gospel in the Parthian Empire – Peter, Thomas, Thaddeus, Bartholomew and Simon Zelotes. (P5)

What happened in the Parthian Empire after the world-shaking events in Jerusalem in the 30's AD shows the *hand of God* at work. The New Covenant was to guide the fate of the Israelites as well as the Jews. Not only are the Israelites being physically guided to their destiny but also their fate will encompass the "spiritual Israelites" as well – Jesus' church that He established – to bring them all to their destiny. (T4)

The evidence we have been able to gather displays an Empire that rose to power during the Greek era and rivaled the Roman Empire but was seldom and only perfunctorily mentioned in passing by contemporary Greek and Roman historians. This Empire is mentioned several times by Josephus but his concentration and bias were always toward Rome. Nevertheless, the data is convincing that Israelites ruled this Empire.

A summary of this new evidence makes it almost undeniable that the Parthian Empire was the center for the "Lost Sheep of the House of Israel".

> ➤ Israelites were in the area in extreme numbers per Josephus
> ➤ The physical appearance of the Parthians was Semitic
> ➤ Their kings and war chiefs were chosen from and *elected* by the members of closely knit royal (Dahae) family that was almost certainly Israelite
> ➤ Their spoken and written language was based on Aramaic (or Hebrew)

---

[122] McBirnie Chapter 12 pg 154

- They consciously followed the pattern of government of Cyrus, the Great who followed the principles established by Deioces of Medea who was an Israelite
- In no other place in the world would there have been this concentration of the "lost sheep of the house of Israel"
- The apostles were given instructions by Jesus to take the Gospel to the "lost sheep of the house of Israel". At least 5 of the apostles spent time in the provinces of Parthia to spread the Gospel
- Church tradition proclaims a great many of the Parthians were converted to Christianity – secular history confirms this to be true
- They, along with the Medes and Persians who were Christian, were persecuted and ejected from Mesopotamia (including Medea, Persia, Syria and Armenia) because of their religious beliefs by the Zoroastrian Sāsānian Empire which succeeded the Parthian Empire (G8) (M4)
- The traditions of the New Covenant and Christianity were carried with them out of their homeland in the Parthian Empire as they helped spread the Gospel of Jesus
- Strangely, because of that forced migration, Ephraim and Manasseh and the rest of the 10 tribes would become the foremost purveyors of Christianity to the whole world.

Amos' and other Prophecy

We've quoted the Amos prophecy several times from which we obtained the word "sifted" for the status of the Israelites after they were taken captive. It is curious that this occurrence of "sifted" in Amos is the only time the Hebrew word נוע [nuwa'] is used with this meaning in the Bible. [123] It indicates something unique to how the Israelites were identifiable even when scattered among various peoples. We now see that includes the long period they were among the Medes and the Parthians up to around 250 AD.

> 9 For, lo, I will command, and I will sift [nuwa'] the house of Israel among all nations, Like as corn is sifted [nuwa'] in a sieve, yet shall not the least grain fall upon the earth. Amos 9:9 (KJV 1900)

Amos prophecy seems to well apply to Israel while living in the Parthian Empire. They were still distinguishable down to the "least grain." They were not so blended as to be unrecognizable.

---

[123] (Niphal) to be tossed about or around. 1C (Hiphil). to cause to wander. Strong, J. (1995). Enhanced Strong's Lexicon. Woodside Bible Fellowship.

Josephus' statement assures us there were large numbers of identifiable Israelites among the Parthian population. This means the blood lines from Abraham to Isaac to Jacob to Ephraim and Manasseh and the 10 tribes of the kingdom of Israel were still distinguishable in the first century AD and likely stayed that way so long as the Parthian Empire stayed intact.

There is other prophecy to help us determine the status of Israel from the start in Assyria in 721 BC up until the 18ᵗʰ century:

> 27 The LORD will scatter you among the peoples, and only a few of you will survive among the nations to which the LORD will drive you. Deuteronomy 4:25–31 (NIV84)

This can apply to the scattering that started after their time as a group "beyond the Euphrates".

> 64 Then the LORD will scatter you among all nations, from one end of the earth to the other. There you will worship other gods—gods of wood and stone, which neither you nor your fathers have known. Deuteronomy 28:64

This has general and longtime application taking Israel through both the BC and AD periods of dispersion.

> 1 When all these blessings and curses I have set before you come upon you and you take them to heart wherever the LORD your God disperses you among the nations, 2 and when you and your children return to the LORD your God and obey him with all your heart and with all your soul according to everything I command you today, 3 then the LORD your God will restore your fortunes and have compassion on you and gather you again from all the nations where he scattered you. Deuteronomy 30:1-3

This seems to apply to the regathering of Israel in the Parthian Empire where God applied his sifting power to restore Israel to their original status as God's people – at least those Israelites who returned to God. As converts to Christianity and the New Covenant of Jesus, the Israelites in the Parthian Empire "returned to the Lord their God" and began to "obey him with all their heart and soul" as they spread the Gospel of Jesus.

In the next chapter we will continue to trace the migration of the Israelites to Central and Western Europe. We can now follow the spread of Christianity as additional criteria to follow their travels. When they complete the journey on which God sent them, He will "restore their fortunes" and gather them "from all the nations" where He scattered them.

* * *

CHAPTER 6

The Second Scattering

From the Parthian Empire to Western Europe (224 - 700 AD)

In Chapter 5 we identified the 10 tribes of the Kingdom of Israel in Medea and environs in 721 BC and then followed their population growth and influence on the Medes and on the Medo-Persian Empire in the 5 centuries before Alexander the Great. Their resistance combined with the Persian armies helped slow the spread of the Greek/Macedonian Empire (GM).

Eventually, around 250 BC, a king from the Dahae expelled the remnants of the GM Empire from the province of Parthia and established the first provinces of the Parthian Empire. At its peak the Parthian Empire extended from the Euphrates River on the west to modern Pakistan on the east and from the Arabian Sea on the south to the borders of southern Russia in the north.

Essentially overlooked by contemporary Greek and Roman historians, the Parthian Empire was the chief rival of the Roman Empire for 350 years. Even to this day its history and influence is minimized by most contemporary historians.

Nonetheless, by examining the histories closely, we found that the Parthian Empire held sway over the most of the Middle-East and controlled the lucrative trade routes from the Far East to the Roman Empire until the 3rd Century AD. By then a majority of the Parthians were Christians. Our newly found evidence convinces us that it was the Christian Israelites in the Parthian Empire that greatly help explain the exponential growth of the early Christian Church.

The Sasanian (Persian) Empire forced the migration of many of the Parthians – Israelites, Scythians, Dahae and Medes who had become Christians. As this new Persian Empire forced most of the Parthians out, the migration possibilities were restricted.

By default, the displaced Parthians had to migrate to the north and northwest.[104]

After leaving the area beyond the Euphrates the people of the 10 tribes of the House of Israel were never again recognized as such by *any* historian. Greek and Roman historians often confused the names of the various peoples migrating into Eastern and Central Europe giving some of them three or more names and calling them all "barbarians".

From now on the trail of the Israelites becomes more like a thousand tributaries leading into small rivers, then to larger rivers and finally into gigantic bodies of water. While this water will contain many of those who have no Israelite blood in them, it will capture the vast majority of Israelite inheritance.

Much of the criteria of Chapter 5 are no longer useful for tracking their movement.

However, four factors will be quite helpful in tracking Israel from the Parthian Empire to Western Europe. These are:

(P) The names and deeds of any people who can be identified as possible Israelites.

(C) The direction of the growth of Christianity from the provinces of the Parthian Empire into Eastern Europe and then into Central and Western Europe. The Parthians took the Gospel of Jesus with them.

(M) The migration paths of the people from the Parthian Empire to Central and Western Europe using the names given them by Greek and Roman historians.

(B) Bible prophecy where it seems appropriate.

This chapter will do two major things. One of these is tracking the migrants from the Parthian Empire. The other is examining the effects of Christianity on the people of the Parthian Empire in the 1st Century AD. It is the latter that is taken up first because not only does it explain the large number of Christians by the 4th century AD but also Christianity is a new concept as a way for tracking Israel.

We have found no researchers who combine the influence of Christianity within the "House of Israel" and the spread of Christianity. Yet, this turns out to be one of the most critical and useful factors for identifying Israel and in explaining the rapid growth of the church.

Furthermore, it graphically illustrates that the *hand of God* is directing the path of His "chosen people", the Israelites. Since the Jews – for the most part, and with the exception of the apostles and Jesus' disciples – rejected Jesus, they had only a minor role in spreading the Gospel. Yet we learn that hundreds of thousands of those other "chosen people" were residing within relatively easy traveling distance of Jerusalem.

1. Christianity and the House of Israel

It is critical to our investigation that we show convincingly that the House of Israel became Christians. This will show prophecies[105] fulfilled through Christ with all Israelites and not just the Jewish converts spreading the Gospel to the gentiles.

In the 1st Century AD Jesus installed the New Covenant. Referring to that covenant, the writer of Hebrews quoted a prophecy from the great prophet Jeremiah that explicitly states that the *New Covenant* would be made with *both* the House of Israel *and* the House of Judah.

> 8 But God found fault with the people and said: "The time is coming, declares the Lord, when I will make a new covenant with the house of Israel and with the house of Judah. 9 It will not be like the covenant I made with their forefathers when I took them by the hand to lead them out of Egypt, because they did not remain faithful to my covenant, and I turned away from them, declares the Lord. 10 This is the covenant I will make with the house of Israel after that time, declares the Lord. I will put my laws in their minds and write them on their hearts. I will be their God, and they will be my people. 11 No longer will a man teach his neighbor, or a man his brother, saying, 'Know the Lord,' because they will all know me, from the least of them to the greatest. 12 For I will forgive their wickedness and will remember their sins no more." Hebrews 8:8–12 (NIV84)

Jeremiah's prophecy also contained promises that God would *never reject the descendants of Israel.*

> 35 This is what the LORD says, he who appoints the sun to shine by day, who decrees the moon and stars to shine by night, who stirs up the sea so that its waves roar— the LORD Almighty is his name: 36 "Only if these decrees vanish from my sight," declares the LORD, "will the descendants of Israel ever cease to be a nation before me." 37 This is what the LORD says: "Only if the heavens above can be measured and the foundations of the earth below be searched out will I reject all the descendants of Israel because of all they have done," declares the LORD. Jeremiah 31:35–37 (NIV84)

Two major factors do much to explain the origin, direction and strength of the Israelite "rivers" which eventually settle into the major body of water making up the masses of the people of Western Civilization, especially Great Britain. This is a crucial collecting point of Israelites in fulfilling the Lord's prophecies for Israel. These are the nations that will make up Western Civilization.

These factors are 1. the exponential growth of Christianity and 2. the evidence for the House of Israel becoming Christian.

The Christianization of the Israelites

Chapter 5 showed considerable evidence (P1, C1) that at least 5 of Jesus' apostles spent decades of the 1st Century in the Parthian Empire preaching the Gospel.

There is substantial history for three of the 5 apostles evangelizing the Parthians and at least minor evidence for a fourth. Peter's (the fifth apostle) influence on the Parthian Empire is indisputable. Peter wrote his first epistle from Babylon[106], the provincial seat of the Babylonian province of the Parthian Empire.

> [12] With the help of Silas, whom I regard as a faithful brother, I have written to you briefly, encouraging you and testifying that this is the true grace of God. Stand fast in it. [13] She who is in Babylon, chosen together with you, sends you her greetings, and so does my son Mark. [14] Greet one another with a kiss of love. Peace to all of you who are in Christ. 1 Peter 5:12–14 (NIV84)

Peter's greeting for the first epistle:

> [1] Peter, an apostle of Jesus Christ, To God's elect, strangers in the world, scattered throughout Pontus, Galatia, Cappadocia, Asia and Bithynia, [2] who have been chosen according to the foreknowledge of God the Father, through the sanctifying work of the Spirit, for obedience to Jesus Christ and sprinkling by his blood: Grace and peace be yours in abundance. 1 Peter 1:1–2 (NIV84)

All these churches[107] to whom Peter was writing were in cities and areas located south of the southern shores of the Black Sea – territory controlled by the Parthian Empire though contested often by the Roman Empire.[108]

The following passage is particularly pertinent to our narrative – it takes on new meaning since we've learned that the House of Israel was residing in the Parthian Empire:

¹ And when He had called His twelve disciples to *Him*, He gave them power *over* unclean spirits, to cast them out, and to heal all kinds of sickness and all kinds of disease. ² Now the names of the twelve apostles are these: first, Simon, who is called <u>Peter</u>, and Andrew his brother; James the *son* of Zebedee, and John his brother; ³ Philip and <u>Bartholomew</u>; <u>Thomas</u> and Matthew the tax collector; James the *son* of Alphaeus, and Lebbaeus, whose surname was <u>Thaddaeus</u>; ⁴ <u>Simon</u> the Canaanite, and Judas Iscariot, who also betrayed Him.

⁵ These twelve Jesus sent out and commanded them, saying: "Do not go into the way of the Gentiles, and do not enter a city of the Samaritans. ⁶ <u>But go rather to the lost sheep of the house of Israel.</u> ⁷ And as you go, preach, saying, 'The kingdom of heaven is at hand.' ⁸ Heal the sick, cleanse the lepers, raise the dead, cast out demons. Freely you have received, freely give. ⁹ Provide neither gold nor silver nor copper in your money belts, ¹⁰ nor bag for *your* journey, nor two tunics, nor sandals, nor staffs; for a worker is worthy of his food. Matthew 10:1–10 (NKJV)

²³ When they persecute you in this city, flee to another. For assuredly, I say to you, you will not have gone through the <u>cities of Israel</u> before the Son of Man comes. Matthew 10:23 (NKJV) ¹⁰⁹

The phrase "house of Israel" is never used in the New Testament to refer to Jews with the exception of their inclusion in one comment by Jesus.[124] Jesus could only have been referring to the 10 tribes of the kingdom of Israel who were deported to Medea and environs in 721 BC *and still there in the Parthian Empire in 94 AD, according to Josephus.*

The description of the crowds of people in Jerusalem celebrating the Pentecost less than two months[125] after Jesus' death and resurrection is relevant:

⁵ Now there were Jews residing in Jerusalem, devout men from every nation under heaven. ⁶ And *when* this sound occurred, the crowd gathered and was in confusion, because each one was hearing them speaking in his own language. ⁷ And they were astounded and astonished, saying, "Behold, are not all these who are speaking Galileans? ⁸ And how do we hear, each one *of us*, in our own native language? ⁹ Parthians and Medes and Elamites and those residing *in* Mesopotamia, Judea and Cappadocia, Pontus and Asia, ¹⁰ Phrygia and Pamphylia, Egypt and the parts of Libya toward Cyrene, and the Romans who were in town, ¹¹ both Jews and proselytes, Cretans and

---

124 Matthew 15:24

125 Pentecost was 51 days after the Sabbath at the end of the Feast of Unleavened Bread [Leviticus 23:15–16]

Arabs—we hear them speaking in our *own* languages the great deeds of God!" Acts 2:5–11 (LEB)

Not only were there religious pilgrimages to Jerusalem by the Parthian Empire citizens but also relatively free trade existed between the Parthian Empire and the provinces of the Roman Empire as well as many nations in Eastern Europe.

Many residents of Jerusalem knew of the "lost sheep of the House of Israel" and even knew where they were.[110] Why is there no mention of any of the apostles other than Peter, James and John after the book of Acts? *Jesus told them specifically to go to "the lost sheep of the House of Israel"!* We know from history that 5 of the apostles went almost immediately into the Parthian Empire to spread the Gospel to "the lost sheep".

By the apostles spreading the Word they likely convinced several hundred thousand Parthians into carrying the New Covenant teaching – the Gospel of Jesus, the Christ – with them when they were forced to migrate from "beyond the Euphrates" into Eastern Europe.

Though there were Jews scattered throughout the Roman Empire as well as many in the Parthian Empire, they were not "dispersed" from their homeland in Palestine at this time.

If Josephus knew where the House of Israel was residing – "beyond the Euphrates", i.e. Parthia, in numbers too big to count – there must have been many other Jews who knew of the Israelites in the Parthian Empire. Jesus would have known of course and perhaps the apostles knew; that would explain their presence in the Parthian Empire within a few years after Jesus was crucified.

An Illustrative Anecdote

The people in Jerusalem at the festival of Tabernacles knew where the "lost sheep of the House of Israel" were located.

In the fall of the year before Jesus was crucified, He was teaching during the Feast of Tabernacles and people were speculating as to whether He was the Messiah:

> [32] The Pharisees heard the crowd murmuring these *things* about him, and the chief priests and the Pharisees sent officers in order to take him into custody. [33] Then Jesus said, "Yet a little time I am with you, and I am going to the one who sent me. [34] You will seek me and will not find *me*, and where I am, you cannot come."

Since these Jews neither recognized that Jesus' saying He was "going to the one who sent me" meant He would return to Heaven to God, the Father who sent Him, nor did they understand that He meant they "cannot come" with Him to Heaven, they were confused. Their reaction is pertinent to our narrative:

> 35 So the Jews said to one another, "Where is this one going to go, that we will not find him? He is not going to go to the Dispersion [diaspora] among the Greeks [Hĕllēn, Greek (-speaking)] and teach the Greeks [Hĕllēn, Greek (-speaking)], is he? 36 What is this saying that he said, 'You will seek me and will not find me, and where I am, you cannot come'?" John 7:32–36 (LEB)

The Parthians spoke Greek in addition to Aramaic. Almost everyone across the Middle East spoke Greek even after the Greek Empire fell as the Greeks had established Greek schools and inculcated Greek culture as part of their ruling of captured peoples. When these Jews spoke of the *diaspora* among the Greeks[111], they could only have been referring to the Israelites from the "lost 10 tribes".

Of what other dispersion could these Jews be speaking before Jesus' death? The scattered Jews across the nations were not lost; their families in Palestine knew where they were. Many years after Jesus' death, Paul had no problem finding the synagogues that were often the first place he visited when entering the various cities on his missionary journeys in the provinces of the Roman Empire.

Exponential Growth of Christianity (40 – 325 AD)

Rodney Stark[126], a sociologist of religion, asked this question: "How did a tiny and obscure messianic movement from the edge of the Roman Empire dislodge classical paganism and become the dominant faith of Western civilization?"

The Orthodox Christian Network blog relates,

> "In the Rise of Christianity, Stark does the math, and shows that a social movement numbering only 1,000 people in 40 A.D. could easily grow to 25 or even 35 million by the fourth century, despite all of the challenges of the ancient world — if the members of the movement lived according to the principles spelled out above. Doing so leads to very tangible demographic results: 40% growth per decade for hundreds of years."[127]

Stark listed those principles:

---

126 The Rise of Christianity Rodney Stark (Princeton, NJ: Princeton University Press, 1996)
127 http://myocn.net/four-reasons-why-early-christian-church-grew-so-quickly/

- ➤ Social networking: Everyday friendships and the personal interactions of average believers are what makes the greatest difference
- ➤ Caring for the sick, widows, and orphans: What distinguished Christians was their response to all-too-frequent calamities. Instead of fleeing to the countryside to escape the most recent plague, they stayed to care for their own
- ➤ Stance against adultery, abortion, and infanticide: Christians spoke out against all of these practices, exhorting the followers of Jesus to remain faithful in marriage (even the men!), and to care for the most vulnerable members of society: little babies
- ➤ A theology of love: The actions described above reflect certain Christian theological principles. The most important one is the insistence that God loves the world He has created and that He desires those who love Him to also love their fellow man

If the early Christians could have actually lived by those principles[112], he is correct. However, he fails to factor in the intense persecution of Christians over those 300 years only lessening slightly when Constantine declared Christianity the official state religion.

Even at the time of Constantine's declaration, the Roman Empire remained mostly pagan. Christians in the Roman Empire over those 300 years in many places could not openly espouse being Christians much less teach others those principles. They certainly taught their children but the public actions described above could not have been made without the actor becoming a martyr. Surely, it happened, but we should remember that feeding Christians to lions or watching gladiators kill Christians were the height of entertainment in the arenas in the Roman Empire.

Robert Louis Wilken, emeritus professor of history at the University of Virginia provides some statistics of the Christian population change from the first century to the 3rd.

> At the end of the first century there were fewer than ten thousand Christians in the Roman Empire. The population at the time numbered some sixty million, which meant that Christians made up one hundredth of one percent or 0.0017 percent according to the figures of a contemporary sociologist.

> By the year 200, the number may have increased to a little more than two hundred thousand, still a tiny minority, under one percent (0.36). By the year 250, however, the number had risen to more than a million, almost

two percent of the population. The most striking figure, however, comes two generations later. By the year 300 Christians made up 10 percent of the population, approximately 6 million.[128]

There are countless other studies that have been conducted to attempt to explain the phenomenal numbers of Christians in the 4th Century AD. *None* of them have truly produced a logical, reasonable explanation but then, *they never considered the possibility of the hundreds of thousands of Parthian Christians.*

What if, instead of starting with 1,000 people in 40 AD, we start in 70 AD – the year the temple in Jerusalem was being razed and the Jewish Christians truly dispersed – with the Christians numbering 200,000 to 500,000 or more when including the Parthian Empire?

The Israelites and other Parthians who were "beyond the Euphrates" were taught the Gospel of Jesus Christ by Holy Spirit filled, eye witnesses of Jesus who routinely healed the sick, made the blind to see, the deaf to hear, the lame to walk and performed other miracles to provide authenticity to their teaching.

Jesus told the apostles concerning the miraculous healing and other miracles He performed:

> [12] I tell you the truth, <u>anyone who has faith in me will do what I have been doing. He will do even greater things than these</u>, because I am going to the Father. [13] And I will do whatever you ask in my name, so that the Son may bring glory to the Father. [14] You may ask me for anything in my name, and I will do it. John 14:12–14 (NIV84)

Moreover, for almost 200 years, the Parthians faced little or no persecution.

The best explanation of the exponential growth of Jesus' church is that God actually planned for the spread of the Gospel to be assisted by the Israelites. *All the tribes of Israel were His chosen people.* For what better purpose could they have been preserved from their demise at the hands of Assyria, sent to a place where they could grow into hundreds of thousands in number again? *Did the apostles remind them of who they were, teach them the Gospel of Jesus so they could take it to the whole world? I think so!*

Although Hosea prophesied the destruction of the Kingdom of Israel by Assyria[129], and their long period away from God, He also offered hope for their future:

---

[128] https://www.thegospelcoalition.org/blogs/justin-taylor/early-church-growth/
[129] Hosea 13:1–14:7

⁴ "I will heal their waywardness and love them freely, for my anger has turned away from them. ⁵ I will be like the dew to Israel; he will blossom like a lily. Like a cedar of Lebanon, he will send down his roots; ⁶ his young shoots will grow. His splendor will be like an olive tree, his fragrance like a cedar of Lebanon. ⁷ Men will dwell again in his shade. He will flourish like the grain. He will blossom like a vine, and his fame will be like the wine from Lebanon. ⁸ O Ephraim, ["Ephraim will say," – KJV] what more have I to do with idols? I will answer him and care for him. I am like a green pine tree; your fruitfulness comes from me." ⁹ Who is wise? He will realize these things. Who is discerning? He will understand them. The ways of the LORD are right; the righteous walk in them, but the rebellious stumble in them. Hosea 14:4–9 (NIV84)

There was ample opportunity for Parthians to spread the gospel within the Roman Empire in the 200 years after the apostles came. The Parthian and Roman Empires were at peace for much of that time. An enormous amount of trade went on between the two empires with the Parthians controlling the trade routes to the east – China, India, Tibet etc. Since the borders were few the Parthians could make use of the Roman infrastructure to carry on their commerce and spread the Gospel.

2. Migration of Christian Israel

After Josephus there is no mention of "Israelites" in secular history; rather they were called by various names by the Greek and Roman historians and it is to the historical record of those various peoples that we must look to find the bloodlines of the Israelites.

To predict their path from now on we must recognize the key points their trail must take to fulfill prophecy. Recall chapter 4 where two critical parts of Daniel's prophecy (B1) are described:

> 1. A Stone Kingdom is to be established and it was to destroy the Roman Empire;
> 2. After the destruction of the Roman Empire the Stone Kingdom was to rise and grow enormously and essentially rule the world.

The Israelites, *now converted to Christianity*, were going on a long journey to a place unknown to them and on that journey, they will help destroy the Roman Empire, spread the gospel to millions upon millions, become a part of the rise of the Stone Kingdom and eventually receive the blessings promised to them. Ephraim and Manasseh would become a nation and a "company of nations" with political and economic hegemony – "possessing the gates of their enemies" and having "nations bow down to them" as a blessing for the people of all the tribes.

The Sasanian Empire (M1) pushed these Israelites along with the rest of the Jewish and Christian citizens of the Parthian Empire out of the land "beyond the Euphrates" but their journey was really just beginning

Sāsānian Empire – the impetus for migration

The political history of Mesopotamia between 320 BC and 620 AD is divided among three periods of foreign rule—the Seleucids to 141 BC, the Parthians to 224 AD, and the Sasanians until the Arab invasions of the 7th century AD. Sources are scarce, consisting mainly of a few notices in the works of classical authors such as Strabo, Pliny, Polybius, and Ptolemy. The available cuneiform sources are mainly incantations, accounts of religious rites, and copies of ancient religious texts.

The Sasanians conducted what Muslims today call a *jihad* against Christians, Jews and even those with no professed religion. One must convert to Zoroastrianism or be persecuted and often killed. Where ever the Christian and Jewish citizens of the Parthian Empire remained in the 3rd Century, they migrated or died.

The magnificent historian George Rawlinson details some of the atrocities against Christians in his massive tome called *The Great Empires of the Ancient East.*[113]

A large number migrated north through Medea and through the passage in the Caucasian Mountains onto the Pontic Steppe. Another group moved due north to the eastern shores of the Caspian Sea living again among the Dahae and reappeared late in the 4th Century as "Huns".

The Sasanian Empire fought the Roman Empire almost continually throughout the 4th, 5th and 6th Centuries devastating much of Mesopotamia. In the 600's the Tigris and Euphrates added floods to the devastation and a plague became widespread.

Shortly thereafter, the Muslim Arabs put an end to the Sasanian Empire.

In 225 AD the inhabitants of the Parthian Empire had nowhere to go but to the north and west. What lay immediately to the northwest? Armenia.

Armenia – the Parthian Empire holdout

Historians cite the year of the fall of the Parthian Empire at 224 AD.[130] However, the Armenian Province of the Parthian Empire did not fall until the reign of Artashes

---

[130] https://www.britannica.com/place/Armenia/Cultural-life#ref44266

IV ended in 428 AD.[131] Armenia was a "magnet" for Christians and those who supported the Arsacid dynasty of the Parthian Empire for at least these two reasons:

(1) Armenia maintained Arsacid royalty as their kings (P2). After hundreds of years of loyalty to the Arsacid kings, settling or even just passing through Armenia would have offered refuge and protection to the tens of thousands being persecuted by the Sasanian Empire.[114]

(2) William McBirnie writes, "(M2, C2) Armenia became the first Christian nation in the world. Christianity was officially proclaimed in 301 A.D. as the national religion of Armenia. King Tiridates, together with the nobility of his country, were baptized by St. Gregory the Illuminator."[132] The Encyclopedia Britannica records that King Tiridates of Armenia (c. A.D. 238314) had already been baptized as a Christian sometime after 261.

This map below shows the boundaries of Woodrow Wilson's Treaty of Sevres (1920). It depicts (in orange) quite well the boundaries of Armenia in the 3rd Century AD. The Roman Empire controlled Syria and the land named Anatolia in this map (Turkey in modern times) as well as the green area labeled Pontus. Though Rome often invaded Armenia they usually left the Arsacid kings in place and more often were expelled by the Armenians sometimes aided by the Sasanians.

Figure 6.1

From places labeled Persia, Assyria and Mesopotamia on this map, a migration to the northwest would have been feasible only through Armenia. However, it could only be a temporary residence for most. The country was (and is) mountainous and

---

[131] Ibid

[132] William Steuart McBirnie, PhD *The Search For the 12 Apostles* ©1973 Tyndale House Publishers, Carol Stream, IL 60188

didn't have the space to add the hundreds of thousands of Parthians to the indigenous population; there was too little arable land to feed that many people. However, it was a gathering place and a place of refuge for the Parthians and for Christians as they migrated from the land beyond the Euphrates.

As they migrated in their tens of thousands – men, women and children – they were a virtual swarm moving through Armenia. The migration pressure continued as the Sasanians tried to establish their control over much of the territory formerly called Medea between the Black and Caspian Seas. The migrants had to move on through the pass in the Caucasian Mountains or following the shore lines of the two Seas.

As conflicts and invasion of Roman territory by these migrants occurred, they began to be recognized by historians but they were not called Parthians. Rome hated the Parthian Empire; their historians never again used the name Parthians. They sometimes referred to them as Scythians or Aryans but more often called them barbarians and sometimes "the Alans".

The Alans (or Alani) (P3) (200 BC – 250 AD)

The name Alan is an Iranian dialectical form of Aryan, a common self-designation of the Indo-Iranians. The Alani were first mentioned in Roman literature in the 1st century AD and were described as a warlike people who specialized in horse breeding. They frequently raided the Caucasian provinces of the Roman Empire. As the former citizens of the Parthian Empire moved into far eastern Europe they joined the Sarmatians and the Alani on the Pontic Steppe. (M3)

They became dominant and soon all were included in the name Alani. The fourth-century Roman historian Ammianus Marcellinus wrote that the Alans were tall, and blond: "Nearly all the Alani are men of great stature and beauty; their hair is somewhat yellow, their eyes are terribly fierce".[133]

The Pontic Steppe covers an area of 994,000 square kilometres (384,000 square miles), extending from eastern Romania across southern Moldova, Ukraine, Russia and northwestern Kazakhstan to the Ural Mountains. The Pontic steppe is bounded by the East European forest-steppe to the north; to the south, the Pontic steppe extends to the Black Sea.

The Pontic Steppe in the 9th Century BC was the land of the Scythians – a band of Eurasian nomads who inhabited the western and central Eurasian steppes until the 1st century BC. Scythia was the Greek term for the grasslands north and east of the

---

[133] https://en.wikipedia.org/wiki/Alans

Black Sea. Moreover, the term Scythian, like Cimmerian, was used to refer to a variety of groups from the Black Sea to southern Siberia and central Asia. We explained earlier why the Scythians of the Parthian Empire were not the same people as the Scythians who inhabited the Pontic Steppe.

This explains why the Alani, the Sarmatians, the former citizens of the Parthian Empire and others were often called "Scythians" by Greek and Roman historians.

Figure 6.2

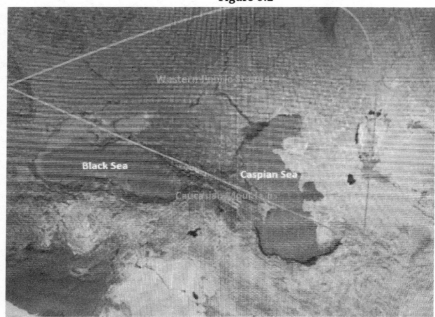

Historians identify 4 different peoples in habiting the Pontic Steppe in the early 200's AD.

> ➤ Sarmatians
> ➤ Alani
> ➤ Aryans
> ➤ Scythians

To Roman and Greek historians these were all "barbarians". They often used the name Scythians when speaking of these people. *Some*, perhaps many, of those people were Israelites.

In 250 AD, the Pontic Steppe was overrun by the Goths[134].

The Goths (250 – 425 AD) (M4)

The Goths were an East Germanic[115] people, two of whose branches – the Visigoths and the Ostrogoths – played an important role in the fall of the Western Roman Empire. (B2)

At their peak of power under the Germanic king Ermanaric, their territory extended all the way from the Danube to the Don River and from the Black Sea to the Baltic Sea. (M5) The Goths "overwhelmed" the Sarmatians, Alani, Aryans and Scythians but after their arrival on the Pontic Steppe, the Goths adopted the ways of the people of the Steppe.

From that point on, all those people who had previously borne other names were now most often called "Goths" by period historians. The Goth's conquered the territory, then intermarried and the conquered men who lived through the conquest enlisted in the Gothic armies.

In 251 AD, the Gothic army raided the Roman provinces of Moesia and Thrace, defeated and killed the Roman emperor Decius, *and took a number of predominantly female captives, many of whom were Christian.* [116]

Christian Goths

The conversion of the Goths to Christianity was a relatively swift process, facilitated by the assimilation of Christian captives into Gothic society. *Within a few generations of their appearance on the borders of the Roman Empire in 238 AD, the conversion of the Goths to Christianity was nearly all-inclusive.*[135] (C3)

According to Philostorgius,[136] a man named Ulfilas became bishop of the Goths in 341 AD. He was the grandson of one such female Christian captive from Sadagolthina in Cappadocia. He continued to serve as bishop to the Christian Goths in Moesia until his death in 383 AD. Ulfilas was ordained by Eusebius, the bishop of Constantinople, in 341 AD.

The Christian cross appeared on coins in Gothic Crimea shortly after the Edict of Tolerance was issued by Galerius in 311 AD, and a Gothic bishop by the name of Theophilas Gothiae was present at the First Council of Nicaea in 325 AD.[137]

---

[134] *ibid*

[135] https://en.wikipedia.org/wiki/Gothic_Christianity

[136] Philostorgius (**Greek**: Φιλοστόργιος; 368 – c. 439 AD) was an **Anomoean** Church historian of the 4th and 5th centuries.

Eusebius of Nicomedia was a pupil of Lucian of Antioch and a leading figure of a faction of Christological thought that became known as Arianism, named after his friend and fellow student, Arius. Between 348 and 383, Ulfilas translated the Bible from Greek into the Gothic language. (C4)

Ulfilas' translation of the scriptures is a good indication of the permeation of Christianity into the Gothic culture.

Ulfilas and His Gothic Alphabet

Ulfilas (or Little Wolf) himself probably a Goth, served as a bishop to the Visigoths in the region beyond the Danube River from A.D. 341 to 348.
With the permission of Emperor Constantine he made the earliest Bible translation into a north-European tongue. Using Greek letters and Gothic runes as raw material, he is credited with being the first man in history deliberately to devise an entirely new alphabet for use by persons who had no written language.
Once his alphabet was completed, Ulfilas translated portions of Scripture into Gothic. The remaining fragments of his translation are the oldest surviving literary work in any Teutonic language. Because he feared that accounts of ancient battles would stir his readers to take up arms, he omitted I and II Kings from his work, which was finished in 380.
Ulfilas' language, itself greatly influenced by the grammatical structure of the New Testament Greek contributed mightily to later Teutonic tongues. But like many other early languages, in the form he used it Gothic has become obsolete and is no longer spoken or written. **Source**: Garrison, Webb, *Strange Facts about the Bible,* 1968 Nashville: Abingdon Press (p. 218-219)

After 493, the Ostrogothic Kingdom included two areas, Italy and much of the Balkans, which had large Arian[138] churches. Arianism had retained some presence among Romans in Italy during the time between its condemnation in the empire and the Ostrogothic conquest. However, since Arianism in Italy was reinforced by the (mostly Arian) Goths coming from the Balkans, the Arian church in Italy had eventually come to call itself "Church of the Goths" by the year 500.

Gothic Migration

The first Greek references to the Goths call them Scythians, since this area along the Black Sea historically had been occupied by a people of that name. The

---

[137] *ibid*

[138] Arian is a person who holds the doctrine of Arianism and is not related to the ethnic term Aryan

application of that designation to the Goths appears to be not ethnological but rather geographical and cultural - Greeks regarded both the ethnic Scythians and the Goths as barbarians.

In episodes of Gothic and Vandal warfare, Germanic tribes (Rugii, Gepids, Vandals, Burgundians, and others) joined the Goths and crossed either the lower Danube or the Black Sea, and led to the Marcomannic Wars, which resulted in widespread destruction and the first invasion of Italy in the Roman Empire period.

In the first attested incursion in Thrace, the Goths were mentioned as Boranoi by Zosimus, and then as Boradoi by Gregory Thaumaturgus. The first incursion of the Roman Empire that can be attributed to Goths is the sack of Histria in 238. Several such raids followed in subsequent decades, in particular the Battle of Abrittus in 251, led by Cniva, in which the Roman Emperor Decius was killed.[139]

The 3rd-century Great Ludovisi sarcophagus depicts a battle between Goths and Romans.

Figure 6.4

After Gallienus was assassinated outside Milan in the summer of 268 in a plot led by high officers in his army, Claudius Gothicus was proclaimed emperor and headed to Rome to establish his rule.

After securing the Roman throne, Claudius was ready to take care of the invasions in the Balkan provinces. Learning of the approach of Claudius, the Goths first attempted to directly invade Italy. They were engaged at the Battle of Naissus.

Aurelian, who was in charge of all Roman cavalry during Claudius' reign, led the decisive attack in the battle. Some survivors were resettled within the empire, while others were incorporated into the Roman army. The battle ensured the survival of

---

[139] https://en.wikipedia.org/wiki/Goths

the Western Roman Empire for another two centuries. In 270, after the death of Claudius, Goths under the leadership of Cannabaudes again launched an invasion on the Roman Empire, but were defeated by Aurelian, who however surrendered Dacia beyond the Danube.[140]

Around 375 AD the Huns overran the Pontic Steppe and then the Gothic territory.

To complete God's plan for the Israelites, a strong, irresistible force was needed to push them all further toward the west.

That force was the Huns.

The Huns (M6) (370 – 455 AD)

The appearance and description of the Huns in secular history includes a surprising new finding for tracing the Israelites into Europe.

To our knowledge, no historian – not even those who have attempted to follow the trail of the Israelites – have paid much attention to the Huns except as to their ferocity and military prowess. The Huns are credited for forcing the migration to central and western Europe of the various peoples mentioned – the Goths, the Vandals, the Anglo-Saxons, the Lombards, the Suebi, the Frisii, the Jutes, the Burgundians, the Alamanni, the Scirii and Franks.

It is almost certain that the Huns carried the bloodlines from the Israelites who were transported to Medea in 720 BC. (C6) That statement is based on these criteria:

> If Deioces (the founder of the Medean Kingdom) was an Israelite;
> if the Israelites revolted against the Medo-Persian rulers and moved to the territory east of the Caspian Sea and became the Dahae, as every indication implies;
> if the Israelites in the Parthian Empire grew to a large population by the First Century AD as stated by Josephus;
> if they acquired the skills of the Medes (who were known for their horses and their skill with those horses and their cavalry[117]) and coupled that with skill in archery;

then the Israelites provide an excellent explanation of the Huns' origin.

This is particularly important since virtually no two historians agree on the origin of the Huns.

---

[140] https://en.wikipedia.org/wiki/Goths

The Huns were a nomadic tribe whose origin is unknown but, most likely, they came from "somewhere between the eastern edge of the Altai Mountains and the Caspian Sea, roughly modern Kazakhstan" (Kelly, 45). They are first mentioned in Roman sources by the historian Tacitus in 91 CE as living in the region around the Caspian Sea and, at this time, are not mentioned as any more of a threat to Rome than any other barbarian tribes. In time, this would change as the Huns became one of the primary contributors to the fall of the Roman Empire, as their invasions of the regions around the empire, which were particularly brutal, encouraged what is known as the Great Migration (also known as the "Wandering of the Nations") between 376-476 CE.[141]

In 91 AD, the "region around the Caspian Sea" was controlled by the Parthian Empire. The "Scythians" or Dahae who lived to the east of the Caspian Sea were the same people from which came Arsaces I, the first king of the Parthian Empire and the founder of the Arsacid dynasty.

Their home was destroyed by the Sasanian Persian Empire in 224 AD and many of the Parthians migrated to the Pontic Steppe. However, about 100 years later, in the late 4th Century, "White Huns" (Ephthalites or Nephthalites) *suddenly* appeared and went to war with the Sasanians. By the beginning of the 5th Century they occupied the regions of Tokharistan and Bactria (Northern Afghanistan). This group of people was exceedingly warlike, and after their emergence they rapidly conquered the territories south of their lands of origin all the way into northern India.[142]

There were at least 4 unique groups identified by various historians as "Huns": 1. The Huns who invaded Europe 372 – 453 AD who's most famous and powerful leader was "Attila the Hun"; 2. The Magyars who entered Hungary in 898 AD; 3. the White Huns or Ephthalites who joined in the invasion of Europe who were originally from the area between the Black and Caspian Seas and 4. The Hunas who invaded India.

Of these 4 groups only the 1st and 3rd are of interest for our quest to understand their roles the migration of the peoples among whom were the Israelites.

In the late 4th Century the Huns invaded Europe.

Historians say *some* of the Huns who invaded Europe were of Oriental or Indian extraction and were not attractive in appearance. But much evidence shows the White Huns became partners with the Kidarite or Kushan people of northern India and that those Kidarite people aided the White Huns militarily when required.

[141] https://www.ancient.eu/Huns/
[142] https://www.ancient.eu/White_Huns_(Hephthalites)/

Before detailing the rulers of the Indian Empire of the White Huns, a distinction should be made about what their role exactly was. The first king of the White Huns in India is known by the name Tunjina or Khingila. However, this name comes with a title of "Tegin" as well. This title denotes governor or warlord. However, there is an entirely different title of the Kagan that is given to the overlord of the White Huns, whose seat is said to be near Bukhara. Evidence suggests that the White Huns who came into India were, although of the same lineage, different in terms of their ruling dynasty and established an outlying independent kingdom in India which was working in tandem with the wider territories in Central Asia. As such, the White Huns can be divided into the Hunas of India, and the Hephthalites of Central Asia. Although they retained separate rule, they nonetheless remained in contact and in alliance, aiding each other militarily when required.[143]

Thus, the ethnic anomaly of the Oriental Huns and the White Huns is readily explained. When the Huns exploded out of the Caucasian Mountains and the Pontic Steppe, they quickly overran the Alani, the Sarmatians, Medes, Israelites, Scythians and moved on to conquer the Goths in the late 4th Century AD. The Huns absorbed and incorporated all these people into their forces. (M7) (C4)

The 6th-century Roman historian Procopius of Caesarea called the majority of the Huns who invaded Europe the Hephthalites or "White Huns" and stated they were the Huns who subjugated the Sassanids and invaded northwestern India. He contrasted the Hephthalites with the nominal description of the Huns as "Asiatic" and "swarthy". The Hephthalites were sedentary, white-skinned, and possessed "not ugly" features.

> The Ephthalitae Huns, who are called White Huns [...] The Ephthalitae are of the stock of the Huns in fact as well as in name, however they do not mingle with any of the Huns known to us, for they occupy a land neither adjoining nor even very near to them; **but their territory lies immediately to the north of Persia** [...] They are not nomads like the other Hunnic peoples, but for a long period have been established in a goodly land... They are the only ones among the Huns who have white bodies and countenances which are not ugly. **It is also true that their manner of living is unlike that of their kinsmen, nor do they live a savage life as they do; but they are ruled by one king, and since they possess a lawful constitution, they observe right and justice in their dealings both with one another and with their neighbours, in no degree less than the Romans and the Persians.**[144] (T4)

---

[143] *ibid*

Figure 6.5

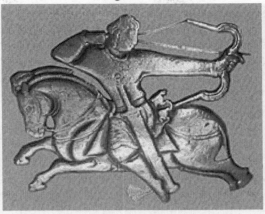

Hephthalite horseman on British Museum bowl, 460–479 CE.

It is interesting that a 6th Century Roman historian would heap such praise upon the Huns – saying they were a moral and upright people when so many of his peers over the years denigrated the Huns at every turn – especially the Gothic Historian Jordanes who claimed the Huns were descended from witches.[118] [145]

The historians were obviously confused. Roman historian Ammianus Marcellinus, who completed his work of the history of the Roman Empire in the early 390s, recorded that the "people of the Huns ... dwell beyond the Sea of Azov near the frozen ocean". Jerome associated them with the Scythians in a letter written four years after the Huns invaded the empire's eastern provinces in 395.

They equated the Huns with the Scythians; a general fear of the coming of the Antichrist in the late 4th century gave rise to their identification with Gog and Magog[146] (whom Alexander the Great had shut off behind inaccessible mountains, according to a popular legend). This demonization of the Huns is also reflected in Jordanes's Getica, written in the 6th century, which portrayed them as a people descending from "unclean spirits" and expelled Gothic witches.[147]

Procopius[148] gave us the "homeland" of the Huns – "immediately to the north of Persia". The land of the Medes to which the Israelites were deported was

---

[144] Procopius of Caesarea (Book I. ch. 3)

[145] https://www.britannica.com/biography/Jordanes

[146] Ezekiel chapters 38 and 39; Revelation 20:7–10

[147] https://en.wikipedia.org/wiki/Huns

[148] https://www.britannica.com/biography/Procopius-Byzantine-historian

immediately to the north of Persia; the land of the Dahae was due north or northeast. It is reasonable to assume that at least *some* of the Huns were Israelites.

Atilla the Hun

Atilla, the most famous and the most powerful Hun, established an empire that stretched from the regions of present-day Russia down through Hungary and across Germany to France and the Atlantic Ocean. He received regular tribute from Rome and, in fact, was paid a salary as a Roman general even as he was raiding Roman territories and destroying Roman cities. His name is still mentioned in military combat training today.

Attila reigned over the Hunnic Empire for almost 20 years (434 – 453 AD). The Huns were part of a vast swarm of nomads who overwhelmed the populations of Eastern and Central Europe and Western Europe as far as the Atlantic coast of France. The continuously held territory of his reign is shown in Figure 6.7

Figure 6.6 Attila the Hun (P5)

Figure 6.7
Empire of Attila the Hun

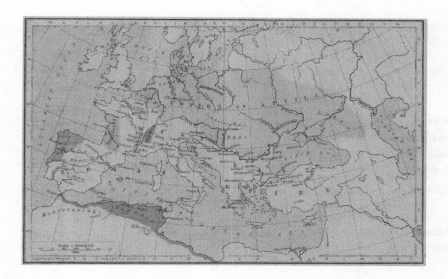

In 434, Attila's first conquest of the Roman Empire was negotiated by envoys of Eastern Roman Emperor Theodosius II. It was "negotiated" because the Eastern Roman Empire armies were defeated sequentially from the beginning and Constantinople was suing for peace and willing to pay tribute.

Attila met with the imperial legation at Margus (Požarevac) seated on horseback in the Hunnic manner, and negotiated an advantageous treaty. The Romans agreed to return the fugitives, to double their previous tribute of 350 Roman pounds (c. 115 kg) of gold, to open their markets to Hunnish traders, and to pay a ransom of eight *solidi* for each Roman taken prisoner by the Huns. The Huns, satisfied with the treaty, decamped from the Roman Empire and returned to their home in the Great Hungarian Plain, to consolidate and strengthen their empire.[149]

During a few years of "peace" with the Roman Empire, the Huns returned to Mesopotamia to punish the Sassanid Empire. After driving them out of Armenia[150], the Huns returned to their conquest of Europe in 440.

In 443 the Huns virtually destroyed the Eastern Roman Army and advanced to the walls of Constantinople. This time when the Romans sued for peace, the terms were harsher than the previous treaty: The Emperor agreed to hand over 6,000 Roman pounds (c. 2000 kg) of gold as punishment for having disobeyed the terms of the treaty during the invasion; the yearly tribute was tripled, rising to 2,100 Roman pounds (c. 700 kg) in gold; and the ransom for each Roman prisoner rose to 12 *solidi*.

---

[149] https://en.wikipedia.org/wiki/Attila#Early_life_and_background
[150] The first nation to declare itself "Christian"

The crushing weight of the tribute to the Huns and the incursions into their markets greatly diminished the Roman Empire's economic and political power. Additionally, the Huns kept raiding the Empire's major cities at will and extracting wealth and captives though the "treaty" was in effect.

By 447, Attila again rode south into the Eastern Roman Empire through Moesia. The Roman army, under Gothic magister militum Arnegisclus, met him in the Battle of the Utus and was defeated, though not without inflicting heavy losses. The Huns were left unopposed and rampaged through the Balkans as far as Thermopylae.

The Eastern Roman Empire never recovered and only survived because its great wealth allowed the payment of tribute to various major chieftains to prevent their total destruction.

In 450 AD Attila proclaimed his intent to attack the Visigoth kingdom of Toulouse by making an alliance with Emperor Valentinian III. He had previously been on good terms with the Western Roman Empire and its influential general Flavius Aëtius. Aëtius had spent a brief exile among the Huns in 433, and the troops that Attila provided against the Goths and Bagaudae had helped earn him the largely honorary title of magister militum in the west. The gifts and diplomatic efforts of Geiseric, who opposed and feared the Visigoths, may also have influenced Attila's plans.[151]

Attila gathered his vassals—Gepids, Ostrogoths, Rugians, Scirians, Heruls, Thuringians, Alans, Burgundians, among others–and began his march west. In 451, he arrived in Belgica with an army exaggerated by Jordanes to half a million strong.

The two armies clashed in the Battle of the Catalaunian Plains, the outcome of which is commonly considered to be a strategic victory for the Visigothic-Roman alliance. Theodoric was killed in the fighting, and Aëtius failed to press his advantage, according to Edward Gibbon and Edward Creasy, because he feared the consequences of an overwhelming Visigothic triumph as much as he did a defeat. From Aëtius' point of view, the best outcome was what occurred: Theodoric died, Attila was in retreat and disarray, and the Romans had the benefit of appearing victorious.[152]

> This was Attila's first and only defeat. In 452 the Huns invaded Italy and sacked several cities, but famine and pestilence compelled them to leave. In 453 Attila died; his many sons divided up his empire and at once began quarreling among themselves. They then began a series of costly struggles

---

[151] Ibid
[152] ibid

with their subjects, who had revolted, and were finally routed in 455 by a combination of Gepidae, Ostrogoths, Heruli, and others in a great battle on the unidentified river Nedao in Pannonia. The Eastern Roman government thereupon closed the frontier to the Huns, who ceased to play any significant part in history, gradually disintegrating as a social and political unit.[153]

The Roman historian Priscus, who was part of an embassy that visited Attila on the Danube left the only eyewitness account that we have of the Hun king and his capital. Priscus offers a picture unlike that recorded by other Roman historians. The discovery of a rich fifth century Hun hoard[154] in Pietrosa, Romania, strongly suggests that the Hun king permitted his subjects to enrich themselves, but it is to Priscus that we owe much of our evidence of Attila's generosity.[155]

The Hun king was capable of mercy—or at least cool political calculation. When he uncovered a Roman plot against his life, Attila spared the would-be assassin from the hideous fate that would have awaited any other man. Instead, he sent the would-be assassin back to his paymasters in Constantinople, accompanied by note setting out in humiliating detail the discovery of the Roman scheme—and a demand for further tribute.[156]

Of all Attila's better qualities, the one that most commends him to the modern mind is his refusal to be seduced by wealth. Priscus, again, makes the point most clearly, describing Attila greeting the Roman ambassadors with a banquet,

> There were tables, large enough for three or four, or even more, to sit at, were placed next to the table of Attila, so that each could take of the food on the dishes without leaving his seat. The attendant of Attila entered first with a dish full of meat, and behind him came the other attendants with bread and viands, which they laid on the tables. A luxurious meal, served on silver plate, had been made ready for us and the barbarian guests, but Attila ate nothing but meat on a wooden trencher. In everything else, too, he showed himself temperate; his cup was of wood, while to the guests were given goblets of gold and silver. His dress, too, was quite simple, affecting only to be clean. The sword he carried at his side, the latchets of his Scythian shoes, the bridle of his horse were not adorned, like those of the other Scythians, with gold or gems or anything costly.[157]

---

[153] https://www.britannica.com/topic/Hun-people

[154] http://www.academia.edu/1572582/Huns_and_other_peoples_archaeological_evidence_in_present-day_Romania

[155] Information from https://www.smithsonianmag.com/history/nice-things-to-say-about-attila-the-hun-87559701/

[156] *Ibid*

To the best of our knowledge, no one has ever suggested that Attila was an Israelite.

But that changes with our narrative. It is not without convincing reasons why this might have been so. He had the light skin and the features of a Semite and the various peoples who followed him were carrying the Israelite bloodline. His system of government was very reminiscent of Deioces' design of government. It also mirrors the Persian Empire of Cyrus, the Great; likewise, it was similar to the Parthian Empire in many aspects – allowing local rule, operating with written codes for government and allowing conquered people to join not only his army but his culture and civilization.

When the Huns defeated and absorbed the Alani, the Ostrogoths, the Visigoths, the Scythians, the Parthians and the Aryans, there were vast numbers among them who carried the blood lines of the Covenant people. They conquered the land all the way to Gaul (France) (M8) before they were stopped.

The Huns disappear from historical reports after 455 AD as if they never existed. Those who invaded Europe evidently became indistinguishable from the people they had conquered. This adds further credence to the assertion that they were Semitic and likely many of them were Israelite.

There is little historical mention of the religion of the Huns other than suggestions that when they were still in the Middle-East they worshipped the sun god. The same could be said of the Israelites until they converted to Christianity in the 1st Century AD. As the Huns absorbed the people they conquered, it is certain some of them converted to Christianity; otherwise they would not have blended so completely with the central and western Europeans.

The Huns are given much of the credit for the destruction of the Roman Empire; the Ostrogoths and Visigoths (who eventually rebelled and defeated the Huns) played a large part in the fall of the Roman Empire. Here then, are two candidate peoples for the Stone Kingdom as foretold by the prophet Daniel – the Goths and the Huns (see Figure 6.10). (B3)

The Huns, of course, did not truly disappear.[119] Instead they *became* Goths or Franks or Anglo-Saxons, or whatever name Roman and Greek Historians chose to call them. They were most likely, based on their character and temperament, the impetus for the beginning of the rise of the Stone Kingdom. The same drive that led them to conquer and destroy the Roman Empire kept them from bowing down to the

---

[157] https://www.britannica.com/biography/Procopius-Byzantine-historian

church in Rome and to a large extent the secular rulers of Central and Western Europe. They were certainly included among those who migrated to the British Isles.

Visigoths and Ostrogoths (M9) (425 – 555 AD)[158]

The Goths remained divided – as Visigoths (west) and Ostrogoths (east) – during the 5th Century. These two tribes were among the peoples who clashed with the Roman Empire during the Migration Period. A Visigothic force led by Alaric I sacked Rome in 410. Honorius granted the Visigoths Aquitania, where they defeated the Vandals and conquered most of the Iberian Peninsula by 475.

In 454 AD, the Visigoths successfully revolted against the Huns at the Battle of Nedao and their leader Theoderic the Great invaded what is now Italy in 488 and settled his people there, founding an Ostrogothic Kingdom which eventually gained control of the whole Italian peninsula.

The Visigothic kingdom persisted until 553 under Teia, when Italy returned briefly to Byzantine control. This restoration of imperial rule was reversed by the conquest of the Lombards in 568. Shortly after Theodoric's death, the country was conquered by the Byzantine Empire in the Gothic War (535–554) that devastated and depopulated the peninsula.

In 552, after their leader Totila was killed at the Battle of Taginae, effective Visigothic resistance ended, and the remaining Goths in Italy were assimilated by the Lombards, another Germanic tribe, who invaded Italy and founded the Kingdom of the Lombards in 567 AD.

Figure 6.8

Migrations and kingdoms of the Goths in the 5th and 6th centuries AD

---

[158] Most of the following information comes from https://en.wikipedia.org/wiki/Goths

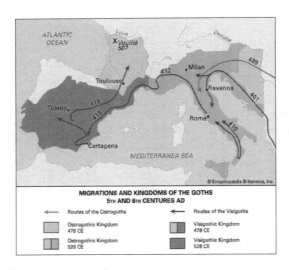

MIGRATIONS AND KINGDOMS OF THE GOTHS
5TH AND 6TH CENTURIES AD

The Goths as were instrumental as were the Huns in the fall of the Western Roman Empire. After they ceased to be a political force or an identifiable nation, they took up residence in Spain, France, Italy and southern Germany. (M9)

When the Franks conquered the Italian peninsula, it was not many years until the hierarchy of the church at Rome began to exert its influence not only upon the religious life of the people of Central and Western Europe but also upon the political structures of that region.

Eventually, for a monarch to have credibility with the "common people" he would obtain the blessing and/or the ordination of the pope in Rome. Thus, came to be the "Holy Roman Empire".

With the national and governmental endorsement of the Catholic Church, most of the residents of Central and Western Europe were Christians and increasingly under not just the religious jurisdiction of Rome but also secular control as well. (M10)

The "Migration Period" – the first millennium AD

Historians often describe the "Migration Period" in which large numbers of people, originating in Western Asia (including the Medean area between the Caspian and Black Seas – the foothills of the Caucasian Mountains) moved into Eastern Europe, the Balkans, middle Europe and eventually into Western Europe.[159]

---

[159] https://en.wikipedia.org/wiki/Migration_Period

The Migration Period was a time of widespread migrations of peoples, notably the Germanic tribes and the Huns, within or into Europe in the middle of the first millennium AD. It has also been called in English by the German loan word *Völkerwanderung* and—from the Roman and Greek perspective—the Barbarian Invasions. Many of the migrations were movements of Germanic, Hunnic, Slavic, and other peoples into the territory of the then Roman Empire with or without accompanying invasions or war.

Scientific consensus has established time frames for the Migration Period as beginning with the invasion of Europe by the Huns in 375 and ending with the conquest of Italy by the Lombards in 568.[160] Along the way the last vestiges of the Western Roman Empire were destroyed.

Various factors contributed to this phenomenon. Starting in 382, the Roman Empire and individual tribes made treaties regarding their settlement in its territory. The Franks, a Germanic tribe which would later found Francia—a predecessor of modern France and Germany—settled in the Roman Empire by whom they were given a task of securing the northeastern Gaul border.

Western Roman rule was first violated with the crossing of the Rhine and the following invasions of the Vandals and Suebi. With wars ensuing between various tribes, as well as local populations in the Western Roman Empire, more and more power was transferred to Germanic militaries.[161] Those "Germanic" militaries were made up of the migrants whose Greek and Roman names we've given so often.

The destruction of the Roman Empire is most important for tracing the Israelite blood lines through all these transitions. Daniel's prophecy predicted that the Stone Kingdom that would rise would first destroy the Roman Empire.

That destruction took several hundred years but if we carefully note the peoples responsible, we'll see people who *could have traced their ancestry to the Kingdom of Israel*. Furthermore, if they were zealous Christians, they knew that the New Covenant made no distinction between Israelites and other nations. But it appears that historians gave little thought to their origins.

The Eastern Roman Empire was less affected by migrations and survived until the Fall of Constantinople in 1453. In the modern era, the Migration Period has been increasingly described with a rather negative connotation. Contemporary historians even declare that the "barbarian" kingdoms that arose in 5th and 6th centuries and

---

[160] *Ibid*
[161] https://en.wikipedia.org/wiki/Migration_Period

came to decisively shape European culture of the upcoming middle Ages were made up of indigenous people.

They fail to mention that these "barbarians" were predominantly Christians and were, in fact, much less barbarian than many of the Romans who maintained their worship of pagan gods and who still at least occasionally persecuted Christians.

The migrants comprised war bands or tribes of 10,000 to 20,000 people, but in the course of 100 years, they averaged not more than 750,000 in total, compared to an average 39.9 million population of the Roman Empire at that time.

Although immigration was common throughout the time of the Roman Empire, the period in question was, in the 19th century, often defined as running from about the 5th to 8th centuries AD. The first migrations of peoples were made by Germanic tribes such as the Goths (including the Visigoths and the Ostrogoths), the Vandals, the Anglo-Saxons, the Lombards, the Suebi, the Frisii, the Jutes, the Burgundians, the Alamanni, the Scirii and Franks; they were later pushed westward by the Huns, the Avars, the Slavs and the Bulgars.[162]

Not only did they destroy the Western capital of the Roman Empire but these same people implementing the destruction also carried the Gospel. With the gospel the church grew. As explained earlier, the migration of Christians out of the Parthian Empire and into Europe, intermingling and trading with the Roman Empire, accounts for the exponential growth of the church in the first three centuries AD.

Although the internecine warfare between the Sarmatians, Medes, Israelites, Scythians, Parthians, and Huns et al would have insured some mixing of genes and ancestry, the Covenant bloodlines were strong in these people.

The Israelite Bloodline in 7th Century AD

We have now traced the migrations from Medea to Western Europe with the Medes, Scythians, Parthians, Aryans, Sarmatians, Alani, Goths, Huns, Ostrogoths, Visigoths, Lombards and Franks blood lines intermingled as they entered the 7th Century AD, moving all the way to Gaul and continuing geographically throughout Western Europe.

There can be little doubt that the descendants of Ephraim, Manasseh and the other 8 tribes were pushed westward in the "great migration" with the various peoples named.

---

[162] https://en.wikipedia.org/wiki/Migration_Period

Additionally, we showed that the Israelites in the Parthian Empire were converted to Christianity in large numbers – large enough to rationally explain the heretofore unexplained exponential growth of Jesus' church in the first three centuries AD.

Though a person with Israelite blood would have been virtually indistinguishable from their neighbors, they nonetheless were "owed" the promises of the Covenants – a "great nation" and a "company of nations" with political and economic hegemony – "possessing the gates of their enemies" and having "nations bow down to them".

By the 7th Century AD hose promises had still not been delivered

Migrations of the Israelites (700 –? AD)

In the 7th Century AD we must add the Angles, Saxons, Jutes, Frisians, Celtics and Germanic people to all those named before – from the Medes and Parthians to the Lombards and Franks. It seems impossible to determine the *real* origins of any of these people with certainty. An intensive study of the recorded history from the 1st Century to the 14th Century will confirm that impossibility.

Those whose writings are reasonably reliable otherwise confused the names and origins of the people of whom they wrote; Roman and Greek historians were biased by their concerns for the Roman Empire. The Catholic Church historians, concerned primarily with the Catholic Church and events that impacted the church, tended to ignore or lose any "barbarian" historians' writings.

So, we ask the question, "How can we be sure of the origins of any of the people of Central and Western Europe over this period?"

When historical records are distorted or run dry, we become limited to connecting the time when that distortion began to the potential times of future fulfillment of historical prophecies.

One connection is a prophecy from the great prophet Isaiah (B4):

> 9 Remember the former things, those of long ago; I am God, and there is no other; I am God, and there is none like me. 10 I make known the end from the beginning, from ancient times, what is still to come. I say: My purpose will stand, and I will do all that I please. Isaiah 46:9–10 (NIV84)

If we look to the "end" of God's purpose we find:

- The destruction of the Roman Empire (see Figure 6.9)
- The establishment of the Stone Kingdom
- The growth of that Kingdom to essentially rule the whole world
- The delivery of the Covenant promises to the descendants of Ephraim and Manasseh
- The delivery of the Covenant promises to the whole world
- The reunification of the children of Israel
- The return of Jesus Christ as "Lord of lords and King of kings
- The *final judgment* of all mankind
- Eternity with God and His people

To this point in 700 AD, we are not yet to fulfillment of the first two predictions, which are the "destruction of the Roman Empire" and the "establishment of the Stone Kingdom."

In the next Chapter we will examine the period from 700 – 1453 AD. The latter is the date most accepted by historians as the final demise of the Roman Empire. We will review the culture, the technology, the growth of knowledge and science, the growth of Christianity, the role of the Roman church and several other factors that fill "the Dark Ages".

We've traced the Israelites to 700 AD – over 1300 years ago. We know when the Roman Empire ceased to exist: in 1453. That was 753 years beyond any clear tracing of the Israelite migration.

Examining those 1300 plus years from 700 AD to today, which are the nations from that time that possibly could have had the physical Covenant promises given to them? For it is among those nations that we will find the descendants of Abraham, Isaac and Jacob. What peoples became a nation and a "company of nations" with political and economic hegemony – "possessing the gates of their enemies" and having "nations bow down to them"? *Although there were several nations that grew to be powerful and established "empires" over those 1300 years, none rivals the British Empire for ruling the whole world.*

In the next chapter, we'll pay special attention to England, Scotland, Wales and Ireland since it is likely that they are the origin of the "company of nations" prophesied in God's Covenant with the Patriarchs and Israel.

Figure 6.8
Daniel's Stone Kingdom Prophecy – Destruction of the Roman Empire – Rise of the Stone Kingdom

Daniel 2:36–43 Prophecy of 4 successive empires:

- ➤ Babylonian
- ➤ Medo-Persian
- ➤ Greek/Macedonian
- ➤ Roman Empire

Daniel 2:34–35, 44-45 Prophecy of the Stone Kingdom to arise upon the destruction of the Roman Empire

Goths

- ➤ 230 AD Goths, supplemented by Parthians, Israelites, Medes, Scythians and Alans begin attacking and significantly weakening the Eastern Roman Empire
- ➤ 260 AD Majority of the Goths are converted to Christianity
- ➤ 270 AD Goths et al attack the Western Roman Empire. Though defeated, they retained Roman Empire provinces and continued to attack
- ➤ 325 AD Gothic bishop Theophilas Gothiae present at the First Council of Nicaea
- ➤ 410 AD Visigoths sack Rome and move on to conquer the Iberian Peninsula
- ➤ 454 AD Ostrogoths revolt against the Huns and invade and conquer Italy
- ➤ 550 AD Byzantine (Eastern Roman Empire) war with the Ostrogoths decimate the population of the Italian peninsula

Huns

- ➤ 370 AD Huns overrun the Gothic Empire and incorporate its people in the army and in their culture
- ➤ 395 AD Huns invade Eastern Roman Empire provinces
- ➤ 434 AD Attila destroyed the army of the Eastern Roman Empire placing that Empire under a truce with annual tribute payment; they destroyed the political and economic power of the whole Empire
- ➤ 450 AD Huns attack the remnants of the Western Roman Empire now allied with the Visigoths and are defeated but the power of the Western Roman Empire destroyed

The Eastern Roman Empire recouped after the Huns disappeared but paid tribute to various Goth chieftains and to the rising Islamic Caliphate to their south and east. The Empire retained some power but continued to decline until the final destruction of Constantinople in 29 May 1453.

34 While you were watching, a rock was cut out, but not by human hands. It struck the statue on its feet of iron and clay and smashed them. 35 Then the iron, the clay, the bronze, the silver and the gold were broken to pieces at the same time and became like chaff on a threshing floor in the summer. The wind swept them away without leaving a trace. But the rock that struck the statue became a huge mountain and filled the whole earth. Daniel 2:34–35 (NIV84)

The Medes, Scythians, Parthians, Aryans, Sarmatians, Alani, Goths, Huns, Ostrogoths, Visigoths, Lombards, Franks, Angles, Saxons, Jutes, Frisians and Celtics destroyed the Roman Empire leaving no trace of its power and dominion. Among those people were the bloodlines of the 10 tribes of Israel. From among those people the Stone Kingdom arose to become a world ruling Empire just as Daniel's prophecy foretold.

* * *

CHAPTER 7

The Final Scattering (700 – 1400 AD)

Migration of the Israelites from Central Europe to Britain

We have traced the path of 10 tribes of Israel from the deportation to Assyria in 721 BC to 469 AD and the dissolution of the Empire of Attila the Hun. Over the next 1000 years, those holding the Abrahamic Covenant birthright were *truly scattered* for the first time. In the first Century AD, the time of Christ, Jesus spoke of them as "the lost sheep of the house of Israel"; Josephus clearly identified them in 94 AD in large numbers in the lands "beyond the Euphrates".

For the next 4 Centuries they were known as Alani, Scythians, and Goths, Teutons, Germanic tribes, Huns etc. but no contemporary historian ever claimed that they were Israelites. Yet we know they were there and that they were spreading Christianity wherever they went.

We recorded that the Goths and Huns were the primary causes of the destruction of the Roman Empire – the Western Empire fell in the 5th Century. A beleaguered Eastern Roman Empire's demise came in 1453 with a little help from the Normans, among whom it is likely were many Israelites.

Chaos in Central and Western Europe

The migrations from Asia to Central and Western Europe of the people among whom the Israelites were scattered were in no way nomadic; they were expansions forced by population increases, wars and conflicts. Because of the loose political structure, tribes did not always migrate *en masse*. Some groups remained in their homelands; some settled and built cities along the migration routes.

Tribes disappeared – at least in the minds of the Greek and Roman historians on whose writings we rely for the scant information available. Thus, Scythians, Sarmatians, Alani, Israelites and Aryans became Goths; many of those same people –

even the Goths – were counted as Huns as the Huns blazed across Europe. Attila incorporated them all and added to the destruction the Goths had wreaked and so weakened the Eastern Roman Empire that it never fully recovered.

These different tribal groups often united for conflicts then split to migrate afterward taking up other wanderers as they traveled. These migrations and conflicts required skilled, strong leadership to keep their people fed and united. This promoted the social and political elevation of an educated, noble or kingly class among these "barbarians".

Because of the military prowess of the Huns and Goth, everywhere within the Roman Empire, towns were fortified – even Rome itself. Franks and Saxons ravaged the coasts of northern Gaul (modern day France) and the British Isles; the incursions of the Visigoths (west) and Ostrogoths (east) kept the Roman Empire from recovering. In fact, it was the only the recruiting of these same tribes – so-called Germanic tribes – by the Roman military paying tribute to their leaders that allowed the Empire to survive as long as it did.

After the Empire of the Huns, none of the migrating tribes were able to coalesce into political unions similar to the Goths or the Huns and their associations were loose at best. The economies of these weak federations were unable to support the steadily growing population and that led to continuing migration and incursions into the Roman Empire both militarily and socially through trade.

This was the beginning of a societal divide that did not coalesce until the complete destruction of the Eastern capitol of the Roman Empire in Constantinople. There were the Greeks, Romans, Egyptians and the remnants of the Persian Empire who were the "Mediterraneans"; a few hundred miles west, north or east were found the land of the "barbarians" (anyone who wasn't Greek or Roman). The Germanic people from north-central Europe were comparatively small in number but they were aggressive.

In 476 AD, a "barbarian" general name Odoacer was declared king of Italy; he deposed the last Western Roman Emperor – Romulus Augustulus – at Ravenna and the Roman Empire of the west was at an end. In the east, the imperial rule remained and Constantinople[120] survived many sieges until its collapse in 1453 AD. "Old Rome" declined into an episcopal center and did not regain its imperial characteristics until the "Holy Roman Empire" appeared.[163]

---

[163] https://www.britannica.com/topic/history-of-Europe/The-Middle-Ages

From the 6th Century onward the migrating "barbarians" clung to their cultures and their version of Christianity (Arianism in part) and resisted assimilation into the Roman Catholic hegemon.[121]

Further migration from the East slowed and essentially stopped for half a century because of a great plague that started in Eastern Europe.

The Plague of Justinian – named for Emperor Justinian of the Eastern Empire – struck Constantinople in 541 AD. From 542 to 594, up to half the population of Europe died – in part, because of the concentration of large populations in fortified cities. The plague spread as far north as Denmark and as far west as Ireland. The plague also spread to Asia, North Africa and Arabia. Millions died.[164] A large majority of the deaths in Europe occurred in the crowded population centers of the Roman Empire.

This further weakened the power and status of what remained of the Roman Empire.

Tracing Israel

From central and western Europe, we can only trace the Israelites as components of many peoples: Goths (including the Visigoths and the Ostrogoths), the Vandals, the Anglo-Saxons, the Lombards, the Suebi, the Frisii, the Jutes, the Burgundians, the Alamanni, the Scirii, Franks and Normans et al.

Furthermore, based on the Seven Times punishment we covered in Chapter 2, more than a millennium lies ahead of them before the physical Covenant promises will be delivered.

As a reminder of the seven-times punishment a figure from Chapter 2 is reproduced as Figure 7.1 with an added specific time calculation:

Figure 7.1
The "Seven Times" Punishment
In the books of Daniel and Revelation there is an expression used – "time, times and half a time" [Daniel 7:25, 12:7; Revelation 12:14]. That this period is 3 ½ years or 42 months or 1,260 days can be seen by these scriptures [Revelation 11:2, 3; 12:6]. In prophecy a "time" is one year – 360 days according to the calendars used during Biblical times.

---

[164] http://listverse.com/2009/01/18/top-10-worst-plagues-in-history/

A "time" is one year; one year is 360 days; and "seven times" is 2,520 days. Using the "day for a year" concept one multiplies 7 X 360 = 2,520 years.

Since we know that the 10 tribes' punishment began in 721 BC with the Israelites kingdom destroyed and up to 200,000 of them deported from their homeland to the "cities of the Medes", simple math will give us the approximate dates of when that punishment will end.

721 BC + 2,520 years = 1799 AD

As a reminder of the Biblical promises the related scripture is reproduced here:

> 40 'But if they confess their iniquity and the iniquity of their fathers, with their unfaithfulness in which they were unfaithful to Me, and that they also have walked contrary to Me, 41 and *that* I also have walked contrary to them and have brought them into the land of their enemies; if their uncircumcised hearts are humbled, and they accept their guilt— 42 then I will remember My covenant with Jacob, and My covenant with Isaac and My covenant with Abraham I will remember; I will remember the land. 43 The land also shall be left empty by them, and will enjoy its Sabbaths while it lies desolate without them; they will accept their guilt, because they despised My judgments and because their soul abhorred My statutes. 44 Yet for all that, when they are in the land of their enemies, I will not cast them away, nor shall I abhor them, to utterly destroy them and break My covenant with them; for I *am* the LORD their God. 45 But for their sake I will remember the covenant of their ancestors, whom I brought out of the land of Egypt in the sight of the nations, that I might be their God: I *am* the LORD.'" Leviticus 26:40–45 (NKJV)

Rome Controlled and Defined Church History

Over the next 700 years – the Dark Ages – the Roman Church gained political power to accompany its religious power. Catholic historians were concentrated in monasteries and their writings were known only to the prelates who monitored what they were writing. Those prelates insured the history recorded did not contradict the doctrines dictated by the hierarchy in Rome. Their descriptions of historical events available to today's historians concentrate on those deemed worthy by the prelates – these were the priests, bishops and other leaders of the Roman Church.

Today's historians and Bible scholars almost without exception accept the premise that only those historical figures and what they said and did represent the Christian church. Any significant Christian leader from this period who deviated from the doctrines of Rome was either denigrated or ignored by Catholic historians and that premise permeates the writings of our current sources of the history of the Dark Ages.

We must remember, however, there were always dissidents and relatively large religious groups who would not bow to the Pope in Rome. Their stories remain untold to this day – they are only hinted at – as one can readily observe by reading contemporary accounts of the Dark Ages. This is one good reason the time is called "the Dark Ages".

From this point forward, new criteria are needed to identify the people carrying the bloodlines of the scattered Israelites. The physical promises of enormous wealth coupled with international hegemony and political power have not yet been delivered to the children of Israel.

The most *important* way of tracking "the lost sheep of the House of Israel" is to observe the spread of the Gospel of Jesus Christ. That Gospel was delivered to the Israelites in their vast numbers in the Parthian Empire by the Apostles. These ambassadors of the Kingdom of God were eye-witnesses of Jesus' life, death and resurrection. Their ears heard His teaching. To add to that credibility, they routinely healed the sick, gave sight to the blind, made the lame to walk and introduced the citizens of the Parthian Empire to God's holy spirit.

The prophecy from Jeremiah[165], repeated in the New Testament book of Hebrews, quoted God saying His New Covenant would be with both the House of Israel and the House of Judah and that He would put His laws "in their minds and write them on their hearts".

History tells us it was not primarily the Jews who spread the Gospel – a large majority of the Jews rejected Jesus as the Messiah. It was the "lost sheep" Israelites who learned of that New Covenant from Jesus' apostles. It was they who were responsible for the exponential growth of the church and its spread throughout Europe. Where that Gospel was concentrated, both inside and outside the auspices of the Roman church, is where Israelites were located – especially when those holding it rebelled against the hegemony of the Pope in Rome.

The Middle Ages

The period from the 6th Century AD to 1400 AD is traditionally known as the Middle Ages, or the Dark Ages.

---

[165] Hebrews 8:8–12 (NIV84)

Though often regarded – with some good reasons – as a time of uninterrupted ignorance, superstition and social oppression, the Middle Ages can also be seen as time during which the people of Europe emerged as a distinct cultural unit. The political, social and economic structures were profoundly reorganized as Roman imperial traditions gave way to those of the descendants of the people who established the Medo-Persian (Achaemenid) Empire, the Parthian Empire, the Gothic Empire and the Empire of the Huns.

These people held to traditions in government first established by Deioces when he united Medea (Chapter 5):

> Local rule (those conquered who lost honorably were allowed to continue to rule albeit under the auspices of and paying taxes to their conqueror)
> Freedom of religion
> Freedom to completely join and be a part of the culture of the conqueror
> Governing by rule of law rather than solely by the whims of the dictator.

They despised the government of the Romans and thought that the Roman system promoted weakness and decadence both in the leaders and the people. That attitude is justifiable when you consider that these "barbarians" destroyed the Roman Empire that had 40+ times their population.

New forms of political leadership were introduced and the population of Europe was gradually Christianized in part by the church in Rome and its local hierarchy of priests but perhaps more so by the "barbarians" who preferred their own ways of worshipping God and spreading the Gospel.

Meanwhile, the church in Rome established monasticism as the ideal form of religious life. The male true believers willingly isolated themselves in monasteries while the females likewise withdrew from society into convents other than when doing "good works".

This led to the reign of Charlemagne in the 9th Century and other rulers of the Carolingian dynasty. A small cultural revival known as the Carolingian renaissance[166] ensued.

However, that minor renaissance was profoundly changed by the Angles, Saxons and the Normans over the succeeding 4 Centuries. They laid the groundwork for the major Renaissance and the Christian Reformation movement a few centuries later – aided by the invention of the printing press making the Bible available to an increasingly literate population.[167]

---

[166] https://www.britannica.com/topic/history-of-Europe/The-Middle-Ages

Middle Ages History (Through Rome's Eyes)

Hierarchy began to form in the Christian churches in the beginning of the 2nd Century AD. As certain church "fathers" began to accumulate the power given to them by their congregations, some began to lust after more power. As their power grew, new peer groups were formed and the concepts of "clergy" and "laity" began to be fixtures in the church.

That concept was and is anathema to the teaching of Jesus.[122]

As the hierarchy of the church in Rome developed after Emperor Constantine declared Christianity the official religion of the Empire, history became more documented *but not more reliable because it was colored by the dogma of the church in Rome.*[123]

Augustine of Hippo[168] (354 -430) posited 6 ages of world history, from creation to the last judgment: 1. Adam and Eve to the flood; 2. From the flood to Abraham; 3. Abraham to David; 4. David to the Babylonian exile; 5. From the exile to Jesus; 6. From Jesus to the second coming and the reign of Christ on earth.

Church "father" Jerome (347-420) and historian Paulus Orosius (? – 417) and others interpreted the Book of Daniel[169] to indicate that the Roman Empire was the 4th of 4 successive world empires – Babylon, Medo-Persian, Greek and Roman. However, they did not relate to the destruction of that Empire as prophesied by Daniel.

Other writers in this tradition added the idea of the *translatio imperii* ("translation of empire"): from Alexander the Great to the Romans, from the Romans to the Franks under Charlemagne in 800, and from Charlemagne to the East Frankish emperors and Otto I. A number of early European thinkers built upon the idea of the translation of empire to define European civilization in terms of scholarship and chivalry (the knightly code of conduct). All these ideas were readily compatible with the Augustinian sequence of the six ages of the world.

These views prevailed until the 14th century when the literary moralist Petrarch (1304–74) introduced a new concept. Francesco Petrarca (commonly anglicized as Petrarch) was an Italian scholar and poet in Renaissance Italy, who was one of the

---

[167] https://en.wikipedia.org/wiki/Normans
[168] Book XXII of *City of God*
[169] Daniel 2:36–45 (reference chapter 4)

earliest humanists. His rediscovery of Cicero's letters is credited with initiating the 14th-century Renaissance. He is often considered the founder of Humanism.

Petrarch was fascinated with ancient Roman history and contemptuous of the time that followed it, including his own century. He divided the past into ancient and new—antiquity and recent times—and located the transition between them in the 4th century when the Roman emperors converted to Christianity.

> According to Petrarch, what followed was an age of Tenebrae ("shadows"), a "sordid middle time" with only the hope of a better age to follow. Although Petrarch's disapproval of the Christianized Roman and post-Roman world may seem irreligious, he was in fact a devout Christian; his judgment was based on aesthetic, moral, and philological criteria, not Christian ones.
> Petrarch's sonnets were admired and imitated throughout Europe during the Renaissance and became a model for lyrical poetry. He is also known for being the first to develop the concept of the "Dark Ages."[170]

His great admiration for the Roman Empire led him to perceive the period before Rome declared Christianity as a culture of great dignity filled with arts and letters and not concerned with "salvation history" or the transfer of Empires.

Petrarch's followers in later centuries focused on the transformative power of education in the arts and letters. They hoped for a renewal of the dignity of earlier Rome with its underpinning of the Greek culture – Plato, Aristotle etc. Petrarch was somewhat reviled in the 1300's but his influence is felt even today in contemporary academia – even in a "religious studies" class[124] – with the ostracizing of religious and moral teaching and a more liberal interpretation of the scriptures.

What these church fathers ignored or failed to understand was the last part of Daniel's prophecy (Chapter 4): *after the fourth kingdom fell, there was to be a fifth kingdom or empire to arise not made by human hands. The Stone Kingdom was to destroy the 4th Empire.* [171]

Across the tenure of Augustine to Petrarch, the destruction of the Roman Empire was taking place but apparently none of them ever considered the origins of the people who were responsible for the destruction to be important.

Perhaps it was because there was nothing momentous in terms of a kingdom rising that was perceived; no significant armies were being raised – few kings other

---

[170] https://en.wikipedia.org/wiki/Petrarch
[171] See Chapter 4

than those approved by the church in Rome were being anointed and crowned. Those leaders considered "dissidents" were denigrated, ignored or killed. Not truly understanding the scriptures and prophecy, they were blind to the Biblical signs. The conditions were ripe for the rise of the Stone Kingdom but it would take many years to become apparent; none of the church leaders or religious historians of that time were even looking for such an event.

In fact, with the rising political power of the church in Rome and the increasing suppression of any dissidents to their religion and authority[125], the church in Rome helped push those who had destroyed the Roman Empire out of Central Europe into the Western Civilization countries – especially the British Isles where they were somewhat isolated from the hegemony of the "Holy Roman Empire".

The Normans and many other Christian groups ignored the strictures of Church authority. They held their own traditional weddings and other societal events with no input from the Catholic clergy.[172]

Middle Ages Cultural and Technical Advances

The migrants from the East – the Huns and their allies – settled in Europe outside the Roman Empire, in the north and all along the European Atlantic Coast.

Between 1000 and 1340 the population of Europe increased from 38.5 million people to 73.5 million. The greatest proportional increase occurred in northern Europe, which trebled its population. Although this did not create a crisis of overpopulation it resulted in a great expansion in agricultural production.

The expansion in population and need for cultivated land also stimulated growth in nonagricultural workers – merchants, tradesmen and support staff – thereby creating a new division of labor and greater economic and cultural diversity.[173]

In the 14th Century, a series of technological innovations came into common usage: use of the horse in agriculture and portage and the harnessing of the power of the water mill and the windmill were among the more important innovations.

The Huns were infamous for their vast herds of horses. It was the Huns who introduced the stirrup allowing the warrior a better seat and greater striking force.[126] The stirrup also made riding horses for work or pleasure more efficient and pleasurable.

---

[172] https://en.wikipedia.org/wiki/Normans
[173] https://www.britannica.com/topic/history-of-Europe/Growth-and-innovation

Europeans now began breeding both the specialized warhorse (complete with stirrups) and the draft horse shod with iron horseshoes that protected the hooves from the damp clay soils of northern Europe. The draft horse was faster and more efficient than the ox, the traditional beast of burden. The invention of the new horse collar in the 10th century, a device that pulled from the horse's shoulders rather than from its neck and windpipe, immeasurably increased the animal's pulling power.[174]

Coupling the water mill with the extensive network of rivers in Western Europe allowed conversion of simple rotary motions into reciprocal motion by the 12th Century. This allowed a powered connection to perform many industrial tasks. This was in addition, of course, to the rapid and inexpensive grinding of grain into flour. The migrants from the East also brought knowledge of windmills for use when rivers were not available spreading the mill to more remote locations.

> In heavily forested and mountainous parts of Western Europe, foresters, charcoal burners, and miners formed separate communities, providing timber, fuel, and metallic ores in abundance. The demands of domestic and public building and shipbuilding threatened to deforest much of Europe as early as the 13th century. Increasingly refined metallurgical technology produced not only well-tempered swords, daggers, and armor for warriors but also elaborate domestic ware. Glazed pottery and glass also appeared even in humble homes, which were increasingly built of stone rather than wood and thatch.
>
> Originally a product of the agrarian dynamic that shaped society after the year 1000, the growing towns of Western Europe became increasingly important, and their citizens acquired great wealth, usually in cooperation rather than conflict with their rulers. The towns helped transform the agrarian world out of which they were originally created into a precapitalistic manufacturing and market economy that influenced both urban and rural development.[175]

Building on these technology foundations, the Stone Kingdom began to arise in the 1400's. These precursor technological innovations and the population growth led to the dispersion of wealth and freedom for those people who had the ambition to learn new technology and apply it to solve old problems. With wealth, freedom and literacy for more people – not just the aristocracy of the post-Roman Empire or the religious hierarchy from Rome – the Stone Kingdom foundation was ready for the "Enlightenment" and the "Renaissance".

The Roman Church Attempt at Control

---

[174] Ibid
[175] https://www.britannica.com/topic/history-of-Europe/Growth-and-innovation

Because they thought common people were not ready for such "advancement", the Roman Church hierarchy attempted to hold back these cultural advances. It took 400 more years (1806) and a new Empire[127] to put an end to the stagnant political hegemony and retrogression of the Roman Church. The secular power of the Roman Church which had been growing since 400 AD was brought to an end by none other than Napoleon Bonaparte.[128]

The Investiture Controversy[176], between Pope Gregory VII and the emperor Henry IV (reigned 1056–1105/06) was one of the more violent conflicts in the reform movement. In this struggle the pope claimed extraordinary authority to correct the emperor; he twice declared the emperor deposed before Henry forced him to flee Rome to Salerno, where he died in exile. Despite Gregory's apparent defeat, the conflicts undermined imperial claims to authority and shattered the Carolingian-Ottonian image of the emperor as the lay equal of the bishop of Rome, responsible for acting in worldly matters to protect the church. The emperor, like any other layman, was now subordinate to the moral discipline of churchmen.

Some later emperors, notably the members of the Hohenstaufen dynasty— including Frederick I Barbarossa (1152–90), his son Henry VI (1190–97), and his grandson Frederick II (1220–50)—reasserted imperial authority and intervened in Italy with some success. But Barbarossa's political ambitions were ended by the northern Italian cities of the Lombard League and the forces of Pope Alexander III at the Battle of Legnano in 1176.

Both Henry VI and Frederick II, who had united the imperial and Lombard crowns and added to them that of the rich and powerful Norman kingdom of Sicily, were checked by similar resistance. Frederick himself was deposed by Pope Innocent IV in 1245.

Succession disputes following Frederick's death and that of his immediate successors led to the Great Interregnum[177] of 1250–73, when no candidate received enough electoral votes to become emperor. The interregnum ended only with the election of the Habsburg ruler Rudolf I (1273–91), which resulted in the increasing provincialization of the imperial office in favour of Habsburg dynastic and territorial interests. In 1356 the Luxembourg emperor Charles IV (1316–78) issued the Golden Bull, which established the number of imperial electors at seven (three ecclesiastical and four lay princes) and articulated their powers.

---

[176] https://www.britannica.com/place/Holy-Roman-Empire/Empire-and-papacy#ref10165
[177] https://www.britannica.com/place/Germany/The-Great-Interregnum

Although the emperor possessed the most prestigious of all lay titles, the actual authority of his office was very limited. Both the Habsburgs[178] and their rivals used the office to promote their dynastic self-interests until the Habsburg line ascended the throne permanently with the reign of Frederick III (1442–93), the last emperor to be crowned in Rome. The imperial office and title were abolished when Napoleon dissolved the Holy Roman Empire in 1806.

Those who had invaded Europe – the Parthians, Israelites, Medes, Scythians, Goths and Alans brought their horses and technology to Central and Western Europe. Now called Angles, Saxons, Jutes, Frisians or just "barbarians" by contemporary historians, they still exhibited the principles followed by Deioces, Cyrus the Great and the Parthian Empire: allowing local rule, operating with written codes for government and allowing conquered people to join not only his army but his culture and civilization. These included the people who incorporated the skills of the Vikings into their European culture and called themselves "Normans".

Based on their character and temperament, the same drive that led them to conquer and destroy the Roman Empire kept them from bowing down to the church in Rome and to a large extent the secular rulers of Central and Western Europe.

That resistance and independence of thought was the bedrock upon which the Enlightenment and the Renaissance would form. Their migration continued.

Western Europe – the Stone Kingdom Grows

The warriors from the East brought their families and their ethnicity with them. Though they had been long separated from the Middle-East, their practices and governments reflected their origins.

Some of these kingdoms, especially that of the Visigoths in southern Gaul and later in Iberia (today's France and Spain), also modeled themselves on the ancient Hebrew kingdoms as described in Scripture. They brought with them certain rituals from the Israelites, such as liturgically anointing the ruler with oil. They reminded the leaders through sermons, prayers, and church council meetings that they were God's servants, with spiritual and political responsibilities that legitimized their power.[179]

As the cultures associated with the new kings and peoples spread throughout western Europe from the 5th to the 8th centuries, they influenced political and religious change in areas that the Roman Empire had never ruled—initially Ireland,

---

[178] https://www.britannica.com/topic/House-of-Habsburg#ref32089
[179] https://www.britannica.com/topic/Visigoth

then northern Britain, the lower Rhineland, and trans-Rhenish Europe (the lands east of the Rhine River). Although many of the "barbarian" kingdoms did not survive, their experiments in Christian kingship, as represented in texts, ritual, pictures, and objects, began a long tradition in European political life and thought.

The Frankish kingdom reached its peak with Charlemagne and after his reign gradually fragmented and by the 10th Century the Saxon dynasty held sway for a time. That dynasty was replaced by the Salian dynasty[180] that lasted until about 1125 AD after which the line disappeared as the Normans came into power. Each of these rather weak dynasties interfaced with the church in Rome and the king sometimes maintained his authority by claiming ordination by the Pope as head of the Holy Roman Empire.

Angles and Saxons

Angles

The Angles, together with the Jutes, Saxons, and Frisians, invaded the island of Britain in the 5th century CE. The Angles gave their name to England, as well as to the word *Englisc*,[181] used even by Saxon writers to denote their vernacular tongue.

The Angles are first mentioned in history by Tacitus (1st century CE). His descriptions in *Germania*[182] are quite interesting:

> [These people] show no traits of intermarriage with other races, being individual, pure, like none other but themselves, such that all, so far as is known with regard to their extensive population, share a common physique: eyes which are fierce and blue in colour, reddish hair, and large frames.
> The chiefs resolve minor matters, the whole tribe major ones, but with this caveat, that even those matters which the people decide are first considered by their leaders. Unless there is some sudden emergency, they gather on particular days when the moon is new or at the full, believing those to be the most auspicious moments to initiate discussion. They reckon not by the days, as we do, but by the nights.
> However, the marriage laws are strictly observed among them, and you will find nothing more laudable in their customs. They, almost alone among

---

[180] https://www.britannica.com/topic/Salian-dynasty

[181] https://www.britannica.com/topic/Angle-people#ref168444 This Anglo-Saxon name for their language became "English"

[182] Tacitus, Publius Cornelius. The Agricola and Germania (Translated, Illustrated) (p. 61) © Copyright 2015 A. S. Kline

barbarians, are content with a single wife: the very few exceptions being embraced not out of libidinous desire, but to strengthen the nobility by multiple ties.

This description of marriage could have come directly from the laws and practices of the Israelites.

According to the Venerable Bede in the Ecclesiastical History of the English People, the Angles settled in large numbers during the 5th and 6th centuries in what became the English kingdoms of Mercia, North Umbria, and East and Middle Anglia.

Saxons

The Roman Empire's decline in the northwest area of the empire was marked by vigorous Saxon piracy in the North Sea. During the 5th century CE the Saxons spread rapidly through north Germany and along the coasts of Gaul and Britain. The coastal stretch from the Elbe to the Scheldt Rivers, however, was held by the Frisians, on whom the Saxons had great influence.

Figure 7.2
Anglo-Saxon England – Encyclopædia *Britannica, Inc.*

The expansion of the Saxons brought collision with the Franks. In 772 the Frankish ruler Charlemagne decided on a campaign of conquest and conversion of the Saxons. With interruptions, the savage Saxon wars lasted 32 years and ended with the incorporation of *the Saxons remaining on the Continent* into the Frankish empire. The majority of Saxons, however, either had already migrated to England or did so because of the Saxon–Frank war.

Thus, England became home to most of the Angles and Saxons.

The Venerable Bede (in Historia Ecclesiastica) described the Germanic invaders of Britain as Angles, Saxons, and Jutes and said that the East, West, and South Saxons (of Essex, Wessex, and Sussex) were descended from the Saxons. However, Bede was not always careful to distinguish Angles and Saxons, and, furthermore, all the invaders of Britain were closely related and spoke dialects similar to each other and to the Frisian language.[183]

---

[183] https://www.britannica.com/biography/Saint-Bede-the-Venerable

The central theme of Anglo-Saxon history in England is the process by which a number of diverse Germanic peoples came to form the centralized kingdom which the Normans inherited from their English predecessors.

According to English traditions, the migration to Britain was preceded by the descent of small companies on different parts of the British coast in the second half of the 5th century. The one contemporary account of these events written by Gildas, *De excidio et conquestu Britanniae* ("The Overthrow and Conquest of Britain"), makes them originate from an invitation sent by an unnamed British prince to certain "Saxon" adventurers to enter his service and defend his country against Pictish and Scottish raiders.[184]

For whatever reasons, by the 8th Century, the Anglo-Saxons who shared a common language and culture dominated England. Over the next 5 centuries they were invaded often. The first of those invaders were from the North.

Rise of the Kingdom of England (797 – 927 AD)

In the last of the 7th Century and into the 8th, central and western Europe had to deal with a new set of invaders.

In the 9th and early 10th centuries a series of invasions from Scandinavia, the lower Danube valley, and North Africa greatly weakened the Carolingian world. The divisions within the Frankish empire impaired its ability to resist the Viking and Hungarian invasions but did not destroy it. Kings and warlords ultimately either turned back the invaders, as Otto I did in 955, or absorbed them into their territories, as the kings of West Francia did with the Vikings in Normandy. In England the invasions destroyed all of the older kingdoms except Wessex, whose rulers, starting with Alfred, expanded their power until they created a single kingdom of England.[185]

Small scattered Viking raids began in the last years of the 8th century; in the 9th century large-scale plundering incursions were made in Britain and in the Frankish empire as well. Though Egbert defeated a large Viking force in 838 that had combined with the Britons of Cornwall and Aethelwulf won a great victory in 851 over a Viking army that had stormed Canterbury and London and put the Mercian king to flight, it was difficult to deal with an enemy that could attack anywhere on a long and undefended coastline. Destructive raids are recorded for North Umbria, East Anglia, Kent, and Wessex.[186]

---

[184] https://www.britannica.com/biography/Saint-Gildas
[185] https://www.britannica.com/topic/history-of-Europe/The-Frankish-ascendancy
[186] *Ibid*

Figure 7.3

Exhumed Viking ship; in the Viking Ship Museum, Oslo, Norway.

A large Danish army came to East Anglia in the autumn of 865 intent on conquest. By 871, when it first attacked Wessex, it had already captured York, been bought off by Mercia, and had taken possession of East Anglia. Many battles were fought in Wessex, including one that led to a Danish defeat at Ashdown in 871. Alfred the Great, a son of Aethelwulf, succeeded to the throne in the course of the year and made peace; this gave him a respite until 876. Meanwhile the Danes drove out Burgred of Mercia, putting a puppet king in his place, and one of their divisions made a permanent settlement in North Umbria. [187]

Alfred was able to force the Danes to leave Wessex in 877, and they settled northeastern Mercia; but a Viking attack in the winter of 878 came near to conquering Wessex. That it did not succeed is to be attributed to Alfred's tenacity. He retired to the Somerset marshes, and in the spring, he secretly assembled an army that routed the Danes at Edington. Their king, Guthrum, accepted Christianity and took his forces to East Anglia, where they settled.

The importance of Alfred's victory cannot be exaggerated. It prevented the Danes from becoming masters of the whole of England. Wessex was never again in danger of falling under Danish control, and in the next century the Danish areas were reconquered from Wessex. Alfred's capture of London in 886 and the resultant acceptance of him by all the English outside the Danish areas was a preliminary to this reconquest.

---

[187] https://www.britannica.com/biography/Alfred-king-of-Wessex

That Wessex stood when the other kingdoms had fallen must be put down to Alfred's courage and wisdom, to his defensive measures in reorganizing his army, to his building fortresses and ships, and to his diplomacy, which made the Welsh kings his allies. Renewed attacks by Viking hosts in 892–896, supported by the Danes resident in England, caused widespread damage but had no lasting success.[188]

When Alfred died in 899, his son Edward succeeded him. A large-scale incursion by the Danes of North Umbria ended in their crushing defeat at Tettenhall in 910. Edward completed his father's plan of building a ring of fortresses around Wessex, and his sister Aethelflaed took similar measures in Mercia.

In 912 Edward was ready to begin the series of campaigns by which he relentlessly advanced into the Danelaw (Danish territory in England), securing each advance by a fortress, until he won back Essex, East Anglia, and the east-Midland Danish areas. Aethelflaed moved similarly against the Danish territory of the Five Boroughs (Derby, Leicester, Nottingham, Lincoln, and Stamford).

She obtained Derby and Leicester and gained a promise of submission from the Northumbrian Danes before she died in 918. Edward had by then reached Stamford, but he broke off his advance to secure his acceptance by the Mercians at Tamworth and to prevent their setting up an independent kingdom. Then he took Nottingham, and all the Danes in Mercia submitted to him.[189]

Athelstan succeeded his father Edward in 924. He made terms with Raegnald's successor Sihtric and gave him his sister in marriage. When Sihtric died in 927, Athelstan took possession of North Umbria, thus becoming the first king to have direct rule of all England. He received the submission of the kings of Wales and Scotland and of the English ruler of North Umbria beyond the Tyne.

Athelstan was proud of his position, calling himself "king of all Britain" on some of his coins and using in his charters flamboyant rhetoric carrying the same message.[190]

The Normans

Earlier it was noted that the most important factor for tracing Israel during the Middle Ages was through the spread of Christianity. *The next* most important factor – in some ways perhaps the greatest factor – since the trail began are the Normans.

---

[188] *Ibid*

[189] https://www.britannica.com/biography/Aethelflaed

[190] https://en.wikipedia.org/wiki/Æthelstan

The Normans more than any other culture brought the world out of the dark ages and into the most modern culture with the greatest good for all since the beginning of time. Their implemented advances in civilization have had no equal before them for their influence on culture, law, music and the common man. So much of what they incorporated into Britain came originally from Israel's laws and practices.

Origins

Recall those Vikings, or Norsemen, or "Normans" who settled in northern France (or the Frankish kingdom)? The Normans founded the duchy of Normandy and sent out expeditions of conquest and colonization to southern Italy and Sicily and to England, Wales, Scotland, and Ireland.

In the course of the 10th century, the initially destructive incursions of Norse war bands into the rivers of France evolved into more permanent encampments that included *local women* and personal property.

As with most marauding armies on foreign soil, they killed the men who resisted but seldom killed the women. The women of the area they conquered were descendants of the Goths and Huns and the various other tribes we've mentioned over and again throughout this narrative. Many of these women were Christians and – just as when the Goths overran the Alani and married their women – these women were instrumental in converting the Vikings to Christianity.

What were the origins of these women? The Empire of the Huns (Figure 6.8) shows that Attila's Empire reached to the Atlantic Ocean and the Baltic Sea. Directly north were the Scandinavian countries. The territory of the Angles and Saxons were the northwestern part of the Hun's Empire. There is no historical record of interaction between the Huns and the Danes or Vikings but it *may* have occurred[129]. Roman and Greek historians would have had little interest.

In 451 AD the Huns attacked the country we call France today – then, it was the home of the "Franks". No one could stand against the Huns. Attila sacked much of France.

What has this to do with the Normans?

The famous Battle of the Catalaunian Plains took place at Chalons (marked by the "scissors" or X in Figure 7.4). The army opposing Attila's forces, ostensibly led by Roman General Flavius Aetius, included Romans, Visigoths, Franks, Alans and Armoricans[191], amongst others.

---

[191]   Amorica   (the   Brittany   Peninsula)   was   where   the   Alans   had   settled

The Alans were placed front and center, opposite the Huns. The Armoricans supplied archers who attacked the Huns' front lines during the main battle and thwarted Attila's night assault on the Roman camp with a hail of arrows "like rain". After the battle was won, Aetius sent the Alans to Armorica and Galicia (Spain).[192]

Attila's raid before the Catalaunian Plains battle brought all those people to France and to northern France where the Viking raiders came a few hundred years later.

After reading chapters 5 and 6, those names should be familiar – Visigoths, Alans, Franks. The whole of Western Europe was populated by descendants of those same people that we traced from the Parthian Empire though Eastern and Central Europe. The descendants of the Huns, Goths, Alans and the others we've mentioned were still there all along the Atlantic Seaboard when the Vikings came. When their husbands, brothers and fathers were killed in the raids, the women were taken as wives by the raiders. The Israelite bloodlines now added Vikings to their heritage.

Figure 7.4

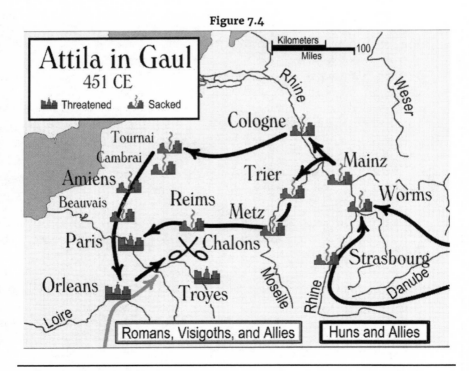

https://en.wikipedia.org/wiki/Armorica
[192] https://en.wikipedia.org/wiki/Brittany

As usual, you'll find no historical research seeking the origin of these people.

At least some of those who rose to power in the 9th Century in England, France and throughout Western Europe harbored the bloodlines of those who were promised the physical blessings of the Covenant God made with Abraham.

The descriptions of the Normans in history sound very much like the descriptions of the Huns, Goths and Alans when each was at their peak.

Norman Conquests

The Duchy of Normandy, which began in 911 as a fiefdom, was established by the treaty of Saint-Clair-sur-Epte between King Charles III of West Francia and the famed Viking ruler Rollo and was situated in the former Frankish kingdom of Neustria. The treaty offered Rollo and his men the French lands between the river Epte and the Atlantic coast in exchange for their protection against further Viking incursions. As well as granting to protect the area of Rouen from Viking invasion, Rollo had to swear not to invade further Frankish lands himself, *accept baptism and conversion to the Christian faith* and swear fealty to King Charles III. [193]

The descendants of Rollo's Vikings and their Frankish wives would replace the Norse religion and Old Norse language with Christianity and the Gallo-Romance language of the local people, blending their maternal Frankish heritage with Old Norse traditions and customs to synthesize a unique "Norman" culture in the north of France.

As their culture was incorporated into the legacy of the Goths and Huns[194], they displayed an unequaled capacity for rapid movement across land and sea, the use of brutal violence and a precocious sense of the use and value of money—these are among the traits traditionally assigned to the Normans. The brutal violence and the use of money by the Normans were also the "trademark" of the Huns albeit the Huns used their horses for that rapid movement rather than Viking ships.[130]

Like the Huns, they exhibited an extreme restlessness and recklessness, a love of fighting accompanied by almost foolhardy courage, and a craftiness and cunning that went hand in hand with outrageous treachery. In their expansion into other parts of

---

[193] https://en.wikipedia.org/wiki/Normans
[194] Who are now called "Franks" by historians

Europe, the Normans compiled a record of astonishingly daring exploits in which often a mere handful of men would vanquish an enemy many times as numerous.[195]

This was one of the blessings promised the Israelites at Mt. Sinai when they established the conditional covenant. This could also be said of the Goths, of the Huns and of the Normans.

> 7 You will pursue your enemies, and they will fall by the sword before you. 8 Five of you will chase a hundred, and a hundred of you will chase ten thousand, and your enemies will fall by the sword before you. Leviticus 26:7–8 (NIV84)

No authoritative source has been found to suggest or imply that the Viking invasions were related to the immense population growth in northern Europe and Britain that occurred after the Viking invasions. They might win battles but they lost a lot of their soldiers in the conflicts; but then the surviving Vikings were absorbed into the indigenous populations. As noted frequently the phenomenon of the victors' assimilation into the conquered populations happened over and over again. Likewise, we have previously noted the fecundity of the Israelite blood line. When the conquests were completed, the survivors assimilated.

In retrospect, the assimilation phenomenon seems purposeful; we have followed the Israelites among the Medes, among the Alani, among the Goths, among the Huns, among the Germanic tribes that originated in the northern parts of Europe. Each assimilation added some facet of that purpose. Through it all, it is fact that to some degree the Israelite blood *almost certainly* was dispersed throughout Western Europe and Britain – *their final scattering.*

Before completely conquering England, the Normans made their presence felt from Western Europe all the way back to the Middle East – the original home of the Israelites.

In 1017, they entered Italy and eventually expelled the Byzantines (Eastern Roman Empire) and the Saracens (Arabs) and conquered the Balkan Peninsula.

In 1038 – 1107, they warred with Byzantium and conquered Armenia, Georgia, the Upper Euphrates Valley and Albania. *This was truly the beginning of the end of the Eastern Roman Empire – the last vestige of that Empire. All prestige was gone from Byzantium and though their fortifications and bribes to local chieftains left Constantinople intact, its eventual demise was inevitable.*

---

[195] https://www.britannica.com/topic/Norman-people

In 1066 – the Battle of Hastings – the Norman King William the Conqueror subdued the entire land of England.

In 1072, William added Scotland into his kingdom with Wales being added gradually over the next few decades though Wales was never invaded. Thus, Great Britain was forming.

Norman Culture

It was not until 1169 that the Normans invaded and settled in Ireland. The Normans had a profound effect on Irish culture and history after their invasion at Bannow Bay.

Initially, the Normans maintained a distinct culture and ethnicity. Yet, with time, they came to be subsumed into Irish culture to the point that it has been said that they became "more Irish than the Irish themselves". The Normans settled mostly in an area in the eastern part of Ireland, later known as the Pale, and also built many fine castles and settlements, including Trim and Dublin Castles.

The cultures intermixed, borrowing from each other's language, practices and outlook. Norman descendants today can be recognized by their surnames. Names such as French, (De) Roche, Devereux, D'Arcy, Treacy and Lacy are particularly common in the southeast of Ireland, especially in the southern part of County Wexford, where the first Norman settlements were established.

Other common Norman-Irish names are Furlong and Morell; Morell (Murrell), derived from the French Norman name Morel. Names beginning with Fitz (from the Norman for son) indicate Norman ancestry. These included Fitzgerald, FitzGibbons (Gibbons dynasty) and Fitzmaurice. Families bearing such surnames as Barry (de Barra) and De Búrca (Burke) are also of Norman extraction.[196]

In 1191, with help from other European countries involved in the Crusades, the Normans conquered Cyprus. The rapid Anglo-Norman conquest of Cyprus proved more important than it might have appeared.

The island occupied a key strategic position on the maritime lanes to the Holy Land, whose occupation by the Christians could not continue without support from the sea. Shortly after the conquest, Cyprus was sold to the Knights Templar where it was subsequently acquired, in 1192, by Guy de Lusignan. After that, it became a stable feudal kingdom[197]. It was not until 1489 that the Venetians acquired full

---

[196] https://en.wikipedia.org/wiki/Normans
[197] https://www.britannica.com/event/Crusades/The-Third-Crusade#ref392436

control of the island, where it remained a Christian stronghold until the fall of Famagusta in 1571.

Norman Law

The term "Norman law" refers to the customary law of the Duchy of Normandy which developed between the 10th and 13th centuries. It survives today in the legal systems of Jersey and the other Channel Islands. Norman law grew out of a mingling of Frankish and Viking customs stemming from the creation of Normandy as a Norse colony under French rule in 911.

There are traces of Scandinavian law in the customary laws of Normandy. A charter of 1050, listing several pleas before Duke William II, refers to the penalty of banishment as *ullac* (from Old Norse *útlagr*). The word was still current in the 12th century when it was used in the Roman de Rou. Marriages were performed *more danico* ("in the Danish manner"), that is, without any ecclesiastical ceremony in accordance with an old Norse custom. The unions were recognized as legal in Normandy and in the Norman church. The first three dukes of Normandy all practiced it. [198]

Norman Music

Normandy was the site of several important developments in the history of classical music in the 11th century. Fécamp Abbey and Saint-Evroul Abbey were centers of musical production and education. At Fécamp, under two Italian abbots, William of Volpiano[199] and John of Ravenna, the system of denoting notes by letters was developed and taught. It is still the most common form of pitch representation in English- and German-speaking countries today.

Also, at Fécamp, the staff, around which neumes were oriented, was first developed and taught in the 11th century. Under the German abbot Isembard, La Trinité-du-Mont became a center of musical composition.[200]

At Saint Evroul, a tradition of singing had developed and the choir achieved fame in Normandy. Under the Norman abbot Robert de Grantmesnil, several monks of Saint-Evroul fled to southern Italy, where they were patronized by Robert Guiscard and established a Latin monastery at Sant'Eufemia. There they continued the tradition of singing.

[198] https://en.wikipedia.org/wiki/Norman_law
[199] https://en.wikipedia.org/wiki/William_of_Volpiano
[200] https://en.wikipedia.org/wiki/La_Trinit-du-Mont

The Common Good

Two of the most unusual and critical developments for the common good attributed to the Normans were The Magna Carta and The House of Commons.

The Magna Carta (1297 AD)

The Magna Carta is perhaps the most important document[201] in the history of Western Civilization – not because it was ever truly enforced but because it introduced certain principles of law that had never before been part of any government.

Among other principles, the Magna Carta proposed the right to a jury trial; the right not to have a person's life, liberty, or property taken without just reason; it guaranteed the right of Habeas Corpus; it mandated a trial if one were arrested; it established the principle that everyone is subject to the law, even the king; it guarantees the rights of individuals, the right to justice and the right to a fair trial. The Magna Carta would provide the foundation for individual rights in Anglo-American jurisprudence.

For the first time, rights were formally granted to "common people".

The background of its development is interesting

> Magna Carta Libertatum, commonly called Magna Carta, is a charter agreed to by King John of England at Runnymede, near Windsor, on 15 June 1215. First drafted by the Archbishop of Canterbury to make peace between the unpopular King and a group of rebel barons, it promised the protection of church rights, protection for the barons from illegal imprisonment, access to swift justice, and limitations on feudal payments to the Crown, to be implemented through a council of 25 barons.
> Neither side stood behind its commitments nor was the charter upheld – it was annulled by Pope Innocent III, leading to the First Barons' War.[202] After John's death, the regency government of his young son, Henry III, reissued the document in 1216, stripped of some of its more radical content, in an unsuccessful bid to build political support for their cause.
> At the end of the war in 1217, it formed part of the peace treaty agreed at Lambeth, where the document acquired the name Magna Carta, to distinguish it from the smaller Charter of the Forest which was issued at the same time. Short of funds, Henry reissued the charter again in 1225 in

---

[201] Other than the Bible

[202] A blatant example of the retrogressive nature of the Roman papacy when it held secular power

exchange for a grant of new taxes; his son, Edward I, repeated the exercise in 1297, this time confirming it as part of England's statute law.[203]

The House of Commons

How did it happen that by 1400 Britain not only had a monarch, a "house of Lords" (all the empires had their "courts" that advised the king) but also *the beginnings of a "house of Commons"?* Had any other empire ever paid substantial attention to the "common man" – that is, its merchants, soldiers and guild people?

> The Parliament of England developed from the Magnum Concilium that advised the English monarch in medieval times. This royal council, meeting for short periods, included ecclesiastics, noblemen, as well as representatives of the counties (known as "knights of the shire"). The chief duty of the council was to approve taxes proposed by the Crown. In many cases, however, the council demanded the redress of the people's grievances before proceeding to vote on taxation. Thus, it developed legislative powers.
>
> The first parliament to invite representatives of the major towns was Montfort's Parliament in 1265. At the "Model Parliament" of 1295, representatives of the boroughs (including towns and cities) were admitted. Thus, it became settled practice that each county send two knights of the shire, and that each borough send two burgesses.[131] At first, the burgesses were almost entirely powerless; while the right to representation of each English county quickly became indisputable, the monarch could enfranchise or disfranchise boroughs at pleasure.[204]

The combination of the influence of the Magna Carta and the increasing wealth of the lower classes set the stage for the rise of a civilization unlike any the world had ever seen.

The Israelite Bloodline in 14th Century AD

With the British Isles united heading into the 14th Century and the might of their armed forces and navy demonstrated throughout Western Europe and the Mediterranean, Western Civilization was beginning to form and Great Britain had laid the groundwork for the rise of the British Empire.

However, a few more very important events were needed for the foundation of that Empire to be solidified and the rise of Western Civilization to reach its zenith. Over the next 400 years the Western World experienced the Enlightenment and the

[203] https://en.wikipedia.org/wiki/Magna_Carta
[204] https://en.wikipedia.org/wiki/House_of_Commons_of_England

Renaissance, the invention of the printing press[205], the Reformation and unprecedented growth in the wealth and literacy of "common people". Those changes and their aftermath would produce The Stone Kingdom.

In the next chapter, we will explore those changes and look at the reasons to believe that Western Civilization – especially Great Britain and the United States – were the recipients of the blessings promised in God's Covenant with Abraham, Isaac, Jacob and the children of Israel.[132]

* * *

---

[205] The first book printed was the Bible

CHAPTER 8

The Rise of the Stone Kingdom (1400 – 1700)

Biased History

Even with the great advances in technology of the past six centuries, historical academia offers little substance on which to base our search for the descendants of Abraham, Isaac and Jacob other than the Jews who at least partially retained their identity.

Historians, for the most part, are biased by the information they work from. Many historians of the past – perhaps most – *tried* to present factual information rather than recording their opinions or trying to please the rulers of the government under which they lived but they *were* biased nevertheless.

Today, the Internet provides easy access to thousands of publications from credible historians but their approach to the past 2500 years is quite similar. Because the sources of factual information prior to 1500 AD are few there is little difference from one narrative to another.

One of the greatest hindrances to understanding that period is the increasing prejudice of contemporary historians toward the Bible and Christianity. There has never been a credible archeological discovery that disproved any significant historical event recorded in the Bible. Quite the opposite is true. There have been many discoveries by archeologists that proved the Biblical accounts to be true.[133]

Only a few have exerted significant effort to use the Bible as a credible source of history. If there were a better understanding of the scriptures and the *true* history of Christianity, the prejudice might be mitigated.

Greek, Roman and Catholic historians provide virtually the sole secular source of information from the 4th Century BC to the fall of the Roman Empire. The Greco-Roman and Catholic historians paid little attention to the actual origin of the people about whom they wrote and dealt more with how those people affected the Greco-Roman empires and the church.

Also, the "church" that historians follow is primarily the Roman church; contemporary historians looking to ancient sources of information about the Christian church have little to go on except for the histories recorded by Roman church historians. There are scattered historical images of those who remained outside the influence of the Roman church, but they are few indeed.

In the 19th Century the concept of "early modern history" – the period from 1400 to 1800 AD –developed in the academic curricula of history in Europe and the United States and was established in university survey courses and research seminars.

> Journals of scholarly historical research began publication in Germany (1859), France (1876), England (1886), and the United States (1895), regularly including studies of one aspect or another of the Middle Ages. Historical documents were edited and substantial scholarly literature was produced that brought the history of the Middle Ages into synchronization with other fields of history. The study of the Middle Ages developed chiefly as a part of the national histories of the individual European countries, but it was studied in the United States as a pan-European phenomenon, with a focus after World War I chiefly on English and French history. The growing influence and prestige of the new academic and professional field of medieval history were reflected in the Monumenta Germaniae Historica ("Historical Monuments of the Germans"), a research and publication institute founded in 1819 and still in operation in Munich, and in the eight-volume collaborative Cambridge Medieval History (1911–36). (The latter's replacement, The New Cambridge Medieval History, began to appear in 1998.) [206]

The Dark Ages, the Middle Ages, the Renaissance, the Reformation and the scientific revolution were subsumed into the period from 1400 – 1800 AD. Classic academia has expended little effort in determining the *true* origins of the people who brought about the Renaissance, the Reformation and the scientific revolution.

> The teaching of academic historians of the Middle Ages still generally reflect either the original tripartite division of European history or the more recent and more common quadripartite division (ancient, medieval, early modern, and modern), *most scholars specialize in only very small parts of a very long period.*[207]

[206] https://www.britannica.com/topic/history-of-Europe/The-Middle-Ages-in-modern-historiography
[207] *Ibid*

What Changed Europe's Culture after the Roman Empire?

Scholars recognized the problem of the obvious differences between the Europe of late antiquity that had been part of the Roman Empire and the culture that arose after the great migration of the first millennium – the 5th to 8th centuries AD. The migrations of the Goths (including the Visigoths and the Ostrogoths), the Vandals, the Anglo-Saxons, the Lombards, the Suebi, the Frisii, the Jutes, the Burgundians, the Alamanni, the Scirii, the Franks and the Huns completely changed the culture of Europe. [134] That change of culture only became more rapid over the next six centuries.

Roman ethnography classified external peoples as distinct and ethnically homogeneous groups with unchanging identities – they were all "barbarians". They most often called the barbarians "Scythians" or Goths or Huns.

19th Century historians adopted this view. Philologists, anthropologists and historians maintained that the "Germanic" tribes that were indigenous to Europe in the 1st Century and before were the ethnic ancestors of the people of the new European culture. Late 20th Century research in ethnogenesis demonstrated those assumptions were false.[208]

Though no ethnogenetic baseline can be scientifically established, there is every reason to believe the migrants from Medea, Mesopotamia, the Caucasian mountains and the Pontic Steppe were the ethnic preponderance of the population of northern and western Europe in the Middle Ages.

The ethnic, racial and cultural history of the migrants from the Middle East made them prone to reject any authority they had not authorized – secular or religious. At least some aspects of the Enlightenment and the Renaissance were created by this inherent resistance to the authority of the Roman Church and those leaders who were ordained by Rome.

In 1400 AD the population of Europe was growing in spite of the Black Death that ravaged Europe and the world in 1347 -1351. That plague caused an estimated 25 – 50 million deaths in Europe and other millions worldwide.[135] Internal warfare brought other deaths but still the population grew.

For the continent as a whole, the population growth under way by 1500 continued over the "long" 16th century until the second or third decade of the 17th century. A

---

[208]https://www.britannica.com/topic/history-of-Europe/Late-antiquity-the-reconfiguration-of-the-Roman-world

recent estimate by the American historian Jan De Vries set Europe's population (excluding Russia and the Ottoman Empire) at 61.6 million in 1500, 70.2 million in 1550, and 78.0 million in 1600; it then lapsed back to 74.6 million in 1650. The distribution of population across the continent was also shifting. Northwestern Europe (especially the Low Countries and the British Isles) witnessed the most vigorous expansion; England's population more than doubled between 1500, when it stood at an estimated 2.6 million, and 1650, when it probably attained 5.6 million. Northwestern Europe also largely escaped the demographic downturn of the mid-17th century, which was especially pronounced in Germany, Italy, and Spain. In Germany, the Thirty Years' War (1618–48) may have cost the country, according to different estimates, between 25 and 40 percent of its population.[209]

Many of the people of Western Europe from Scandinavia to Gibraltar and from the British Isles to the Baltics were those carrying the bloodline of Ephraim and Manasseh and the eight other members of the "10 lost tribes".

In the 1700's the population numbered more than 125 million including England's and Wales' 5.7 million. By 1850, Europe was home to 208 million and England and Wales population was 18 million.[210]

The territory that would become the United States was home to 1.17 million people in 1750; by 1850 that number grew to 23.19 million people.[211]

The God-given birthright of Ephraim and Manasseh – they would become a nation and a "company of nations" with political and economic hegemony, "possess the gates of their enemies" and have "nations bow down to them" – was among the people of Western Europe and Great Britain in the 14th through the 17th Centuries.

If this is true, we should find the leaders of the Stone Kingdom and their confederates in Western Civilization joining them in reaping the benefits of a birthright promised to Abraham, Isaac and Jacob more than 4,000 years ago.

Preparation for the Stone Kingdom

In the 14th Century, the last remnant of the Roman Empire was destroyed. Christianity permeated all of Europe. Great Britain was united under the Normans and its power displayed. The Israelites were scattered among the nations of Western

---

[209] https://www.britannica.com/topic/history-of-Europe/Demographics

[210] Source: Durand, 1967; Mitchell, 1998; United Nations, 2000; McEvedy and Jones, 1978; Livi-Bacci, 1992.

[211] https://en.wikipedia.org/wiki/Demographic_history_of_the_United_States

Europe and in the British Isles. The improvements in technology and agriculture and relative peace in Europe allowed for a large increase in population.

Seven cultural and geographic developments contributed to the foundation of the Stone Kingdom:

- ➢ 1. The Renaissance
- ➢ 2. The Reformation
- ➢ 3. The Scientific Revolution
- ➢ 4. The Enlightenment
- ➢ 5. The rise of the British Empire
- ➢ 6. Discovery of the Americas and British control of the seas
- ➢ 7. The American Revolution

The Renaissance

The term Renaissance is a label for the period after the end of the Roman Empire in the 14th Century. In Southern Europe – Italy in particular – the Renaissance included a cultural recovery of the heritage of ancient Greece and Rome. There was a sweeping transformation from medieval universalism personified in the Papacy and the Holy Roman Empire to a renewed reverence for the classic Greek literature and the "dignity" and government of the Roman Empire. This was expressed in the cultural convulsions of the 17th Century.

The Renaissance in southern Europe was mainly in literature and art, influenced by the latest and most successful of a long series of medieval Classical revivals. Classical scholarship and publication of vernacular literatures helped spread the effects of the Renaissance.

For all but exceptional individuals and a few marginal groups, the standards of behavior continued to arise from traditional social and moral codes. Identity derived from class, family, occupation, and community, although each of these social forms was itself undergoing significant modification.[212]

In Northern and Western Europe in this period, new technologies and ideas about government brought by the migrants from the Middle East resulted in a revival of urban life and the use of many innovations brought with those migrants: commercial enterprise based on private capital, banking, systematic investigation of the physical world, and the formation of states with local rule. City-states, regional and national

---

[212] https://www.britannica.com/topic/history-of-Europe/The-Renaissance

principalities supplanted the hegemony of the Roman Empire and the Papacy and eliminated the feudal jurisdictions that had covered Europe.

By the end of the 15th century, such northern cities as London, Paris, Antwerp, and Augsburg were becoming centers of Renaissance activity rivaling or exceeding Italy's. By making books cheaper and more plentiful, the development of printing allowed "common" people to discuss and take part in the transformation.

In Northern Europe and in Great Britain, the Renaissance was essentially Christian in spirit and purpose though some scholars refer to it as simple "humanism". This was in contrast to the essentially secular nature of Italian humanism.

However, Italian Lorenzo Valla, one of the founders of classical philology, showed how the critical methods used to study the classics could be applied to problems of Biblical exegesis and translation as well as church history.

> That this program only began to be carried out in the 16th century, particularly in the countries of northern Europe (and Spain), is a matter of chronology rather than of geography. In the 15th century, the necessary skills, particularly the knowledge of Greek, were possessed by a few scholars; a century later, Greek was a regular part of the humanist curriculum, and Hebrew was becoming much better known, particularly after Johannes Reuchlin published his Hebrew grammar in 1506. Here, too, printing was a crucial factor, for it made available a host of lexicographical and grammatical handbooks and allowed the establishment of normative Biblical texts and the comparison of different versions of the Bible.[213]

Some of today's historical texts refer to this desire to adhere to the Biblical descriptions of Christianity as "Christian humanism". However, this was fundamentally a conception of the Christian life that was grounded in the rhetorical, historical, and ethical orientation of the Bible itself.

> By restoring the gospel to the center of Christian piety, the humanists believed they were better serving the needs of ordinary people. They attacked scholastic theology as an arid intellectualization of simple faith, and they deplored the tendency of religion to become a ritual practiced vicariously through a priest. They also despised the whole late-medieval apparatus of relic mongering, hagiology, indulgences, and image worship, and they ridiculed it in their writings, sometimes with devastating effect.

[213] https://www.britannica.com/topic/history-of-Europe/Northern-humanism

According to the Christian humanists, the fundamental law of Christianity was the law of love as revealed by Jesus Christ in the Gospel. Love, peace, and simplicity should be the aims of the good Christian, and the life of Christ his perfect model. The chief spokesman for this point of view was Desiderius Erasmus, the most influential humanist of his day. Erasmus and his colleagues were uninterested in dogmatic differences and were early champions of religious toleration. The Roman Catholics said of Erasmus, "he laid the egg that Luther hatched" [214]

The 16th century saw a true renaissance of national literatures. In Protestant countries, the Reformation had an enormous impact upon the quantity and quality of literary output.

If Luther's rebellion destroyed the chances of unifying the nation politically— because religious division exacerbated political division and made Lutherans intolerant of the Catholic Habsburgs—his translation of the Bible into German created a national language.

Biblical translations, vernacular liturgies, hymns, and sacred drama had analogous effects elsewhere. On all sides of the religious controversy, chroniclers and historians writing in the vernacular were recording their versions for posterity.

The Reformation

Jesus, the founder of Christianity, clearly taught that hierarchies and positions of rulership among Christians were anathema. Jesus taught that power corrupts.[136]

> 8 "But you are not to be called 'Rabbi,' for you have one Teacher, and you are all brothers. 9 And do not call anyone on earth 'father,' for you have one Father, and he is in heaven. 10 Nor are you to be called instructors, for you have one Instructor, the Messiah. 11 The greatest among you will be your servant. 12 For those who exalt themselves will be humbled, and those who humble themselves will be exalted. Matthew 23:8–12 (NIV)
>
> 42 Jesus called them together and said, "You know that those who are regarded as rulers of the Gentiles lord it over them, and their high officials exercise authority over them. 43 Not so with you. Instead, whoever wants to become great among you must be your servant, 44 and whoever wants to be first must be slave of all. 45 For even the Son of Man did not come to be served, but to serve, and to give his life as a ransom for many." Mark 10:42–45 (NIV)

---

[214] *Ibid*

24 "No one can serve two masters; for either he will hate the one and love the other, or else he will be loyal to the one and despise the other. You cannot serve God and mammon.[215] Matthew 6:24 (NKJV)

The *hierarchy* of the Roman Catholic Church in the 16th Century was corrupt. Over the centuries the church became ever more deeply involved in the political life of Western Europe. There were political intrigues and manipulations. Increasing power and wealth contributed to the denigration of the church's spiritual authority.

Such abuses as the sale of "indulgences" [216] by the clergy and other charges of corruption caused political authorities to curtail the secular role of the church and this brought increasing tension in all areas.

Another factor was the Inquisition. The Inquisition began in 1231 when Pope Gregory IX assigned the Dominicans responsibility for combating heresy. The list of atrocities over the next six centuries – until 1834 when the Spanish Inquisition was abolished – is still astonishing today.[217]

Figure 8.1
The Inquisition

1231. The Inquisition begins as Pope Gregory IX assigns Dominicans responsibility for combating heresy.

- ➤ 1252. Torture used. Absolution of torturers promised by the church hierarchy.
- ➤ 1415. Jan Hus, Bohemian preacher and follower of Wycliffe, burned at stake in Constance as heretic.
- ➤ 1415. John Wycliffe died in 1384. His body was exhumed in 1415 and his remains burned as a ruling of the Council of Constance.
- ➤ 1431. Joan of Arc leads French against English, captured by Burgundians and turned over to the English, burned at the stake as a witch after ecclesiastical trial.
- ➤ 1478. Ferdinand and Isabella establish Spanish Inquisition
- ➤ 1492. Tourquemada, Grand Inquisitor, forces conversion or expulsion of Spanish Jews
- ➤ 1499. Forced conversion of Moors
- ➤ 1531. Inquisition in Portugal
- ➤ 1543. First Protestants burned at the stake in Spain
- ➤ 1561. Persecution of Huguenots (Calvinist Protestants) in France stopped by Edict of Orleans.
  - • 1572. French religious wars begin again with massacre of Huguenots at Vassy.

---

215 "Mammon" is not specifically "money" but the accumulation of wealth and power by oppressing others.

216 church permission to sin could be purchased

217 https://en.wikipedia.org/wiki/Inquisition

- 1573. St. Bartholomew's Day Massacre—thousands of Huguenots murdered. Amnesty granted by the Roman church.
- 1598. Persecution continued periodically until Edict of Nantes gave Huguenots religious freedom until 1685.

➢ 1633. The Inquisition forced Galileo (astronomer) to recant his belief in Copernican theory
➢ 1834.Spanish Inquisition abolished
➢ No reliable records are available but somewhere between 50,000 and 200,000 people died

Martin Luther

Martin Luther is often credited with starting the Reformation; he deserves ample credit for his actions and teaching but others before him paid a price for attempting reform (See Figure 8.1)

> The Reformation of the 16th century was not unprecedented. Reformers within the medieval church such as St. Francis of Assisi, Valdes (founder of the Waldensians), Jan Hus, and John Wycliffe addressed aspects in the life of the church in the centuries before 1517. In the 16th century Erasmus of Rotterdam, a great humanist scholar, was the chief proponent of liberal Catholic reform that attacked popular superstitions in the church and urged the imitation of Christ as the supreme moral teacher. These figures reveal an ongoing concern for renewal within the church in the years before Luther is said to have posted his Ninety-five Theses on the door of the Castle Church, Wittenberg, Germany, on October 31, 1517, the eve of All Saints' Day—the traditional date for the beginning of the Reformation.[218]

What made Luther different from previous reformers was that he went to the theological root of the problems with the church – the perversion of the doctrine of redemption and grace. Others mostly attacked the corruption in the church and many of the teachings of the church that the reformers thought to be in contradiction of Biblical doctrines.

In his Ninety-Five Theses, Luther attacked the indulgence system declaring the Pope had no authority over purgatory[137] and that the doctrine of the merits of the saints had no foundation in the Bible.

> Here lay the key to Luther's concerns for the ethical and theological reform of the church: Scripture alone is authoritative (sola scriptura) and justification is by faith (sola fide), not by works. While he did not intend to break with the Catholic Church, a confrontation with the papacy was not

---

[218] https://www.britannica.com/event/Reformation

long in coming. In 1521 Luther was excommunicated; what began as an internal reform movement had become a fracture in western Christendom.[219]

The Reformation movement spread throughout Germany. Huldrych Zwingli built an organization in Zürich which joined the church directly to the state in service to God. Zwingli agreed with Luther on some points but had a different understanding of the Holy Communion.[138]

Another group believed that baptism should be performed on adults who had professed their faith in Jesus – not children. Called Anabaptists, they survive today as the Mennonites and Hutterites. Opponents of the Catholic Trinitarian dogma called the Socinians established congregations in Poland.

After his conversion to the Protestant cause, John Calvin was forced to leave France for Switzerland where he brought out the first edition of his *Institutes of the Christian Religion*[139] in 1536. This was the first systematic, theological treatise of the new reform movement. His movement eventually merged with Zwingli's and they published the Second Helvetic Confession of 1561.

> The Reformation spread to other European countries over the course of the 16th century. By mid-century, Lutheranism dominated northern Europe. Eastern Europe offered a seedbed for even more radical varieties of Protestantism, because kings were weak, nobles strong, and cities few, and because religious pluralism had long existed.

> In England the Reformation's roots were both political and religious. Henry VIII, incensed by Pope Clement VII's refusal to grant him an annulment of his marriage, repudiated papal authority and in 1534 established the Anglican Church with the king as the supreme head. In spite of its political implications, the reorganization of the church permitted the beginning of religious change in England, which included the preparation of a liturgy in English, the Book of Common Prayer. In Scotland, John Knox, who spent time in Geneva and was greatly influenced by John Calvin, led the establishment of Presbyterianism, which made possible the eventual union of Scotland with England. [220]

John Wycliffe

In England, John Wycliffe (1320s – 1384) was an English scholastic philosopher, theologian, Biblical translator, reformer, and seminary professor at the University of

---

[219] *Ibid*
[220] **Ibid**

Oxford. He was an influential dissident within the Roman Catholic priesthood during the 14th century and is considered an important predecessor to Protestantism.

Wycliffe was the first to translate the Bible into English from the Vulgate[140] version.

Wycliffe attacked the privileged status of the clergy, which was central to their powerful role in England. He then attacked local parishes for their luxury and ceremonial pomp.

Wycliffe was also an advocate for translating the Bible into the vernacular. He completed a translation directly from the Vulgate into Middle English 1382. Known now as Wycliffe's Bible, it was completed by 1384.

Figure 8.2 John Wycliffe

Known as Lollards, Wycliffe's followers took his lead in advocating predestination, iconoclasm, and the notion of caesaropapism,[141] while attacking the veneration of saints, the sacraments, requiem masses, transubstantiation, monasticism, and the very existence of the Papacy.

The Inquisition was incensed over Wycliffe making a Bible available to "common" people. Their concerns worsened when Wycliffe's Latin writings greatly influenced the philosophy and teaching of Czech reformer Jan Hus.

Jan Hus was burned at the stake for his "heresy" in 1415 which sparked a revolt and led to the Hussite Wars.[221].

John Wycliffe died the same year his Bible was finished in 1384. After they executed Hus, Wycliffe's body was exhumed and his remains burned as a ruling of the same Council of Constance that condemned Hus.

Wycliffe was a "hero" to the "restoration" movement in the United States (1790 – 1840) because Wycliffe gave "common people" their first real access to the Holy Scriptures. His translation is still valued highly among today's churches that sprang from that movement.[142]

The Scientific Revolution

During the 15th, 16th, and 17th centuries, scientific thought underwent a revolution. A new view of nature emerged, replacing the Greek view that had dominated science for almost 2,000 years. Science became a separate discipline, distinct from both philosophy and technology, and it came to be regarded as having utilitarian[222] goals.

Out of the ferment of the Renaissance and Reformation there arose a new view of science, bringing about the following transformations: the reeducation of common sense in favor of abstract reasoning; the substitution of a quantitative for a qualitative view of nature; the view of nature as a machine rather than as an organism; the development of an experimental method that sought definite answers to certain limited questions couched in the framework of specific theories; the acceptance of new criteria for explanation, stressing the "how" rather than the "why" that had characterized the Aristotelian search for final causes.[223]

The scientific revolution began with astronomy.

Copernicus

In 1543 Polish astronomer Nicolaus Copernicus was the first to develop the theory that the earth and planets revolved around the sun. He also developed mathematical proof of his theory and for this discovery was threatened with excommunication from the Catholic Church.[143]

---

[221] https://en.wikipedia.org/wiki/John_Wycliffe

[222] Rather than esoteric "science" like alchemistry, the new science was finding things that could be used by everyone.

[223] https://www.britannica.com/science/physical-science

At the beginning of the 17th century, the German astronomer Johannes Kepler provided proof of Copernicus' theories and added two new "laws" describing the motion of the planets and mathematics to determine their orbit. In so doing he joined Englishman William Gilbert in searching for the reason the planets stayed in place thus being precursors to Newton's theory of gravity.

Galileo

Italian Galileo Galilei used the telescope – an invention of Dutch lens grinders – to prove Aristotle wrong in claiming the moon's surface was smooth. He observed the moons of Jupiter and demonstrated that the phases of Venus showed that planet orbiting the sun rather than the earth.

Figure 8.3 Galileo Galilei

Galileo introduced a new physics founded on mathematics and explained the math behind free fall, inertia and why one does not experience the rotation of the earth.

Newton

The work of Sir Isaac Newton represents the culmination of the scientific revolution at the end of the 17th century.

Newton's monumental Philosophiae Naturalis Principia Mathematica (1687; Mathematical Principles of Natural Philosophy) solved the major problems posed by the scientific revolution in mechanics and in cosmology. It provided a physical basis for Kepler's laws, unified celestial and terrestrial physics under one set of laws and established the problems and methods that dominated much of astronomy and physics for well over a century. By means of the concept of force, Newton was able to synthesize two important components of the scientific revolution, the mechanical philosophy and the mathematization of nature.[224]

Figure 8.4 Isaac Newton

The technologies, innovations and marvels of science – such as radio, television, computers, space travel, aviation and the Internet et al would not have been possible but for the foundations laid by these pioneers and many others who developed the "scientific method".[144]

The Enlightenment[225]

The first recorded treatises on the powers and uses of reason were created by the philosophers of ancient Greece. The Romans adopted and preserved much of the Greek culture including the ideas of "natural order" and "natural law" in our world and the universe.

As Christianity spread across Europe with the aid of the hundreds of thousands of converts descended from the people of the Parthian Empire, the Roman Empire persecuted the Christian church for 300 years. Even after Constantine made

---

[224] *Ibid*
[225] French *siècle des Lumières* (literally "century of the Enlightened")

Christianity the official religion of the Empire persecutions continued. With the turmoil and terror that arose with the military incursions of the Goths and the Huns, the leaders of the church found uses for their Greco-Roman heritage.

The system of thought known as Scholasticism, culminating in the work of Thomas Aquinas, resurrected reason as a tool of understanding but subordinated it to spiritual revelation and the revealed truths of Christianity. The intellectual and political edifice of Christianity, seemingly impregnable in the Middle Ages, fell in turn to the assaults made on it by humanism, the Renaissance, and the Protestant Reformation.

Humanism bred the experimental science of Francis Bacon, Nicolaus Copernicus, and Galileo and the mathematical investigations of René Descartes, Gottfried Wilhelm Leibniz, and Sir Isaac Newton. The Renaissance rediscovered much of Classical culture and revived the notion of humans as creative beings, and the Reformation, more directly but in the long run no less effectively, challenged the monolithic authority of the Roman Catholic Church.

For Martin Luther as for Bacon or Descartes, the way to truth lay in the application of human reason. Received authority, whether of Ptolemy in the sciences or of the church in matters of the spirit, was to be subject to the probing of unfettered minds.[226]

The intellectual and scholarly leaders found faith in the human capacity to gain knowledge. With Newton's capturing in a few mathematical equations the laws that govern the motions of the planets and the idea of the universe as a mechanism governed by a few simple and discoverable laws had a subversive effect on the belief in the rigid dogmas of the Catholic Church.

Most of the Enlightenment pioneers retained a strong faith in God but some withdrew from Christianity and became Deists. For the Deist, a very few religious truths sufficed – those that were manifest in rational thinking: the existence of one God, the existence of a system of rewards and punishment administered by that God and the obligation of humans to virtue and piety. God was often conceived as an architect or designer who had created this world and the universe.[145]

Some carried the idea of application of reason to religion further and became skeptics, materialists or atheists. Much of the anti-Christianity thought in today's culture is derived from the writing of these anti-religion thinkers of the Enlightenment.

Modern psychology and ethics were first produced by the Enlightenment.

John Locke conceived of the human mind as being at birth a tabula rasa, a blank slate on which experience wrote freely and boldly, creating the individual character according to the individual experience of the world. Supposed innate qualities, such as goodness or original sin, had no reality. In a darker vein, Thomas Hobbes portrayed humans as moved solely by considerations of their own pleasure and pain. The notion of humans as neither good nor bad but interested principally in survival and the maximization of their own pleasure led to radical political theories.[227]

Where the state was considered as a flawed approximation of the eternal order, it came to be seen as an arrangement among humans that protected the natural rights and self-interest of each person.

The reality of the states in existence at that time contrasted with the possibilities of their imaginations and they became even more critical, demanding reform and if reform failed revolution.

Locke and Jeremy Bentham in England, Montesquieu, Voltaire, Jean-Jacques Rousseau, Denis Diderot, and Condorcet in France, and Thomas Paine and Thomas Jefferson in colonial America all contributed to an evolving critique of the arbitrary, authoritarian state and to sketching the outline of a higher form of social organization, based on natural rights and functioning as a political democracy.[228]

Figure 8.5 Thomas Jefferson   **Figure 8.6 Thomas Paine**

However, the more the Deists extracted their religion from Christianity with only the simplest explanations for our existence and purpose, the less it offered to those seeking comfort and salvation in religion. The rejection of the Deists' religion led to exploration of a world of sensation and emotion in the cultural movement known as Romanticism.

---

[227] https://www.britannica.com/event/Enlightenment-European-history
[228] *Ibid*

The Enlightenment expired as the victim of its own excesses. The Reign of Terror that followed the French Revolution severely tested the belief that an egalitarian society could govern itself. The high optimism that marked much of Enlightenment thought, however, survived as one of the movement's most-enduring legacies: the belief that human history is a record of general progress[229]

By the 17th and 18th Centuries, those who ran from the influence of the papacy in Rome were entering their interpretation into the history of the "Holy Roman Empire" and the secularization of the influence of the Roman church. Some were trying to reform the Catholic Church; others were advocating a return to the religion of the Bible without Catholic dogma; still others pulled away from religion in general while some were happy with the Church the way it was.

The rise of the British Empire

In this era – 1400 to 1800 – amidst the political and cultural turmoil the Dutch, the Portuguese and the Spanish saw their hegemonies shrink until the political reach of each was essentially within their national borders. The French were the last of the Europeans to hold Empire aspirations but they too fell behind the British as they were rising to their peak as an Empire. It was to become the greatest Empire in world history, almost doubling their closest rivals in terms of the power, wealth and reach of Empires.

16th and 17th Centuries[230]

England, Spain and Portugal began exploring beyond the oceans in the 1490's. In 1497 John Cabot was sent across the Atlantic Ocean by English King Henry VII to look for a trade route to China. Cabot reached the coast of what became the Americas – probably in Newfoundland but no settlement was established.

During the early 1500's, British seamen led by Francis Drake discovered that piracy paid much better than hauling potential colonists across the seas. Not only did they successfully loot vessels on the Spanish Main but they also honed their skills as seamen.

Walter Raleigh sponsored two attempts to settle Roanoke Island off the coast of what is now North Carolina; both were disastrous. Other attempts met with similar fates and the English became more active in the East. In 1600 Queen Elizabeth I

---

[229] *Ibid*
[230] Much of the following information comes from http://www.historyworld.net/

granted a charter to the organization that became the East India Company – the longest lasting of Britain's colonial enterprises.

Competition with the Dutch – who joined England, Spain and Portugal in exploration – sparked a massacre of the English in the Spice Islands in 1623 causing the English to concentrate on developing their trade with India. This proved profitable and soon the British were firmly established in that country in Bombay, Madras and Calcutta.

The first successful British settlement in the Americas came in 1609 by accident. Castaways from a ship headed for Virginia found safety on the island of Bermuda. The Spanish had removed most of the indigenous people to the island they called Hispaniola – today comprised of the Dominican Republic and Haiti. The Spanish found lucrative gold mines on the section that became Haiti and imported the Arawak Indians as slaves to do the mining. Today Haiti's language is Creole while the Dominican Republic's native language is Spanish.

The British foothold in the Caribbean Islands were their settlements in St. Kitts, Barbados, Antigua, Nevis and Montserrat as of 1636. The French settled parts of St. Kitts, Dominica, Martinique and Guadeloupe and the two eventually expelled Spain from the Caribbean. An English fleet invaded and captured Jamaica and the French occupied half of Hispaniola (Haiti) while the British controlled the other half (Dominican Republic today).

The natives of the Caribbean were virtually eliminated by the Spanish exploitation and the diseases brought by the Europeans. It was to these Caribbean Islands that the first African slaves were brought first by the Dutch, then by the Portuguese and then later by the British.

There were frequent sea battles between the British and the French, both of whom pirated the ships of Spain transporting the gold and other wealth garnered in Mexico and Peru.

Most of the military (naval) friction between France and Britain in the 17th Century was related to Newfoundland and Nova Scotia (New Scotland) with the French gradually accepting British sovereignty. The last French fortification was captured by a volunteer militia from New England in 1745. The French and Indian War in 1754 expelled the French from the Ohio valley.

The French East India Company gained a foothold and profited for a few years but the two East India Companies soon found themselves at war. The rivalry in India fought by proxies of several powerful Indian states but the British eventually prevailed.

In the Paris peace treaty in 1763, France conceded all territory in the Americas. Britain had ceded the land between the Mississippi River and the Rocky Mountains to Spain. The United States reacquired much of that territory in 1803 with the Louisiana Purchase.

Great Britain was humiliated in the United States war of independence as France joined the USA in 1778 and defeated the British. Britain recovered rapidly with the election of William Pitt in 1784 and the speed of the recovery was enhanced by the transformation of the Industrial Revolution.

The 18th Century

The Dutch Boers had occupied the southern tip of Africa but the French invaded and conquered the land in 1795 only to lose control to the British in 1806. The Boers or Afrikaans clashed with the British. In 1807 as the influence of Christianity grew, the British Parliament enacted the abolition of the slave trade which did not sit well with the Afrikaans.

An early statute of the British in the Cape colony became known as the Hottentot Code (officially the Caledon Code, 1809). It required written contracts to be registered for the employment of tribal servants and provided safeguards against their ill treatment. But it also enshrined one familiar condition of serfdom; servants could only leave a farm if a pass was signed by their employer.

British missionaries, led by John Philip, soon protested this restriction. From 1826 Philip campaigned vigorously back in Britain and in 1828 the house of commons passed a resolution for the emancipation of the Cape tribes. In the same year the governor of the Cape colony guaranteed complete liberty of movement to 'free persons of colour'.

From the point of view of the Afrikaners, worse was to come. In 1833 the reformed parliament in London passed the Emancipation Act. All slaves in British colonies were to be freed after a period of 'apprenticeship', which in the Cape colony ended in 1838.

The Afrikaners inevitably felt that alien ways were being imposed upon their long-established culture by a new colonial power, and their sense of isolation was increased by other changes. In 1820 British families, numbering about 5000 people, were shipped to the Cape and are given 100-acre plots of land.

Under the new regime English became the language of the law courts. British teachers set up village schools where the lessons were in English. But above all it was British interference in the relationship between the races in South Africa which gave the most profound offence to the traditionally-minded Boers - and prompts the Great Trek.

> An Afrikaner woman, Anna Steenkamp, later records in forthright terms her people's complaint. The British had placed slaves 'on an equal footing with Christians, contrary to the laws of God and the natural distinctions of race and religion, so that it was intolerable for any decent Christian to bow down beneath such a yoke; wherefore we withdrew in order thus to preserve our doctrines in purity.'[231]

The British attempted to establish their rule over Afghanistan but failed to win two wars in 1838 -1842 and 1878 -1881. They finally established a regime friendly to the British and withdrew from the territory in 1881.

Cecil Rhodes was the driving force behind the British expansion in Africa. His discovery of the diamond mines in Kimberly in 1871 and later gold fields in Transvaal left his De Beers Consolidated Mines and Gold Fields of South Africa producing almost unimaginable wealth for the British Empire. Much of Africa came under the dominion of Great Britain.

By the end of the 18th Century as Queen Victoria's reign came to a close, the Golden Jubilee in 1809 – marking 50 years of her rule – celebrated the British Empire at its height.

The British Empire at its peak was an empire like no other in the history of the world.

The Greatest Empire in World History

The British Empire began with overseas colonies and trading posts and in the end comprised dominions, protectorates, and mandates, as well. It was made up of 13 million square miles of land - more than 22% of the earth's land-mass. In 1922, the Empire had a population of 458 million people or about 20% the global population.

The wealth and power of the British Empire was so phenomenal that even after its decline and its political power shrunk to today's status – essentially England, Scotland, Ireland and Wales – it remains one of the wealthiest nations in the world

---

[231] http://www.historyworld.net/ History of the British Empire page 7

and it still has a significant amount of authority on the world scene. In almost every area of measurement, its closest rivals in history are almost doubled. See Table 8.1

Figure 8.7
The British Empire

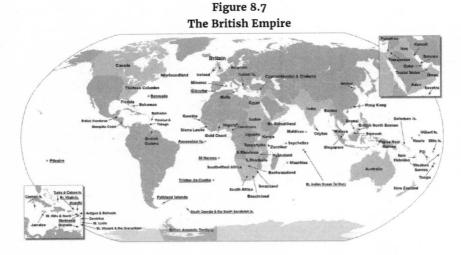

Historians have long debated how and why the British were able to amass such a formidable and expansive empire in the years from 1400 to 1800. Why were the British able to supplant the Portuguese, Dutch and Spanish Empires in the Seventeenth and eighteenth Centuries and effectively fend off French, Russian and German challenges over the nineteenth and early twentieth Centuries?

The combination of commerce, civilization and Christianity were factors in the rise of the British Empire in the late nineteenth and early twentieth Centuries.

The Protestant aspect of Christianity was seen by many within the British Empire as part of the larger battle with the more 'Catholic' nations of Continental Europe. Ever since the Reformation, religion represented not merely a spiritual difference between the Catholic and Protestant churches but was part of a far larger cultural and political competition between deadly rivals.

Portugal, Spain and France were the Catholic nations who developed successful commercial empires before the English (and Dutch) were able to do so. Religion gave an excuse for this commercial rivalry to turn into military and political competition. The very success of the Protestant nations in challenging the Catholic hegemony in the New World and the East Indies seemed to confirm that God might be on the side of the British.[232]

---

[232] http://www.britishempire.co.uk/*Christianity, Commerce and Civilisation*

The British had no monopoly on technological innovation. Gunpowder, the printing press and navigational equipment were all developed and improved on the continent. Western Europe was a place of innovation and new ideas but Britain benefited more from the progress and sill made significant contributions to the Renaissance and the Age of Enlightenment.

The Industrial Revolution

However, some fortunate innovations gave Britain an unprecedented advantage. One of those major innovations changed the world. *Britain was the first nation to harness the power of steam.* This was the key to the Industrial Revolution in which high quality, mass-produced British goods flooded the markets all over the world.

Mass production – available because of Britain's expertise in the use of steam provided a technology gap with which non-European nations could not compete. Precision-made muskets, rifles, machine guns, train locomotives, steam ships would provide the relatively small and British armed forces with unparalleled advantages.

Control of the Seas

The British controlled the seven seas.

In 1688 Dutch King William of Orange took control of the English crown. This reduced the rivalry between the Dutch and English and gave the English access to the sophisticated Dutch banking techniques. This allowed the British to borrow money to build a huge Navy during the Seven Years war of 1756 to 1763 with which they took on the far richer and supposedly more powerful Kingdom of France.

The idea of this investment was to pay back the loans once Britain had been victorious in the war. The French Navy had no such infusion of investment and so they were hard pressed to see off the challenge from the Royal Navy especially on the global scale of what was really the first 'World War' in that it stretched over all corners of the globe.

In some ways, the French were able to get an element of revenge by helping the American Revolutionaries in the 1770s and 1780s in their humiliation of the British. But this in itself would be a false dawn for the French Monarchy. They had invested huge quantities of money to challenge the Royal Navy (and help the Americans to win the Revolutionary War) but without the benefit of receiving tangible assets to recoup this investment.[233]

---

[233] http://www.britishempire.co.uk/maritime advantages

The massive spending by the French during that war lead indirectly to the defeat of Napoleon and later to the French Revolution.

> Napoleon would concentrate on his land campaigns, but he would be constantly frustrated or harassed by the Royal Navy. For example, Nelson destroyed Napoleon's fleet at anchor off Egypt in 1798 which killed off his Pyramid Campaign. Napoleon would try to combine the French and Spanish fleets to lure the Royal Navy across the Atlantic to allow him to launch an invasion force against England. The resulting battle of Trafalgar in 1805 became the defining naval battle for the next century. The British did not fall for the lure and ended up blockading the French and Spanish fleets instead. Once these fleets set sail, Nelson directed an aggressive assault that would destroy them and leave the Royal Navy ruling the waves until World War One and beyond. For the rest of the Nineteenth Century, there was no maritime power who could come close to challenging British domination of the maritime communication and trade routes.[234]

The great power and wealth accumulated by the British Empire is unparalleled in human history. With control of the seas, with steam power yielding the ability to produce goods for the markets of the world, with British rule bringing British law and customs to the nations they ruled, the cultures of many nations were changed forever.

Though Great Britain exploited the people of some nations using them as slaves, Christianity eventually eliminated that practice and the people of the dominions ruled by Britain had access to education, medical advances and legal systems that most often produced some rights for the "common man" in those dominions. The legacy of the British Empire is truly astounding.

The legacy of the British Empire includes many stable democracies, often modeled on the Westminster Parliament. English Common law remains the basis of legal systems throughout the former colonies.

Schools, colleges, and universities founded by the British have developed into institutions of excellence. Protestantism, with its accompanying secular values such as the dignity and rights of the individual, has been planted widely. The many railways that were constructed improved communications and enabled people to develop a sense of national identity as well as a feeling of belonging to the wider civilized world. English remains a lingua franca, often popular even where it is not an official language (as in India).

---

[234] *Ibid*

The greatest legacy is probably the Commonwealth of Nations – a voluntary association of 53 former colonies who wanted to maintain close ties with Britain and with each other. The head of the Commonwealth is the Queen. She is still the Head of State of sixteen Commonwealth realms such as Canada, Australia, and Barbados.[235]

The Stone Kingdom: Great Britain – a nation and a "company of nations"; The United States of America – a great nation; The creation of Western Civilization

The British Commonwealth described above is truly a nation and a company of nations.

Canada, Australia and South Africa were given "dominion" status – made free and independent nations – and with all the other nations the British controlled, the British Empire truly became a "company of nations" joined together by the throne of England.

There is little need to delve into the Revolution from which came the United States of America. Libraries of books are available detailing the growth of the USA and the writings of the founders of this country.

Today, as always, one must take into consideration that all historians are biased to some degree but it is obvious that the USA was founded upon Christian principles though freedom of religion was much on the minds of those founders. The USA and Great Britain remain the closest of allies. One might say they act as "brothers" on the world stage.

From the time of the captivity of the 10-tribed kingdom of Israel (which included Ephraim and Manasseh to whom the birthright was promised) in about 721 B.C. until the rise to dominance of the "company of nations" and the "great nation" in the early 1800's was the prophesied time span – 2,520 years. God's punishment was carried out exactly as He promised and for the time He promised.

At the beginning of 1800 A.D., Britain and the United States were two relatively small nations in international terms and yet they began to grow into vast national riches and power unmatched in the history of the world. Soon the British Empire had spread around the world and the "sun never set" on her possessions.

---

[235] http://www.newworldencyclopedia.org/entry/British_Empire/Legacy

In 1803 Napoleon, the emperor of France sold all of Louisiana and the territories held by France as far north as the Canadian border to the United States for what was really a very small sum of money. The famous "Louisiana Purchase" more than doubled the territory of the United States.

President Thomas Jefferson within the next few years ordered the similarly famous "Lewis and Clark" expedition that opened the rest of the territory all the way to the Pacific Ocean allowing for an almost never-ending flood of immigrants to the United States and to its western territories.

Historically, only Great Britain allied with the United States qualifies as the "Stone Kingdom". Great Britain spawned a "company of nations" and another "great nation".

Western Civilization itself can be said to be "a company of nations" that quarrel but generally agree on many things. The core of the culture of Western Civilization started as one nation and one people. The descendants of those people received the physical blessings promised to Abraham, Isaac and Jacob and those blessings have been spread around the whole world.

Rationale

Since the 1500's, from where came all the great advances in the things that make life better for the "average man"? From where have the great advances in agriculture, medicine, transportation, clothing, housing, and the other every day needs of the "common man" come?

How is it that the average lifespan of all of humanity has more than doubled in the past 300 years? From where came the knowledge and techniques to eradicate or at least treat most of the diseases that were a sure death sentence in the 1500's?

Which was the first country to eliminate and outlaw slavery? Which nation and "company of nations" spread the laws of Western Civilization (based largely on Bible principles) throughout the world? Which nation has become the greatest exporter of Christian "missionaries" to the world?

Which nation and "company of nations" set up the principles of private property coupled with a banking system that allows free trade throughout the world placing the accumulation of personal wealth within reach of the "common man"?

Which nation and "company of nations" defeated the Axis powers in World War II thereby ending the extermination of not only the Jews but also dozens of other peoples considered "inferior races" by the Axis powers?

Which powerful nation is the first on the scene with aid wherever natural disasters strike throughout the world, thereby forestalling the many diseases that usually follow in the aftermath of those disasters?

Which nation and "company of nations" have literally taught millions throughout the world to improve their agricultural techniques and supplied food for starving populations during drought and other famine conditions? Which nation and "company of nations" advocate freedom for the "common man" throughout the world?

All the people of the world have been greatly blessed by the advances of Western Civilization and the mostly benevolent hegemony of that nation and "company of nations" beginning with the British Empire and continuing currently with the world's only "superpower" – the United States.

The "company of nations" – the British Commonwealth nations – beginning in the 18th Century – became the most geographically extensive empire in world history and they were for a time the foremost global power, superseded only by the United States after World War II with the nation and "company of nations" remaining the closest of allies.

The British Empire literally controlled the "gates of their enemies" – the British dominated the sea-lanes of the world and no one could travel far without passing through one of the land or sea "gates" controlled by the British. Even today, no country and few people are long without some influence of Western Civilization, dominated by Britain and the United States.

Along with the other promises, the final four promises made by God to Abraham have been fulfilled in Great Britain and the United States.

4. That Abraham, Isaac and Jacob's descendants would "possess the gates of their enemies";
5. That Abraham, Isaac and Jacob's descendants would spread over the whole world

---

6. That Abraham, Isaac and Jacob's would become "a nation and a company of nations"

7. That all the people of the world would be blessed through those descendants.

If you wish to discuss God's timing I suggest that you take that up with Him. However, as this book shows, 4,000 years ago He set in motion His plan to present the "good news", the Gospel of Jesus Christ, to the entire world and all the people in it.

Just as He planned and as He revealed to Abraham at the beginning, Abraham's descendants (the Israelites) would be a blessing to the whole world.

What has been missing from history is that the main task for those "10 lost tribes of Israel" was to spread that Gospel.

The "lost 10 tribes" – the Israelites – did so by participating in forming Western Civilization in which Great Britain and the United States developed their hegemony. They and their allies were the first nations and first culture in history to have global communication, global outreach, near-universal language (English) and near universal international law based on Western Civilization standards.

All this to allow and encourage the rapid spreading of the Gospel to the whole world – something never possible before.

Their conversion in the 1st Century AD through their migration and eventual formation of Western Civilization demonstrates the hand of God as no other sequence in history. Now it is truly clear why the Israelites were the "chosen people" – not because they were inherently "better" than any other people but because they were the people who would build Western Civilization and help spread God's plan of salvation for all people.

Table 8.1 Comparison of Empires
From a list of 100

Rank	Empire	Max. land area (million mi2)	% of world land area	Year
1	British Empire	13.71	23.84%	1920

2	Mongol Empire	9.27	16.11%	1270
3	Russian Empire	8.8	15.31%	1895
4	Qing dynasty	5.68	9.87%	1790
5	Spanish Empire	5.29	9.20%	1810
6	Second French colonial empire	4.44	7.72%	1920
7	Abbasid Caliphate	4.29	7.45%	750
8	Umayyad Caliphate	4.29	7.45%	720
9	Yuan dynasty	4.25	7.39%	1310
10	Portuguese Empire	4.02	6.98%	1815
11	Xiongnu Empire	3.47	6.04%	176 BC
12	Brazilian Empire	3.22	5.60%	1889
13	Eastern Han dynasty	2.51	4.36%	100
14	Ming dynasty	2.51	4.36%	1450
15	Rashidun Caliphate	2.47	4.30%	655
19	Achaemenid Empire	2.12	3.69%	500 BC
21	Macedonian Empire	2.01	3.49%	323 BC
22	Ottoman Empire	2.01	3.49%	1683
23	Maurya Empire	1.93	3.36%	250
24	Roman Empire	1.93	3.36%	117 BC
29	Hephthalite Empire	1.54	2.69%	470
30	Hunnic Empire	1.54	2.69%	441
33	Seleucid Empire	1.51	2.62%	301 BC
34	Italian Empire	1.47	2.55%	1938
39	Sasanian Empire	1.35	2.35%	550
41	First French	1.31	2.28%	1670

	colonial empire			
	German			
44	colonial empire	1.24	2.15%	1912

* * *

PART III
THE STONE
KINGDOM

CHAPTER 9

Israel and The Stone Kingdom (1700 –)

After 721 BC the Kingdom of Israel was no more. After 586 BC the Kingdom of Judah was no more. The last vestige of the Old Covenant – the Covenant between God and the children of Israel at Mount Sinai – was destroyed by the Roman Army in 67 – 70 AD as they razed Jerusalem and the temple, captured and dispersed the Jews.

Sometime around the beginning of the first millennium AD God was born as a human baby, Jesus of Nazareth. He was executed on the stake outside the walls of Jerusalem in the 30's AD. Jesus was resurrected three days later as witnessed by His apostles and hundreds of His followers[236]. Jesus gave the ambassadors[237] of the Kingdom of God – His apostles – special powers to spread the word of His New Covenant.

Jesus promised His apostles to not only give them special powers – healing the sick, raising the dead, either speaking foreign languages or giving their listeners the ability to understand the apostles' speech and other miracles – but also the power of God's Holy Spirit. The Spirit[146] gave them credence and courage and taught them everything they needed to know to spread the Gospel of Jesus.

That power was seen and demonstrated about 50 days after Jesus' crucifixion during the Pentecost Festival in Jerusalem.[238]

The New Covenant with the House of Jacob and the House of Judah was the one prophesied[239] by Jeremiah et al. The New Covenant was made not only with the children of Israel but also with all of mankind.

Jesus established His *ecclesia*[240] – His church – to include all mankind and its mission was clear: they were to spread the Gospel of Jesus to the whole world.[241] The

---

[236] 1 Corinthians 15:3–8

[237] ἀπόστολος [apostolos /ap·os·tol·os/] literally, one sent forth with orders, i.e., an "ambassador"

[238] Acts 2:1–21

[239] Jeremiah 31:31–34

New Covenant was one in which God's laws would be written on the hearts of His followers[242] and was foretold in the first Covenant between God and man in the person of Abraham.[243]

We traced the passage of that Covenant birthright to Abraham's son Isaac and to Isaac's son Jacob[244] and from Jacob to his sons who would become the 12 tribes of Israel. We found that some of the promises of that Covenant were delivered to the children of Israel during Bible times. The most important promise – the spiritual part of that Covenant – was delivered in the person of Jesus and His implementation of the New Covenant. However, some quite specific physical promises were never delivered during Bible times.

For as long as possible we used the Bible as our primary guide to Israel's history. With the cessation of the scriptures in the 1st Century AD, we sought evidence from secular historians beginning with the 4th Century BC Greek historian Herodotus and ending with the accounts of contemporary historians that are available in our time in encyclopedias and in those historians' own writings.

We've shown the trail of the Israelites through 1800 AD with as much credibility and clarity as possible and in the process have tied the narrative of the Holy Scriptures to our present time.

Others have previously made the attempt to forge that tie. It has been one of the most controversial subjects of the past 350 years with many honest and sincere people disagreeing vehemently over both history and the concept of Israelites (other than Jews) having anything to do with the formation of our world today.

As my friend and bother in Christ, Hal Booher[245], reminded me from the time, this work would not be complete unless the concept of "British-Israelism" were discussed and a place found within the thesis of this book.

Differing Opinions

For many years, hundreds of people including some highly esteemed scholars, have speculated about the fate of the "10 lost tribes" of Israel. Quite a few have attempted to make the connection between Israel and Great Britain and the USA.

---

[240] An assembly of ones called out from their homes for a public meeting or deliberation
[241] Matthew 28:18–20
[242] Joel 2:28–32
[243] Genesis 22:15–18
[244] God changed Jacob's name to Israel
[245] See Acknowledgement

A great majority of historians deny any genealogical connection between our modern culture and the Israelites. [246] Instead, they assert that all the Israelites who lived through the fall of the Kingdom of Israel in 721 BC either disappeared completely into other nations or returned to the Kingdom of Judah and became "Jews".

That narrative has become accepted as factual truth in many scholarly circles and by most of the Christian people of the world. Thus, you'll hear Christian preachers and teachers and contemporary historians referring to "the Jews coming out of bondage in Egypt" or "the Jews establishing the Covenant at Mount Sinai" as if all of the Israelites were called Jews. Many scholars know that the term Jews should only be used with reference to the tribe of Judah or the citizens of the Kingdom of Judah yet they still use the term Jews as all-inclusive of Israel.

This "accepted truth" blinds many to understanding Old Testament prophecy[147] – especially the meaning of God's covenants with mankind and the inheritance promised the children of Israel. It has resulted in little true scholarly examination of the fate of the "10 Lost Tribes" of Israel.

In this chapter we examine some of the history and research gathered by those who believed strongly that Israel *became* Great Britain and the USA. Those believers first appeared in historical records about the same time as the Renaissance, the Enlightenment and the Reformation. There have been sects of Christianity in which that concept formed a major doctrine of their human religious organizations. Many books – some with credible references and reasonable, logical speculation – have expounded that theory.

We will also present some compelling thought and writing supporting the argument against that theory of the 10 tribes. We will present the assertion that Israelites had little if anything to do with the formation of Great Britain, the USA or any part of Western Civilization.

We will then compare those two broad theories with the thesis of this book: The Bible *is* the story of God's Covenants with Israel and through those Covenants God has dramatically shaped the world we live in today.

---

[246] Other than the Jews, of course, who never lost their identity as Israelites.

Our position on the British-Israelism theory is that the Kingdom of Israel does not exist, has not existed since 721 BC and will never exist again as a political or social entity.

The Hand of God used the Israelites to change the world; the "lost sheep of the House of Israel" were reattached to the Vine that is Jesus[148] in the 1st Century AD and were the prime force in the exponential growth of the church. They contributed to the Renaissance, the Enlightenment, the scientific revolution and the Reformation. To a large extent, they were responsible for the spreading of the spiritual and physical blessings of Abraham's Covenant to the whole world.

The Israelites today are part, and maybe a large part, of the Stone Kingdom[247]. What is important now is not genetic inheritance but the personal relationship of each Christian – whatever their genetic heritage – with the Almighty God.

The Kingdom of Judah exists today and calls itself the nation of Israel. The Jews also are part of the Stone Kingdom and are held in high esteem among many Christians. The staunchest supporters of the nation of Israel outside of that country are the Christians labeled as "evangelical" by the more "main stream" Christian churches. Some of those main stream churches are only a step or two removed from the Catholic Church.

British-Israelism/Anglo-Israelism

British-Israelism or Anglo-Israelism is a theory that the "10 lost tribes" of Israel migrated to Western Europe and eventually to the British Isles as the Anglo-Saxon race. Almost all recognized[248] historians from Herodotus to this day either do not mention the concept. Those who do mention the Israelites dismiss that concept with some amount of contempt.

But some impressive scholars have done extensive and scientific research on the theory.

The search for the "10 lost tribes" has a long history.

---

[247] See previous chapters for prophecy of and explanation of the "Stone Kingdom"
[248] Accepted by modern scholars as credible

In the 9th Century Eldad ben Mahli ha-Dani wrote an account that claimed he was a descendant of Dan[249] and that Danites together with the tribes of Naphtali, Asher, and Gad established an Israelite kingdom in Cush, variously interpreted as Ethiopia or present-day Sudan.[250]

The British-Israelism theory first appeared in the 15th Century. The French Hugenot magistrate M. le Loyer's *The Ten Lost Tribes*, published in 1590, provided the first expression that "Anglo-Saxon, Celtic, Scandinavian, Germanic, and associated cultures" were direct descendants of the ancient Israelites.

Anglo-Israelism has also been attributed to Francis Drake and the British King James VI and I[149], who believed he was the King of Israel.

Adriaan van Schrieck (1560-1621), who influenced Henry Spelman (1562-1641) and John Sadler (1615-1674), wrote in the early 17th century about his ideas on the origins of the Celtic and Saxon peoples. In 1649, Sadler published *The Rights of the Kingdom*, "which argues for an 'Israelite genealogy for the British people'".[251]

Others have made claims that Israelites have been found in many places from Japan to the North American continent in the person of the American "Indians".

Manasseh ben Israel (1604–57) used the legend of the lost tribes in pleading successfully for admission of Jews into England during Oliver Cromwell's regime. Peoples who at various times were said to be descendants of the lost tribes include the Nestorians, the Mormons, the Afghans, the Falashas of Ethiopia, the American Indians, and the Japanese.[252]

Prior to the 18th Century, there were genealogical claims of Israelite heritage among the British people but our research found no one claiming that Britain and/or the USA *were* the Kingdom of Israel.

That would change in the 18th Century with the publications that claimed the monarch of England was *descended* from the royal line of King David of Israel. Others found fables in Ireland that told of the prophet Jeremiah bringing a young woman to Ireland named Tea Tephi who was a daughter of the last King of Judah. According to that legend, after her arrival she married a young ruler in Ireland who was himself a descendant of King David thus uniting two branches of the royalty of Judah himself.[253]

---

[249] One of the "10 lost tribes"

[250] https://www.britannica.com/biography/Eldad-ben-Mahli-ha-Dani

[251] https://en.wikipedia.org/wiki/British_Israelism

[252] https://www.britannica.com/topic/Ten-Lost-Tribes-of-Israel

[253] Genesis 38:1–30

Those who believe this theory today are said to number more than two million with most residing in Britain or the British Commonwealth nations and the United States. At one time they included a member of the English House of Lords and a Colonial Bishop of the Church of England.[254]

There is no exclusive sect of Christianity that holds this belief; adherents are found among many Christian denominations and independent churches and some are found among non-mainstream Catholics.

Richard Brothers

The first published document pertaining to this theory was by Richard Brothers (1757-1824) who proclaimed himself to be a descendant of King David. His treatise *Revealed Knowledge* was published in 1794 where Brothers prophesied that he would be revealed as a "prince of the Hebrews" on November 19, 1795.

Figure 9.1 Richard Brothers

Brothers began to attract quite a following, but due to his rejection of organizational work, and eccentric nature, he did not develop any sort of social movement. As a consequence of prophesying the death of the King and the end of the monarchy, he was arrested for treason in 1795 and imprisoned on the grounds of being criminally insane. His case was, however, brought before Parliament by his ardent disciple, Nathaniel Brassey Halhed, an orientalist and a member of the House of Commons. As a result, Brothers was removed to a private asylum in Islington where he died in 1824. [255]

---

[254] http://www.jewishencyclopedia.com/articles/1524-anglo-israelism
[255] https://en.wikipedia.org/wiki/Richard_Brothers

Brothers asserted that God had called him to make the Israelites in Britain aware of their genealogical heritage and that afterward they would return – along with the Jews – to Palestine where Brothers would rule over them until the return of Christ. In 1822 Brothers published his *Correct Account of the Invasion of England by the Saxons, Showing the English Nation to be Descendants of the Lost Ten Tribes*, which many regard as the foundation of the British-Israeli movement.

Sharon Turner

Turner was born in 1768 in Pentonville, Yorkshire, England. At the age of 15 he left school to become an attorney but left that profession when he became interested in the study of Anglo-Saxon literature. He settled in Red Lion Square near the British Museum and wrote for sixteen years. Some of his manuscripts were written almost illegibly in the margins of letters, on the inside covers of magazines, or on discarded wax paper.

Figure 9.2 Sharon Turner

Turner researched extensively in the collections in the British Museum and the manuscripts of Sir Robert Cotton. In doing so he obtained a working knowledge of Anglo-Saxon. Turner's *History of the Anglo-Saxons* appeared in four volumes between 1799 and 1805.

Turner's *History* had a profound impact on historiography[150] for the succeeding fifty years. Robert Southey said that "so much new information was probably never laid before the public in any one historical publication".

However, the Edinburgh Review in 1804 criticized Turner for a lack of discrimination and for the romantic parts of the work. Sir Walter Scott acknowledged his debt to Turner for his historical work in his Dedicatory Epistle to his novel Ivanhoe. In 1981 J. W. Burrow said Turner produced "the first modern full-length history of Saxon England ... It was a genuinely pioneering work, and was much admired, and not without reason."[256]

These histories were works of real research, developing a new field of inquiry in the area of Anglo-Saxon history. For example, Turner quoted Herodotus stating that the Persians called the Scythians "Sakai". Turner identified these very people as the ancestors of the Anglo-Saxons. In carefully determining their origins in the Caucasus, Turner wrote: "The migrating Scythians crossed the Araxes[151], passed out of Asia, and suddenly appeared in Europe in the sixth century B.C. ... The names Saxon, Scythian and Goth are used interchangeably."[257]

Many advocates of British-Israelism based their claims on Herodotus's statement and Turner's assertion that the Sakai became known as Scythians and later as Saxons. They conflate Saxons with "Isaac's Sons" and refer to a prophecy in Genesis[258] as "proof" that those people were Israelites.

John Wilson

Wilson was born in 1799 in Scotland. He began studying at the Library of Trinity College in Dublin in 1837 and within a year gave a series of lectures which drew large audiences. In 1840 he published *Our Israelitish Origin* – a book of his lectures – in which he claimed that the people of the 10 lost tribes had found their way across Europe to the British Isles.

He brought evidence from Ptolemy and the works of Diodorus[152] supporting the earlier history of the Israelites. He studied the works of historians Rawlinson, Herodotus and Josephus and quoted extensively from Sharon Turner, the eminent scholar who was Wilson's contemporary.

His lectures attracted the attention of, among others, Charles Piazzi Smyth, Astronomer Royal for Scotland and one of the first Pyramidologists. It was in

---

[256] https://en.wikipedia.org/wiki/Sharon_Turner
[257] *Ibid*
[258] Genesis 48:16

Wilson's house in St. Pancras, London, that the Anglo-Israel Association was founded in 1874.[259]

The list of publications of the British-Israelism theory from the 18th Century to the 1920's is quite long. Here are a few samples arranged chronologically:

Figure 9.3

> 1827 On the Asiatic Origin of the Anglo-Saxons. —Sharon Turner
> 1840 Our Israelitish Origin. —John Wilson
> 1861 Where Are The "Lost 10 Tribes" Today? —F.R.A. Glover
> 1871 Identification of the British Nation with Lost Israel—Edward Hine
> 1877 Sixty Anglo-Israel Difficulties Answered. —John Wilson
> 1880 Heir of the World—G. W. Greenwood
> 1881 The Lost Ten Tribes of Israel in England and America—E. K. Tullidge
> 1885 The Queen's royal descent from King David the Psalmist—A. B. Grimaldi
> 1902 Judah's Sceptre and Joseph's Birthright—J. H. Allen
> 1918 Tamar Tephi: or The Maid of Destiny, —John Dunham-Massey
> 1920 The House of Israel and The House of Judah by F. F. Bosworth

In the 1890's the "Anglo-Israel Association" had 300 members. It was formed by physician George Moore who later promoted the idea in the United States.

Adherents of British Israelism dug up parts of the Hill of Tara in Ireland in the belief that the Ark of the Covenant was buried there. The Hill of Tara located near the River Boyne, is an archaeological complex that runs between Navan and Dunshaughlin in County Meath, Ireland. It contains a number of ancient monuments and, according to tradition, was the seat of the High King of Ireland.

A legend associated with the Hill of Tara claims it was the capital of the *Tuatha Dé Danann*, whom some adherents of British-Israelism believe were from the Israelite tribe of Dan. The tribe of Dan was said to contain Israel's ship-builders based on one indefinite Biblical reference[260]. During Solomon's reign there are many references[261] to Israelites exploring many parts of the world in ships. However, nothing there is no definite reference to Dan building a navy in the Bible. Nonetheless, some British-Israelism adherents believe the *Tuatha Dé Danann* were from the tribe of Dan.

---

259 https://en.wikipedia.org/wiki/John_Wilson_(historian)
260 Judges 5:17
261 I Kings 9:26; 10:11, 22; II Chronicles 8:18; 9:21

Figure 9.4
Hill of Tara, Lia Fáil and surrounding landscape

Atop the hill stands a stone pillar that is called the Irish *Lia Fáil* (Stone of Destiny) on which the High Kings of Ireland were crowned. The Hill of Tara seems to have political and religious influence and remains a major tourist attraction rivaling the famous Stonehenge monument to the south.

The Anglo-Israel Almanac in 1914 listed a large number of British-Israelism groups operating in the British Isles, Australia, New Zealand, South Africa, Canada and the United States.

The British-Israel World Federation was founded in London in 1922 and dispensed information though Covenant Publishing.

The organization was patronized by several prominent people including Princess Alice, Countess of Athlone[153], William Massey the prime minister of New Zealand. Howard Rand[154] was the head of the Anglo-Saxon Federation of America in 1928. He published a bulletin called *The Messenger of the Covenant* which he later renamed *Destiny*.

During its heyday in the early 20th century, British Israelism was also supported by John Fisher[155], 1st Baron Fisher. A prolific author on British Israelism during the later 1930s and 40s was Alexander James Ferris.

The BIWF continues to exist, with its main headquarters located in Bishop Auckland in County Durham in northeast England. It also has chapters in Australia, Canada, The Netherlands, New Zealand and South Africa.[262]

For those who are interested in fully understanding the British-Israelism theory, The Jewish Encyclopedia[263] lists the history of the movement, the chief arguments, the Biblical texts, the historic connection and the philological arguments that are shared by many of those who believe the British-Israelism theory. It is the most succinct yet encompassing description we have found in our research.

---

[262] https://en.wikipedia.org/wiki/British_Israelism
[263] http://www.jewishencyclopedia.com/articles/1524-anglo-israelism

British-Israelism in America

The 1902 wide-spread publication of *Judah's Sceptre and Joseph's Birthright* by J. H. Allen[156] influenced several others who wrote and taught the British-Israelism concept in the United States. Allen's sincere approach and Bible references lend credibility to the writing. The book is available on the Internet in several websites and is downloaded frequently to this day.

Some have suggested that Allen's work was heavily plagiarized by Herbert W. Armstrong.

Armstrong was the best-known advocate for British-Israelism in the United States in the middle of the 20th Century. Armstrong added new material, but several passages of *The United States and Britain in Prophecy* published in 1954 appear almost identical to passages from Allen's book.

Figure 9.5 Herbert W. Armstrong

Armstrong was founder and Pastor General of the Worldwide Church of God. The British-Israelism theory was heavily promoted by Armstrong and his son, Garner Ted Armstrong, on their widely-syndicated radio program called *The World Tomorrow*.

Armstrong believed that the teaching was the key to understanding biblical prophecy: "One might ask, were not biblical prophecies closed and sealed? Indeed, they were—until now! And even now they can be understood only by those who possess the master key to unlock them."[264]

Armstrong believed that he was called by God to proclaim the prophecies to the Lost Tribes of Israel before the "end-times". Armstrong's belief caused his separation from the Church of God Seventh Day because of its refusal to adopt the teaching. Armstrong created his own church, first called the "Radio Church of God" and later renamed the "Worldwide Church of God". He described British Israelism as a "central plank" of his theology.[265]

At its zenith, estimated membership in the Worldwide Church of God was over 500,000.

After Armstrong's death in 1986, many "splinter" organizations of the WWCG were formed and still teach British Israelism, including the Philadelphia Church of God, the Living Church of God, and the United Church of God.

One of the best-written, most carefully researched series of books on British-Israelism was written by a former member of the WWCOG, Steven M. Collins, who published *"The Lost" Ten Tribes of Israel...Found!* In 1992. There are at least 6 other related books written by Collins with publishing dates in the 2000's available on Amazon today.[266] These books are well-written and interesting reading if you wish to understand British-Israelism and they provide as good an argument for the theory as you're likely to find.

Rebutting British-Israelism

Evangelical perspective

There were at one time many of the so-called "Evangelical" movement who considered British-Israelism to be truth. It was so wide-spread that it caused problems in the movement. The more mainstream evangelicals today either ignore the theory or at least do not teach the theory in their congregations.

An evangelical website partially explains British-Israelism but ties it to several secret societies – primarily with the Freemasons – and declares that the doctrine has faded within the evangelical movement. The website declares that all the references within the New Testament related to the nation of Israel refer to the Christian church and have nothing to do with genealogy.

---

[264] https://en.wikipedia.org/wiki/Herbert_W._Armstrong

[265] *Ibid*

[266] https://www.amazon.com/Steven-M.-Collins

As we examine British Israelism teaching we are required of God to test it by the Scriptures. The fact is, every doctrine must be tested by such to see if it is biblical or not. British Israelism has probably waned enormously over this past hundred years. It was once an extremely popular doctrine within the British Isles with countless devotees, whereas today it is sparse.[267]

Among those secret Masonic societies the site claims follow the British-Israelism doctrine are the Orange Order, Royal Black Knights of the Camp of Israel and Royal Arch Purple degree. In exposing these secret societies, evangelicals denounce British-Israelism.

Evidently, this chosen nation is NOT a physical earthly nation but a spiritual heavenly nation. This is clearly seen in the Lord's wording – it would be a nation that brings forth the spiritual fruits of the Kingdom of God. Undoubtedly, Christ is talking about the Church. British Israelism is therefore wrong to relate spiritual truths to a physical temporal earthly nation.[268]

Moriel Ministries[269] makes a cogent argument against the "two-house" theology associated with the British-Israelism movement and demonstrates that those who follow that movement have fallen into replacement theology.

In its simplest terms, "replacement theology" holds that the descendants of the "10 lost tribes" have replaced the ecumenical church Jesus established. Moriel declares the New Covenant is open to all people regardless of genealogy, race or color and it is wrong to suggest that salvation belongs to Israel alone.

While replacement theology effectively displaces Israel, Two House Theology denies and displaces the ekklesia. Moriel Ministries writes:

Two House Theology, consistent with its other errors, sees the ekklesia as simply "new covenant Israel":"(Your Arms To Israel Doctrinal Statement)": Ã,. It teaches that supposedly Gentile believers within the ekklesia are in fact mostly unrecognised Ephraimites, Israelites) Ã,:"(Your Arms To Israel Doctrinal Statement)": Ã,. These "Israelites", by uniting with the believing Jews in the church "Judah", are reuniting both houses of Israel -hence Two-House Theology. One error leads to another. Confusion regarding origin and terminology inevitably creates confusion regarding the identity of Israel and of the church.

---

[267] http://www.evangelicaltruth.com/british-israelism-exposed
[268] *Ibid*
[269]https://www.moriel.org/component/k2/item/179-a-brief-assessment-of-two-house-theology.html?ml=1

Scripture teaches that the ekklesia or church is a truly new entity. Paul speaks of Jewish and Gentile believers united in one body:" (I Cor 12:13; Eph 2:16) ": Union of this kind was impossible before Messiah's death:"(Col 2:14; Eph 2:14, 15) ": We are now heirs together and sharers together:"(Eph 3:6)"[270]

Moriel claims that the people of the Northern Kingdom of Israel had mostly moved into the Kingdom of Judah and eventually all became known as "Jews".

The northern kingdom was invaded by the Assyrians around 722BC and many of its people deported:" (II Kings 17:6) ": However, prior to the invasion many of the Israelites (...from every tribe of Israel...) were living in the southern kingdom among the people of Judah and Benjamin (I Kings 12:17; II Chronicles 11:3, 16). Large numbers from Ephraim, Manasseh and Simeon had moved to the southern kingdom (II Chronicles 15:9). Even following the Assyrian exile many Israelites were recorded as still dwelling among the people of Judah and Benjamin (II Chronicles 30:25; 34:9; 35:18).[271] [157]

Moriel also asserts that the terms Israelites and Jews were used interchangeably throughout the New Testament.

As should be expected, the New Testament continues to use the terms Israelite and Jew interchangeably. Peter, In Acts 2, addressed his kinsmen as fellow-Jews in verse 14 but men of Israel in verse 22. Paul explicitly calls himself both an Israelite:"(Romans 11:1; II Corinthians 11:22)": and a Jew:"(Acts 21:39; 22:3) ": Throughout Romans, Paul uses Israel and Jew interchangeably. He freely moves between statements distinguishing Jew and Gentile:"(e.g. Romans 1:16; 2:9-3:1; 3:28-30; 9:24; 10:12; 15:8,9,27)": and Israelite and Gentile:"(e.g. 9:30; 11:11-14; 11:25-26) ": If these terms are given the meanings assigned by Two House Theology some of Paul's propositions become meaningless or confused :"(e.g. Rom 11:11 ...through their, Israel's, fall, salvation has come to the Gentiles to provoke them to envy... THT teaches that most Gentiles who come to saving faith are in fact Israelites. As such, Paul's statement is rendered meaningless.) ":.

None of the twelve tribes was considered lost in the first century. James knew that there were believers among all twelve tribes and that many were living in the Diaspora (dispersion). He began his letter to those Jewish believers ...to the twelve tribes scattered among the nations, greeting...:"(James 1:1) ": Jesus' listeners in John 7 clearly understood that many of their people remained scattered among the Gentiles:"(John 7:35) ":

---

[270] Ibid
[271] Ibid

The prophetess Anna, mentioned by Luke, was of the tribe of Asher, one of the supposedly lost tribes:"(Luke 2:36) ". The notion of lost tribes is found to be without biblical basis.[272] [158]

Anglican perspective

An article[273] written by C. T. Dimont, D.D, the principal of Salisbury Theological College Chancellor and Canon of Salisbury Cathedral, lays out perhaps the most cogent rebuttal of British-Israelism to be found on the web.

Dr. Dimont clearly states that "the Ten Tribes were never lost" and thus all the British-Israelism adherents should find their beliefs without foundation.

> First, then, we may state a fact which if we were so disposed might dispense us from further troubling about the matter. The British cannot be the descendants of the Lost Ten Tribes, because no such body of lost tribes exists or ever has existed. The assertion that all the Ten Northern Tribes were carried away to Assyria is contrary to Scripture and to the testimony of the monuments. Sargon, the King of Assyria, says that he carried away from Israel 27,290 captives. It is quite obvious that this was but a fragment of the whole population of the Northern Kingdom (cp. 2 Sam. xxiv. 9, which puts the men of military age in North Israel at 800,000). From the account in 2 Kings xvii. 6 and xviii.11 they appear to have been deported in two groups, one of which was placed in Western Mesopotamia, and the other in the far eastern parts of the Assyrian Empire. And this, as Dr. McCurdy says in his book, History, Prophecy and the Monuments (sec. 363), "is the whole story of the famous 'Dispersion of the Ten Tribes.' " The number stated by Sargon is not likely to have been put too low. Assyrian kings were not in the habit of minimising their exploits. Yet it comes to no more than the present population of Salisbury. A few years later more than seven times this number were carried away from Judah without destroying the southern and smaller kingdom.[274] [159]

Dimont also calls attention to the flaws in the various British-Israelism theories regarding the Scythians turning into Saxons, Druids, Celts, Teutons or Welsh.

> British-Israel finds in these also some of the Lost Tribes, and proceeds to see in them the ancestors of the Welsh, Cymry. Welsh, it is alleged, is largely derived from Hebrew, and the Druids spoke Hebrew. This theory

---

[272] *Ibid*
[273] https://theologicalstudies.org.uk/article_legend_dimont.html
[274] *Ibid*

certainly presents us with a curious historical situation. Apparently one section of the Ten Tribes, the Kimmerians, had no sooner found a new home and settled down comfortably than they were thrust out by others of their brethren who followed them, and who for some strange reason preferred to be called Scythians.

Those who are familiar with both Hebrew and Welsh assure us that the derivation of the second of these from the first is a vain imagination, and that there is no connection between the two languages. Equally unhappy is the suggestion that the name British is compounded of the Hebrew words berith and ish, meaning "man of the covenant." A glance at any philological dictionary will be enough to dispose of this absurdity. As regards the name Saxon we are given a choice in British-Israel manuals between finding the source of it either in Isaac, or in the Sacæ, an obscure race, who seem to have drifted about in Asia. It seems to be only necessary to find two words which have two letters alike to declare them to be cognate. Ordinary textbooks inform us that Saxon is derived from a word meaning a dagger.[275]

Church of Christ[160] perspective

Foy Wallace[276] gives one of the most lengthy and detailed rebuttals of British-Israelism. Wallace follows the tenets of British Israelism almost point by point beginning with the historical background of the movement.

His best points are those that rebut the movement as a *political* movement, which Wallace sees as potentially subversive. Wallace sees British-Israelism to some extent in the same political context as Nazism – the Anglo Saxons being the "master race" with their special connection to God.

The claim that Great Britain *is* the Kingdom of Israel and holder of God's Covenants with man raises racial issues also. Wallace points out that some adherents specifically deny that the Jews of today are Israelites.

Lutheran perspective

Like many of those rebutting British-Israelism, the Evangelical Lutheran Synod faults the movement for its "millennialism" connotations equating the movement to some extent with "fundamentalism" like that taught by Jerry Falwell, Billy Graham and Oral Roberts. The ELS also considers the *political* aspects of the movement to be dangerous to our national independence.

---

[275] *ibid*
[276] http://www.bible.ca/pre-british-israelism-foy-wallace.htm

British Israelism is simply millennialism with a slightly different twist to it. Adherents of this movement believe that the Anglo-Saxons make up two of the lost tribes of Israel, one in England, the other in the United States. They maintain that when the northern kingdom of Israel was taken captive by the Assyrians, these tribes escaped and emigrated to the British Isles. They feel that the Anglo-Saxons and not the ostensible Jews, were the chosen people of God; that by destiny they have been selected to rule the world; that this will be accomplished by the merger of Britain and America into one common citizenship.

Herbert W. Armstrong (who just recently died) and his Worldwide Church of God has been one of the leading and visible proponents of British Israelism. But this non-Trinitarian cult is not the only pusher of this pernicious doctrine; even many Trinitarian groups have incorporated this kind of millennialism into their theological system. It is hard to expose the British Israel World Federation, since they have no membership as such, visibly speaking. It is the invisible, though, that makes this movement so dangerous to our Christian faith, as well as to our national independence.[277]

The ELS dismisses British-Israelism as having no more proof or foundation for its tenets than the Mormon claim "that the captives of the northern kingdom of Israel immigrated to American and their descendants are now American Indians."

Baptist perspective

Dr. Michael S. Heiser, presently the Scholar-in-Residence for Logos Bible Software and previous adjunct professor at several Baptist Seminaries and colleges, gives a brief definition of the British-Israelism theory and recommends a book by former Worldwide Church of God member Greg Doudna. Doudna is quite well known for his scholarly work on the Dead Sea scrolls.

Doudna traces many of the points of British-Israelism made by Herbert Armstrong to their sources and shows the inconsistencies, the misuse and faulty interpretation of esoteric Old Testament prophecies. He completely demolishes the Tea-Tephi fable[161] claimed to be found in ancient Irish annals declaring that the fable was intentionally fabricated from its beginning.

Doudna's book "Showdown at Big Sandy" also records the many foibles of the Worldwide Church of God but the British-Israelism rebuttal is worth the read.

Further information on British-Israelism

---

[277] http://els.org/resources/answers/british-israelism/

At last glance there were more than 60 titles related to BI available from Amazon.com. There are hundreds of articles both pro and con on the subject available through any of the search engines on web browsers. Some of the articles cited above have URL's listed as footnotes.

Comparing our thesis with British-Israelism

The thesis for this book: *The Bible is the story of God's Covenants with Israel and through those Covenants God has dramatically shaped the world we live in today.*

Agreement with British-Israelism

> The nation of Israel was formed by God's Covenant with Abraham
> The Covenant was unconditional and guaranteed by God
> The Covenant birthright passed from Abraham to Isaac to Jacob (Israel)
> There were two parts to the Covenant: 1. Physical and 2. Spiritual
> The spiritual part was bestowed upon Judah along with national royalty
> The physical birthright was bestowed upon Ephraim and Manasseh, Joseph's sons
> After the unified Kingdom of Israel – under Saul, David and Solomon – the nation divided
> The northern 10 tribes were called the Kingdom of Israel – Israelites
> The tribes of Judah and Benjamin and most of Levi formed the Kingdom of Judah – Jews
> The northern kingdom was destroyed and many of its people deported in 721 BC
> The deported Israelites eventually migrated across Europe
> The Israelite nation was created and guided by God across its entire history
> The physical Covenant blessings were bestowed primarily upon Great Britain, its commonwealth nations and the USA

Disagreement and Differences with British-Israelism

> The Israelites retained their identity until the 1st Century AD
> The spiritual and royalty blessings were delivered in the person of Jesus, the Son of God
> A very large number of the Israelites were converted to Christianity in the 1st Century AD by Jesus' apostles Peter, Thomas, Bartholomew, Thaddeus and Simon Zelotes

- As the Israelites migrated across Europe they converted the peoples among whom they were "scattered" to Christianity, which explains the exponential growth of the church
- The "scattered" Israelites were called various names by Greek and Roman historians including Scythians, Aryans, Sarmatians, Alani, Goths, Huns, Ostrogoths, Visigoths, Angles, Saxons, Lombards, Franks and Normans. No historian called them Israelites; they assimilated among the Europeans with no retention of their ancient identity
- The Israelites and the people with whom they assimilated helped create the Renaissance, the Enlightenment, the scientific revolution and the Reformation
- As a result of these massive cultural shifts, the descendants of the Israelites rebelled against the church in Rome and its hierarchy; with the invention of the printing press and the translation of the Bible into the language of the "common" people, Christianity diversified and could be understood to some extent by "ordinary people" thus setting the stage for its global dissemination.
- Throughout their history, the Israelites disobeyed God more often than not; still, their descendants were due the physical blessings and political hegemony in an *unconditional* Covenant promise from God to Abraham, Isaac, Jacob and the children of Israel. The blessings were given, not because they were *good* people or especially deserving, but because God keeps His word.

Steven M Collins is the most cogent advocate for British Israelism. Collins is a very good writer and systematic in his presentations. It is possible that some of his highly interesting *theories* and scriptural interpretations are valid. However, he and many of his predecessors (Armstrong, J. H. Allen et al) who wrote of British-Israelism rely upon two very weak links in following the Israelites.

- First is using the sound of certain words to make their connection – Saxons is equated with "Isaac's sons"; Scythians were called *Sakae* again referencing "Isaac's sons". When Jacob was "adopting" and bestowing their birthright[278] upon Ephraim and Manasseh[279], Jacob said "may they be called by my name, and the names of my fathers Abraham and Isaac." They were called "Israelites" (Jacob's name given by God was Israel) but nowhere in the scriptures are they referred to as "Isaac's sons". There are two references to the "children of Abraham"[280] in which the people so designated are Jews. They also infer that the various geographic names

---

[278] Genesis 48:16
[279] Joseph's two sons
[280] Acts 13:26; Galatians 3:7

were given by the tribe of Dan – Danube River, Dneister River, Denmark ("Danmark").

➢ Second is their accepting as truth an Irish fable of "a wise man from the East who brought a "princess" to Ireland to begin the dynasty of a descendants of King David that would rule over Israel (Great Britain) until the return of Jesus. The necessity of there being a descendant of David ruling over Israel forever is based on one prophecy by Jeremiah. [162]

Based on those connections they add in ancient history to support their theories. The connections are tenuous and scores of critics have rebutted the theories at great length.

> [7] For if that first *covenant* had been faultless, occasion would not have been sought for a second. [8] For in finding fault with them he says, "Behold, days are coming, says the Lord, when I will complete a new covenant with the house of Israel and with the house of Judah, [9] not like the covenant which I made with their fathers on the day I took hold of them by my hand to lead them out of the land of Egypt, because they did not continue in my covenant and I disregarded them, says the Lord. [10] For this *is* the covenant that I will decree with the house of Israel after those days, says the Lord: I am putting my laws in their minds and I will write them on their hearts, and I will be their God and they will be my people. [11] And they will not teach each one his fellow citizen and each one his brother, saying, 'Know the Lord,' because they will all know me, from the least of them to the greatest. [12] For I will be merciful toward their wrongdoings, and I will not remember their sins *any* longer." Hebrews 8:7–12 (LEB)

Agreement with critics of British-Israelism

➢ The assignment of Israelite identity based on the sound of certain words, i.e. *Sacae* and *Saxon* = Isaac's Son, leads to multiple assignment of Israelite identity when there are no other supporting historical criteria.

➢ The British-Israelism tendency to exclude Jews from contemplation as Israelites is not only non-sensical but also in direct contradiction with the Bible concepts of the New Covenant.

➢ The tendency of certain proponents of British Israelism to include only Israelites in receiving the physical Covenant blessings is evidence of a racism specifically condemned throughout the Bible

➢ The attempts by British-Israelism to prove genealogy by conflating certain names, the words of various languages with the Hebrew/Aramaic language are specious

➢ Asserting that the Israelites were by nature a superior people in terms of morals, ethics and cultural tendencies ignores the nature of the Israelites as shown clearly in the Bible

- The incorporation of the tenets of British-Israelism into secret societies is troubling; the incorporation of those tenets into the activities of political leaders – their assuming that God will bless them whatever they might do – is *dangerous* and should be called to account.
- The concept that the monarchy in Britain is comprised of the descendants of King David of Israel is without historical proof and carried to extreme is also politically and culturally *dangerous*.
- The only Israel that exists today is *spiritual Israel* which includes the genetic Israelites (including the Jews) and all races and colors.

Disagreement with the critics of British Israelism

- The concept of all the people of Israel amalgamated into the Jews is not historically accurate; referring to all Israelites as Jews shows not only a lack of Biblical understanding but also a lack of historical research. The New Covenant Jesus established was to be with the "House of Israel" and the "House of Judah".
- Failure to comprehend the working of the *Hand of God* causes these critics to overlook God's plan for spreading His Gospel to the whole world through the Israelites that were in existence in 94 AD in the Parthian Empire. Josephus' statemen is clear and ample proof that the Israelites were "beyond the Euphrates" in large numbers at the end of the 1st Century AD
- That Jesus sent His apostles to the "lost sheep of the House of Israel" in the Parthian Empire in the first Century AD is clearly stated in the Bible and is confirmed by the exemplary research of William Steuart McBirnie, PhD in his book "The Search for the Twelve Apostles"[281]. [163]
- Almost all the critics assert that the New Testament uses the words Jews and Israelites interchangeably. This is a gross error and often shows a lack of in-depth knowledge of both the Old Testament and New Testament scriptures and the Covenants God made with mankind.
- C. T. Dimont bases his claims that there were only about 27,000 Israelites taken captive and deported to "the cities of the Medes" on the records of Sargon, the ruler of Assyria. Documents found in the Assyrian cuneiform library in excavated Ninevah quote Sargon's successor on the throne of Assyria, Sennacherib, as stating that the number was *much* larger – more than 200,000 Israelites – and the Bible seems to agree. [164] When one considers that it was common in that day to only count the grown men when numbering, the actual number could easily have been twice that 200,000.
- Foy Wallace fails to comprehend the Biblical history cited in previous chapters of this book and declares that the terms Jews and Israelites are

---

[281] William Steuart McBirnie, PhD *The Search For the 12 Apostles* ©1973 Tyndale House Publishers, Carol Stream, IL 60188

used interchangeably in the Bible – in particular in the New Testament. Like most of those rebutting British-Israelism, Wallace is unaware of the Parthian Empire and the role the "lost 10 tribes" played in the 1st Century spread of Christianity

> Critics fail to understand Biblical history and prophecy – not of the Israelites becoming British – but of the future of Israel and Judah.
> Critics fail to understand the Covenant with Abraham – that it is clearly split into a spiritual side and a physical side – and that those two sides were separated when Ephraim was given the physical birthright and Judah was given the spiritual and royalty birthright.

This book has shown that the following are *quite likely* to be true:

> The Israelites were scattered throughout Europe with large numbers concentrated in Western Europe
> There was a significant concentration of the descendants of Ephraim and Manasseh in Great Britain and the USA so that the physical blessings of great wealth and political and economic hegemony fell upon those people.
> These blessings allowed the rise of the largest Empire the world has ever known followed by the most powerful single nation ever to exist.
> Together, the British Empire, the commonwealth nations, the United States of America and the rest of the nations that comprise Western Civilization today formed the Stone Kingdom as prophesied by Daniel.
> The world today has been shaped by Abraham's Covenant with God. The Covenant blessings and promises have all been delivered.
> The only Covenant that remains in effect is the New Covenant installed by Jesus; the only Israel that remains is "spiritual Israel" and the Jews.
> The New Covenant is for both:

Summary

It is a common failing of humanity to underestimate the power and scope of what God is doing and to see His influence in terms of the way humans would do things.

There are many ways in which the British-Israelism concept has been detrimental to understanding how the *Hand of God* has been working in this world. Among those ways are the racial aspects – some people's belief that the nation of Israel still exists and that its existence negates the concept of the New Covenant established by Jesus. That Covenant is for all people, all races, all ethnicities – for every human being on the face of this earth. The British-Israelism concept has led many to believe that Great Britain, its commonwealth nations and the United States remain favored in God's eyes. But is that true? The people of Western Civilization have "ruled" the rest of the world since the late 1700's.

We've shown that the *Hand of God* preserved the nation of Israel until the 1st Century AD; that He preserved the laws of God down to the time of Jesus and the establishment of the New Covenant for the House of Israel and the House of Judah. That Covenant expanded the special status of the nation of Israel to include all those who believe in Jesus as a new "spiritual Israel".

We've shown how it is possible – and almost certain – that the *Hand of God* used Israel to destroy the remnants of the Babylonian Empire, the Medo-Persian Empire, the Greek Empire and the Roman Empire.

Those same Israelites – converted to Christianity – were responsible for the phenomenal, exponential growth of Jesus' church. With God's guidance, the descendants of the Israelites changed the culture of the whole world with the social, political, economic and intellectual influence of the Renaissance, the Enlightenment, the scientific revolution and the Reformation.

The hand of God brought about the power and hegemony of the British Empire and the United States by the bestowal of the great physical blessings of Abraham's Covenant. Those physical blessings allowed the spreading of that wealth and knowledge and the Gospel of Jesus to the whole world with the spiritual blessings of Abraham's Covenant as well.

Both the spiritual and physical promises and blessings of Abraham's Covenant have been delivered as promised. A New Covenant was installed by Jesus that is no longer exclusive to the Israelites. The Israelites served their purpose and – as always – the will of God has prevailed. There is little reason today to believe that genetic Israelites hold any special place in God's eyes other than as citizens of the "Stone Kingdom".

God has formed His Stone Kingdom and promised it would never fall. That does not mean that genetic Israelites have any advantage over the other people who make up Western Civilization.

The Stone Kingdom citizens comprise all of the people who believe the Gospel of Jesus, love God with all their hearts, souls and minds and love their neighbors as themselves.

> *The advantage under the New Covenant belongs to Jesus' ecclesia – spiritual Israel.*

We've now brought our narrative to our present time. So where do we go from here? In the next chapter we will offer some suggestions based on what has gone before.

$$* \quad * \quad *$$

CHAPTER 10

Retrospective

> [10] I make known the end from the beginning, from ancient times, what is still to come. I say, 'My purpose will stand, and I will do all that I please.' Isaiah 46:10 (NIV)

Our journey in this book started at the *beginning* with Abraham. What did God make known "from the beginning"?

1. Abraham's descendants would be as numerous as the stars in the sky
2. God's Covenant with Abraham would be inherited by Isaac
3. His descendants would possess the territory from the river of Egypt to the Euphrates
4. Kings and a "company of nations" would come from Isaac's progeny
5. Abraham and Isaac's descendants would possess "the gates of their enemies"
6. Other nations would "bow down" to Abraham and Isaac's descendants.
7. All the people of the world would be blessed through Abraham

We followed the Covenant to Isaac, then to Jacob and then to the children of Israel. We followed Israel through slavery to the Promised Land and the Kingdom of Israel. We followed the Israelites after the destruction of both the Kingdom of Israel and the Kingdom of Judah. We followed the Israelites to Medea, through the rise and fall of the Empires of Babylon, Medo-Persia, Greece and Rome. We followed them across Europe as they helped spread the Gospel of Jesus, as they helped destroy the Roman Empire and as they helped form Western Civilization.

The Bible displays the work of the *Hand of God*. In retrospect, we can see the panorama of the beauty and awesome majesty of His work over the 2,000 years from Abraham to the time of Jesus. For too long now, many if not most Christians have *assumed* that the story that began with Abraham more than 4,000 years ago ended with the last chapter of the book of Revelation.

One continuing theme of this narrative has been to show that *not all* of God's plan for Israel and mankind ended with the Holy Scriptures. There has been no lull in that plan for the last 2,000 years. The movement of people, kings and nations by the *Hand of God* has never slacked; it has brought about His will. It is still unfolding just as it was in the days of Abraham.

Is God still working with the Israelites? The Jews are well known among us and the bloodlines of all 12 tribes still exist scattered within the nations of Western Civilization.

Two Theses

It is the firm belief of the author that God, who knows the end from the beginning, planned for the Israelites to spread the Gospel of Jesus and to be instrumental in delivering not only the spiritual blessings but also the physical blessings of that Covenant to the whole world through the rise of Western Civilization. If this is true, we have found the true origin of Western Civilization.

This book was written based upon two theses:

1. The Bible – from Genesis to Revelation – is the story of the Covenant God made with Abraham, the guidance of Abraham's descendants until the 1st Century AD – the time of Jesus – and the delivery of many of the blessings and promises made by God in that holy pact.

2. God's plan for Israel and mankind has continued to unfold from the 1st Century AD to the present; that guidance and the delivery of the blessings and promises *not* made during Biblical times can be shown to have a direct correlation not only to the rise and hegemony of the nations of Western Civilization but also – and even more importantly – the growth of God's church and the delivery of the Gospel of the Christ to the whole world.

The First Thesis Part 1, chapters 1 – 4

Part 1 provides a synopsis of the first thesis based solely on the Bible with, of course, my personal understanding of those scriptures. However, other than for my interpretation of certain prophecies, the basics are there for anyone to follow by a close examination of the scriptures.

That the hand of God guided the patriarchs and the nation of Israel from the time of Abraham to the time of Jesus is beyond question unless you deny the authenticity of the scriptures; that God chose the Israelites to be a holy[165] people and guided their fate throughout the times covered by the Bible is likewise unassailable.

That the Bible shows many of the promises of God were kept and can be verified by secular history and archeology is also fact. Examples include their possession of the land of Canaan – the "Promised Land" – the rise of the kingdom of Israel under Saul, David and Solomon and the great national power and wealth accrued under the latter two kings. Under David and Solomon, the kingdom of Israel extended from the "river of Egypt to the Euphrates" just as God promised Abraham[282].

The most important Covenant spiritual blessing was the birth, life, death and resurrection of Jesus and the installation of a New Covenant that incorporates all people and all nations[283].

Libraries are filled with the writings of others concerning the story of the Bible. There is, in fact, very little within this narrative of Biblical times that could be said to be "new" in terms of not having been written and taught before.

However, the succinct nature of this narrative is somewhat new in that the story of the Covenant over nearly 2,000 years as related in the 66 books of the Canon is compressed into just 4 chapters. There was no intent to provide extensive scholarly documentation as such can be found in the thousands of books written on the subject. Our narrative is devoted foremost and primarily to tracing the Covenant rather than elaborating upon the history of the Israelites. Only enough information is given to allow one to follow that narrative and gain the background to understand and follow the next 5 chapters.

It is in those 5 chapters of Part 2 that some new and, I hope, highly interesting concepts are presented; it is Part 2 that ties Bible times to our time.

The Second Thesis

Part II, Chapters 5 – 8 is likewise a compression of almost 2,000 years into just 4 chapters. In this part of the narrative, there is historical information not commonly known even among Bible scholars and ignored or overlooked by secular historians.

---

[282] Genesis 15:18
[283] Genesis 12:3

The information missing from the narratives of most Christian teachers and ignored or overlooked by secular historians is the direct result of our culture's tendency to accept the traditional teaching that all Israelites are Jews.

As we discussed several times in Part I, at the end of King Solomon's reign, there was an abiding separation of the Israelites into the Kingdom of Israel – 10 of the 12 tribes led by the tribe of Ephraim – and the Kingdom of Judah – the tribes of Judah, Benjamin and most of Levi. The former retained the name of Israel while the latter became known as Jews.

The unquestioning acceptance of traditional teaching on this matter is "hard set" in our culture. Today's Christian teachers refer to the Jews being led out of Egyptian bondage by Moses; they refer to God's giving the 10 Commandments to the Jews; throughout the Old Testament history, these teachers speak of Jews as if all the Israelites carried that name.

When the Kingdom of Israel was destroyed and 200,000 Israelites were taken captive by the Assyrian Empire and deported to the "cities of the Medes", the traditional teaching proclaims that the Israelites either disappeared into the populations of the areas into which they were deported or returned to the Kingdom of Judah where they all became "Jews".

This tradition is so ubiquitous that you find virtually no *recognized* major historians who even mention the fate of those deported Israelites; much less will you find any legitimate historical research by those historians.

Instead, those who have attempted to provide that research have been marginalized and ridiculed *or ignored* by those same historians. Some of that ridicule and ignoring *may have been deserved*! However, *some* of their work concerning the last two millennia should have been incorporated into our historical narrative.

The failure to do so has blinded otherwise astute Bible scholars and historians to the working of the *hand of God* over that period.

Chapter 9 of this book addresses that historical error directly by giving a synopsis of some of that work and the converse efforts to denigrate some truly significant historical writing.

A New Concept

What should be of considerable interest to Christians today is tracing the work of the *hand of God* in preparing the Israelites to spread the Gospel of Jesus Christ. This information, so far as we've been able to determine, is a new concept of how the church that Jesus established was able to grow from the 12 apostles and a few thousand converts in the first century AD to nearly 40 million Christians in the next 275 years.

Most Christians, it seems, are under the impression that the 12 apostles, the apostle Paul and the relatively few Jewish believers were somehow able to convert enough "gentiles" to carry the gospel to the rest of Europe after the death of the apostles – most of whom had died or were martyred by the time Jerusalem and the temple was destroyed in 70 AD.

By recognizing that the *hand of God* was still at work with Israel we found not only Biblical clues but secular historical clues as to what really happened. Our magnificent God who "knows the end from the beginning, had sequestered a large number of Israelites in the Parthian Empire in the 1st Century AD.

The first and what should have been the most obvious clue to that fact is a statement by the Jewish historian Josephus who in 94 AD stated that the 10 tribes were still located "beyond the Euphrates" in numbers too large to count and that only the two tribes (Judah and Benjamin) were under the rule of the Roman Empire. A few historians quibble with various parts of Josephus' writing but virtually none question his statements about his personal time period.

Josephus, in 94 AD (~60 years after Jesus' death) proclaims the location of the 10 tribes of Israelites, indicates they were known to be Israelites (not "Jews") and that there were a great many of them.

When we read in Matthew's Gospel that Jesus sent His apostles to "the lost sheep of the House of Israel"[284], most Christians assume that He meant the Jews scattered abroad among the gentiles in the Roman Empire. We read and marvel – and rightly so – at the missionary journeys of Paul, the "apostle to the Gentiles"[285], and all his persecution, many trials and tribulations.

However, if you count the cities in which Paul helped establish congregations, and *generously* allow for perhaps 300 to 500 conversions in each of the 14 locations described in Acts, add some number of Christians to account for the Jews who converted to Christianity and round the total number to 30 congregations, there were perhaps as many as 20,000 Christians in the Roman Empire in 70 AD[166]. It's not an

---

[284] Matthew 10:5–23
[285] Romans 11:13; Galatians 2:8

insignificant number but with all the persecution Christians faced in the Roman Empire – described in the Bible *and* in secular history – it does not explain the exponential growth of the church to 35 *million* by 400 AD[286].

We learned from many historical sources (including Eusebius and other "church fathers") and the magnificent research of William Steuart McBirnie[287] that there were at least five of the original apostles – holy spirit-filled, eye-witnesses of the life, death, burial and resurrection of Jesus of Nazareth – who spent from 10 to 30 years in the Parthian Empire establishing congregations and preaching the Gospel.

The apostle Peter, whose first epistle was written from Babylon – a province of the Parthian Empire – was joined by Thomas, Thaddeus, Bartholomew and Simon Zelotes and perhaps others. The New Testament narrative does not mention these apostles (other than Peter) after the 1st chapter of the book of Acts. Have you noticed that fact and how would you explain that 8 of Jesus' 12 ambassadors to the world are not mentioned elsewhere in the New Testament canon?

Secular historians give no credit to their being 500,000 to 1,500,000 Israelites in the Parthian Empire who would – just as prophesied by Old Testament prophets – return to the worship of the one Creator God of their ancestors[167]. They already carried with them the ancestral knowledge of the "law of Moses" and the Ten Commandments though for centuries many of them had been worshipping the false Gods of the nations into which they were dispersed in 721 BC.

Some of them were present on the day of Pentecost about 50 days after Jesus ascended back to God, the Father. It was that day when God poured out His spirit upon the apostles and they began performing the task to which they had been appointed by Jesus[288]. Read for yourself of the "Parthians, Medes, residents of Mesopotamia and Asia" – all parts of the Parthian Empire – who were present for the proclamations of Peter and the other apostles on that day.

Secular history confirms, as does McBirnie, the conversion of many in the Parthian Empire with one province of that Empire – Armenia – declaring Christianity as the official religion of that province in 301 AD, long before Emperor Constantine declared Christianity the official religion of the Roman Empire.

As a result of the efforts of the apostles there may have been several million Christians in the Parthian Empire by the middle of the 2nd Century AD. There was

---

[286] *The Rise of Christianity* Rodney Stark (Princeton, NJ: Princeton University Press, 1996)

[287] William Steuart McBirnie, PhD *The Search For the 12 Apostles* ©1973 Tyndale House Publishers, Carol Stream, IL 60188

[288] Acts chapter 2

little if any persecution of Christians in the Parthian Empire, which had free trade with the Roman Empire as well as many of the nations of eastern Europe.

Those Christian Parthians traded with the Romans and many other outlying countries in eastern Europe. Some of those Christians were no doubt among the many military mercenaries *hired* by the Roman Empire and sent to remote areas to protect the borders of the Empire. There were many opportunities to spread the Gospel even before the Israelites and many of their Gentile neighbors were forced to migrate from the Parthian Empire into eastern Europe.

When the Zoroastrian Sasanian Empire of Persia began their pogrom against Christians and Jews near the end of the 2nd Century, the Israelites and others became part of the grand migration into eastern and central Europe. That migration is covered extensively in secular history.

Although all these migrants were known as "barbarians" to the Greek and Roman historians and were called by many different names, the Israelites were among them joined by all the others who converted to Christianity and became "spiritual Israel".

Europe and the Roman Empire were predominantly Christian by the 5th Century AD.

We followed the spread of Christianity and the migrants from the east as they spread throughout central and western Europe weakening and then destroying the Roman Empire. The Western Roman Empire headquartered in Rome was destroyed in the middle 400's AD while the Eastern Roman Empire remained extant until the 1400's AD.

We then covered the preparations for the rise of Western Civilization showing that Christian principles and the migrants from the East participated in and contributed to the Renaissance, the Enlightenment, the scientific revolution, the Reformation and the general spread and sustained growth of Christianity.

These social convulsions resulted in a casting off of the political and religious oppression of the Roman Catholic hierarchy and the rise of Protestantism and other religious movements that were almost totally separated from the Catholic Church. Many Christians wanted no absolute leader of the church other than Jesus.

The invention of the printing press resulted quickly in the translation of the holy scriptures into the language of "common people" and there was no holding back the spread of the Gospel both through the Catholic Churches and through those who owed no allegiance to Rome.

As Great Britain established the largest Empire the world has ever known and with America becoming the greatest nation the world has ever known – both of these in terms of political, economic and social hegemony – the world as we see it today came into being.

With the template of the Bible showing the work of the hand of God, it's no radical interpretation that the last 2,000 years likewise demonstrate His handiwork.

One major purpose of this book is to help people to see that it's all one continuing story – from Abraham directly to the 21st Century in America. The author has a list with some of these historial moments highlighted – when he thinks certain events and the actions of people had an outcome that likely demonstrate the result of the direction of the Hand of God. The author will not share that list with you in this book. Make up your own mind.

The Hand of God

2260 [289]* BC	God calls Abram in Haran
2240 * BC	God establishes His Covenant with Abram
2130 * BC	Isaac is born to Abram and Sarai
2110 * BC	God tests Abraham and makes the Covenant unconditional
1975* BC	The Covenant passes to Isaac
1935* BC	The Covenant passed to Jacob
1840* BC	Joseph, 2nd in Command in Egypt, provides food for Jacob's family
1845* BC	Jacob and his sons enter Egypt and reunite with Joseph
1860* BC	Jacob passes the Covenant to Ephraim, Manasseh and Judah
1445 BC	The Exodus from Egypt
1445 – 1405	Moses and children of Israel wander in the wilderness
1405 BC	Joshua and children of Israel enter the Promised Land
1398 – 1050	Judges lead Israel (1085 -1053 Samuel)
1050 – 1010	King Saul

---

[289] All the dates marked by an asterisk (*) are arbitrary

1010 – 970	King David
970 – 930	King Solomon (966 -965[290] Solomon begins building the

temple)

930 BC   Israel splits into the Kingdom of Israel and the Kingdom of Judah

721 BC   200,000 Israelites are deported from their destroyed Kingdom of Israel and many were transported to the cities of the Medes

700 – 647 BC   Deioces, who likely was one of those deported Israelites, is *elected* King of Medea, builds the capital at Ecbatana, unites the Medes and forms the Medean Empire

605 BC   Nebuchadnezzar, King of Babylon attacks Jerusalem. Daniel taken prisoner

586 BC   Nebuchadnezzar besieges and destroys Jerusalem and the temple there taking thousands of Jews captive deporting them to Babylon

559 – 530 BC   Cyrus the Great, descendant of Deioces, forms the Medo-Persian Empire using the system of government designed by Deioces. Cyrus the Great issues the edict that not only allows the captive Jews to return from Babylon but *pays the costs* of rebuilding the temple and Jerusalem but gave them back most of the temple treasure stolen by Nebuchadnezzar.

516 BC   Jerusalem and the temple are rebuilt

330 BC   Alexander the Great conquers Persia and most of the known world

247 BC – 225 AD   The Parthian Empire is formed with many of its leaders and its ruling class almost certainly being Israelites

175 BC   Antiochus IV Epiphanes of the Seleucid Empire begins to force Greek culture into Judea.

147 BC   Maccabees gain independence for Jews

63 BC   Roman soldiers occupy Palestine

27 BC   The Roman Empire is established and controls most nations in Europe and the middle east other than the Parthian Empire

5 BC – 36 AD   Jesus is born, lives and dies on the cross

40 AD   James and other Christians in Jerusalem face persecution with James being killed by Herod in 42 AD. Peter, Thomas, Thaddeus, Bartholomew, Simon Zelotes and others take the Gospel to the "lost sheep of the House of Israel" – the thousands of Israelites living the Parthian Empire

66 AD   The apostle Paul is martyred in Rome

70 AD   Jerusalem and the temple are destroyed by the Roman Empire. Many Jews are taken captive to Rome where some were murdered in the Roman arenas and the rest killed or made slaves

---

[290] This date is verified by secular history and archeology

100 AD   Christianity spreads throughout the Parthian Empire with converts in the tens of thousands. The great work of the apostle Paul bears fruit in many thousands of Gentiles being converted in the Roman Empire

225 AD   The Zoroastrian Persian Empire commits "jihad" against Christians, Jews and all who will not covert to Zoroastrianism forcing their migration into eastern Europe

250 AD   Tens of thousands of Israelites and their Gentile companions migrate through Armenia and the Caucasian Mountains into the Pontic Steppe, the original home of the Scythians. Greek and Roman historians call them Alani, Scythians or Barbarians

275 AD   The Goths invade the Pontic Steppe and control all of eastern Europe outside the Roman Empire

300 AD   The Goths conversion to Christianity is nearly all-inclusive

301 AD   Armenia declares Christianity the official religion of that nation

375 AD   The Huns overrun the Pontic Steppe and then the Gothic Empire forcing the Goths, the Vandals, the Anglo-Saxons, the Lombards, the Suebi, the Frisii, the Jutes, the Burgundians, the Alamanni, the Scirii and Franks to become part of the Hun Empire or migrate to western Europe

410 AD   Western Roman empire disintegrates under weak emperors. Alaric, king of the Visigoths, sacks Rome.

450 AD   Attila the Hun's Empire that stretches from the Pontic Steppe to the Atlantic Ocean in northern Europe comes to an end

475 AD   Visigoths rule from Italy to Spain

496 AD   Clovis, ruler of the Franks (French), is converted to Christianity

542 - 594 AD Bubonic plague spreads through Europe; kills half the population

560 AD   Lombard Kingdom established in Italy

597 AD   St. Augustine of Canterbury brings Christianity to Britain

650 AD   Medes, Scythians, Parthians, Aryans, Persians, Sarmatians, Alani, Goths, Huns, Ostrogoths, Visigoths, Angles, Saxons, Lombards, Franks *et al* blood lines intermingled as they entered the 7th Century AD, moving all the way to Gaul (France) and continuing geographically throughout Western Europe.

771 AD   Charlemagne becomes king of the Franks

800 AD   Charlemagne crowned first Holy Roman Emperor in Rome; the Roman Church establishes political and religious hegemony over much of Europe

859 AD   Vikings (Norsemen) attack as far south as the Mediterranean

871 AD   Alfred the Great becomes king of Britain

936 AD   Otto I becomes King of Germany

960 AD	Mieczyslaw I becomes first ruler of Poland
987 AD	Hugh Capet elected King of France; dynasty rules till 1328
1000 AD	Hungary and Scandinavia converted to Christianity
1054 AD	Final separation between Eastern (Orthodox) and Western

(Roman) churches

1066 AD　　　　　　William of Normandy invades England, defeats last Saxon king, Harold II, at Battle of Hastings, crowned William I of England ("the Conqueror")

1095 AD　　　　　　At Council of Clermont, Pope Urban II calls for a holy war to wrest control of Jerusalem from Muslims, which launches the First Crusade (1096), one of at least 8 European military campaigns between 1095 and 1291 to regain the Holy Land

1189 AD　　　　　　Richard I ("the Lionhearted") succeeds Henry II in England

1215 AD　　　　　　King John forced by barons to sign Magna Carta at Runneymede, limiting royal power.

1231 AD　　　　　　The Inquisition begins as Pope Gregory IX assigns Dominicans responsibility for combating heresy. Torture used (1252). Ferdinand and Isabella establish Spanish Inquisition (1478). Tourquemada, Grand Inquisitor, forces conversion or expulsion of Spanish Jews (1492). Forced conversion of Moors (1499). Inquisition in Portugal (1531). First Protestants burned at the stake in Spain (1543). Spanish Inquisition abolished (1834).

1273 AD　　　　　　Thomas Aquinas stops work on Summa Theologica, the basis of all Catholic theological teaching; never completes it.

1295 AD　　　　　　English King Edward I summons the Model Parliament

1325 AD　　　　　　The beginning of the Renaissance in Italy: writers Dante, Petrarch, Boccaccio; painter Giotto

1347–1351　　　　　At least 25 million people die in Europe's "Black Death" (bubonic plague)

1376–1382　　　　　John Wycliffe, pre-Reformation religious reformer, and followers translate Latin Bible into English

1418–1460　　　　　Portugal's Prince Henry the Navigator sponsors exploration of Africa's coast

1428　　　　　　　Joan of Arc leads French against English, captured by Burgundians (1430) and turned over to the English, burned at the stake as a witch after ecclesiastical trial (1431).

1453　　　　　　　Turks conquer Constantinople, end of the Byzantine empire, beginning of the Ottoman empire

1455　　　　　　　Having invented printing with movable type at Mainz, Germany, Johann Gutenberg completes first Bible

1493　　　　　　　Columbus becomes first European to encounter Caribbean islands, returns to Spain

1497	Vasco da Gama sails around Africa and discovers sea route to India; John Cabot, employed by England, reaches and explores Canadian coast
1509	Henry VIII ascends English throne
1513	Balboa becomes the first European to encounter the Pacific Ocean
1517	Martin Luther posts his 95 theses denouncing church abuses on church door in Wittenberg—start of the Reformation in Germany
1519	Ulrich Zwingli begins Reformation in Switzerland
1520	Luther excommunicated by Pope Leo X; Magellan reaches the Pacific, is killed by Philippine natives (1521). One of his ships under Juan Sebastián del Cano continues around the world, reaches Spain (1522)
1524	Verrazano, sailing under the French flag, explores the New England coast and New York Bay
1532	Pizarro marches from Panama to Peru, kills the Inca chieftain, Atahualpa, of Peru
1535	Reformation begins as Henry VIII makes himself head of English Church after being excommunicated by Pope. Sir Thomas More executed as traitor for refusal to acknowledge king's religious authority. Jacques Cartier sails up the St. Lawrence River, basis of French claims to Canada
1536	John Calvin establishes Reformed and Presbyterian form of Protestantism in Switzerland, writes Institutes of the Christian Religion. Danish and Norwegian Reformations
1541	John Knox leads Reformation in Scotland, establishes Presbyterian church there (1560)
1543	Publication of On the Revolution of Heavenly Bodies by Polish scholar Nicolaus Copernicus—giving his theory that the earth revolves around the sun
1545	Council of Trent to meet intermittently until 1563 to define Catholic dogma and doctrine, reiterate papal authority.
1553	Roman Catholicism restored in England by Queen Mary I.
1558	Queen Elizabeth I ascended the throne (rules to 1603), restores Protestantism, establishes state Church of England (Anglicanism). Renaissance reaches its height in England—Shakespeare, Marlowe, Spenser
1560	Presbyterian church established by John Calvin
1561	Persecution of Huguenots in France stopped by Edict of Orleans. French religious wars begin again with massacre of Huguenots at Vassy. St. Bartholomew's Day Massacre—thousands of Huguenots murdered (1572). Amnesty granted (1573). Persecution continues periodically until Edict of Nantes (1598) gives Huguenots religious freedom (until 1685).
1568	Protestant Netherlands revolts against Catholic Spain; independence acknowledged by Spain in 1648
1570	Queen Elizabeth I excommunicated by Pope

1580   Francis Drake returns to England after circumnavigating the globe; knighted by Queen Elizabeth I

1588   Defeat of the Spanish Armada by English. Henry, King of Navarre and Protestant leader, recognized as Henry IV, first Bourbon king of France. Converts to Roman Catholicism in 1593 in attempt to end religious wars.

1597   Lutheran Church established

1600   Giordano Bruno burned as a heretic. English East India Company established

1607   Jamestown, Virginia, established—first permanent English colony on American mainland. Pocahontas, daughter of Chief Powhatan, saves life of John Smith

1609   First Baptist church established in Amsterdam; first Baptist church in America in 1638 by Roger Williams

1610   Galileo sees the moons of Jupiter through his telescope

1611   King James Version of the Bible published in England

1618   Start of the Thirty Years' War. Protestants revolt against Catholic oppression; Denmark, Sweden, and France will invade Germany in later phases of war

1620   Pilgrims, after three-month voyage in Mayflower, land at Plymouth Rock

1630   Massachusetts Bay Colony

1633   Inquisition forces Galileo (astronomer) to recant his belief in Copernican theory

1660   English Parliament calls for the restoration of the monarchy; invites Charles II to return from France

1664   British take New Amsterdam from the Dutch. English limit "Nonconformity" with re-established Anglican Church. Isaac Newton's experiments with gravity

1682   Pennsylvania founded by William Penn

1685   James II succeeds Charles II in England, calls for freedom of conscience (1687). Protestants fear restoration of Catholicism and demand "Glorious Revolution." William of Orange invited to England and James II escapes to France (1688). William III and his wife, Mary, crowned. In France, Edict of Nantes of 1598, granting freedom of worship to Huguenots, is revoked by Louis XIV; thousands of Protestants flee

1689   Beginning of the French and Indian Wars (to 1763), campaigns in America linked to a series of wars between France and England for domination of Europe

1701   War of the Spanish Succession begins—the last of Louis XIV's wars for domination of the continent. The Peace of Utrecht (1714) will end the conflict and mark the rise of the British Empire. Called Queen Anne's War in America, it ends with the British taking Newfoundland, Acadia, and Hudson's Bay Territory from France, and Gibraltar and Minorca from Spain

1707   United Kingdom of Great Britain formed—England, Wales, and Scotland joined by parliamentary Act of Union

1730   First "Great Awakening" in Britain and the 13 colonies; Great Britain, Spain, Portugal, the Netherlands and later the United States begin in earnest to spread the Gospel to the whole world. Catholic, Protestant and Independent Christian churches send missionaries all over the globe.

1732   Benjamin Franklin begins publishing Poor Richard's Almanack. James Oglethorpe and others found Georgia

1738   Methodist Church established by John and Charles Wesley

1746   British defeat Scots under Stuart Pretender Prince Charles at Culloden Moor. Last battle fought on British soil

1756   Seven Years' War (French and Indian Wars in America) (to 1763), in which Britain and Prussia defeat France, Spain, Austria, and Russia. France loses North American colonies; Spain cedes Florida to Britain in exchange for Cuba

1757   Beginning of British Empire in India as Robert Clive, British commander, defeats Nawab of Bengal at Plassey

1765   James Watt invents the steam engine. Britain imposes the Stamp Act on the American colonists

1773   The Boston Tea Party

1774   First Continental Congress drafts "Declaration of Rights and Grievances."

1775   The American Revolution begins with battle of Lexington and Concord. Second Continental Congress

1776   Declaration of Independence. Gen. George Washington crosses the Delaware Christmas night. Adam Smith's Wealth of Nations. Edward Gibbon's Decline and Fall of the Roman Empire. Thomas Paine's Common Sense

1787   The Constitution of the United States signed

1789   In U.S., Washington elected president with all 69 votes of the Electoral College, takes oath of office in New York City. Vice President: John Adams. Secretary of State: Thomas Jefferson. Secretary of Treasury: Alexander Hamilton

1790   Philadelphia temporary capital of U.S. as Congress votes to establish new capital on Potomac. U.S. population about 3,929,000

1791 – 1840   The second "Great Awakening"; the Restoration Movement[168]. The pioneers of this movement were seeking to reform the church from within and sought "the unification of all Christians in a single body patterned after the church of the New Testament."

1791   U.S. Bill of Rights ratified

1800   Federal government moves to Washington, D.C.

1803	U.S. negotiates Louisiana Purchase from France: for $15 million, U.S. doubles its domain, increasing its territory by 827,000 square miles, from the Mississippi River to the Rockies and from the Gulf of Mexico to Canada
1804	Lewis and Clark expedition begins exploration of what is now northwest U.S.
1812	In the U.S., war with Britain declared over freedom of the seas for U.S. vessels
1824	Mexico becomes a republic, three years after declaring independence from Spain
1828	Church of Latter Day Saints (Mormon) established by Joseph Smith
1840	Seventh Day Adventist church established by William Miller
1865	Gen. Lee surrenders to Grant at Appomattox; the Civil War is over
1887	Queen Victoria's Golden Jubilee (50 years of the British Empire)
1893	New Zealand becomes first country in the world to grant women the vote
1900	Pentecostal movement established

The Stone Kingdom

> 34 You watched while a stone was cut out without hands, which struck the image on its feet of iron and clay and broke them in pieces. 35 Then the iron, the clay, the bronze, the silver, and the gold were crushed together, and became like chaff from the summer threshing floors; the wind carried them away so that no trace of them was found. And the stone that struck the image became a great mountain and filled the whole earth. Daniel 2:34–35 (NKJV)

From the 35th verse we understand that the fifth kingdom – the Stone Kingdom – would destroy the Roman Empire, and that any trace of it and the three prior historical kingdoms would be like "chaff" that "the wind carried away." Further the stone kingdom became so great that it filled the entire earth.

With Great Britain and the United States leading the way, the Stone Kingdom is personified in Western Civilization. The Roman Empire was defeated and destroyed; the attempt to reestablish that Empire – the Third Reich[169] – was defeated and destroyed in World War II. So far, no serious successor has appeared.

How many people in the world profess Christianity? As of 2010, the latest year for which figures are available, there are an estimated 2.2 billion Christians around the world.[291]

How many people in the United States profess Christianity? As of 2014, there were roughly 245 million adults in the United States, including 173 million Christians.[292]

How many Christian denominations (including those non-affiliated churches which don't consider themselves to be "denominations"? Around 1500 sects in North America. Many of these, although technically the same denomination, believe very different things from each other as that is the nature of how sects form: groups that believe something different from the main body splinter off and form their own sects.[293]

Has the Gospel been preached to the whole world? No. It has been preached to much of the world, but not all of it. Of course, there are still many people in "Christian" nations who do not know what the Gospel is really about, even if they have some vague idea of God and Jesus. On top of that, though, there are many places where the Gospel still has had very little impact. At this point, if such is the case, it is mostly due to political influences. Places like China, Myanmar, Saudi Arabia, etc. either ban or heavily discourage the preaching of alternative religions. We will not reach the point at which the Gospel has been preached to the whole world until every nation has been opened to it.[294] There are Internet web sites that track the progress of reaching people with the Gospel. This image comes from The Joshua Group:

---

[291] https://www.yahoo.com/news/many-christians-world-113630753.html
[292] www.pewresearch.org/
[293] https://www.quora.com/How-many-Christian-denominations-are-there-in-the-U-S
[294] https://www.quora.com/Has-the-gospel-been-preached-to-the-whole-world   Ronald Kimmons

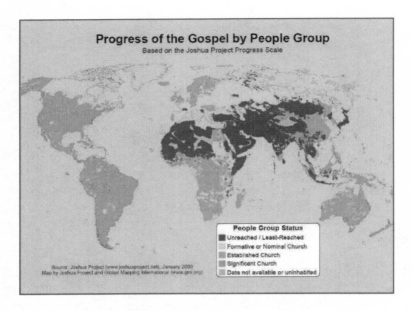

The Joshua Project[295] provides this graph:

Global Summary
An overview of the people groups of the world
People Groups:17,017
Unreached Groups:7,087
% Unreached Groups:41.6%
Population:7.59 Billion
Population in Unreached:3.14 Billion
% Population in Unreached:41.4%

As these items graphically illustrate, there are still 41% of the people alive today who have not heard the Gospel of Jesus Christ.

Points for consideration

> God foretold Western Civilization – its spiritual and physical blessings for the whole world – *in the beginning* with Abraham's Covenant
> The Stone Kingdom (Western Civilization) has been established
> The prophecy says the Stone Kingdom will never be destroyed
> The New Covenant is in effect for all people everywhere
> The *Hand of God* is still at work

---

[295] https://joshuaproject.net/

- ➤ In the natural cycles of culture, are we due for a world-wide "great awakening"?
- ➤ This book has shown you the *beginning*
- ➤ The Bible teaches that *the end* will come when Jesus returns to establish His Kingdom

---

What if The Hand of God is about to move the people of this time to reverse the cultural trends of the last 100+ years and turn to Him? What if we Christians could put aside our minor differences and concentrate on just being Christians? God's purpose will stand and He will do all that He pleases.

If so, what a wonderful time to be alive!

[10] I make known the end from the beginning, from ancient times, what is still to come. I say, 'My purpose will stand, and I will do all that I please.' Isaiah 46:10 (NIV)

* * *

Epilogue

The promises, prophecies and blessings of God's Covenant with Abraham and his descendants have been fulfilled and bestowed.

The spiritual parts of the Covenant culminated in the birth of God as a human, Jesus of Nazareth, the endowment of all humanity with the New Covenant and the spreading of the Gospel of Jesus with its promise of salvation to the whole world. Jesus' life, death and resurrection has the power to eliminate the fear of death if our faith is strong.

The physical or "birthright" parts of the Covenant were realized in the Israelites' occupation of the Promised Land, the Kingdom of Israel under Saul, David and Solomon and the formation of Western Civilization with the "double portion" of that blessing creating the British Empire – the largest Empire in world history by more than two times its closest competitor.

Thus the "end" God revealed "from the beginning" with Abraham has come to pass.

Is God through with dealing with humanity?

No analogy is ever perfect; no human can fathom the mind of God.

However, after observing the *hand of God* at work over the past 4,000 years as recorded in the Bible and in secular history one might form this analogy:

This earth was created as a laboratory to produce children for God.

Individual human beings must live through the crucible[296] of human existence to eliminate those who are defective. Others will grow spiritually from life's experience and learn to become what God made them capable of becoming – His children.

One who comes to understand who and what he is; one who recognizes the existence of his Creator; one who not only survives the trials of life but also prospers spiritually; one who learns God's laws and lives by them to the best of his ability; one who, of his own free will, comes to love God with all his heart, soul and mind; one who, of his own free will, comes to love his neighbor as himself; that individual will reap the rewards promised by God including eternal life.

One who cannot rise above thinking that he, himself is the ultimate arbiter of truth and reality; one who refuses to see that all that exists requires the intelligent design of a Creator; one who cannot rise above the selfish, intolerant nature of all human beings; one who despises and takes advantage of those who are weaker than he; one who seeks to amass fortune and fame by gaining power over others and abusing that power; one who comes to know God and then rejects Him; that person is defective and will be destroyed (not tormented or tortured).

It's simple, straightforward and it is the truth. I suggest that you adjust your life accordingly.

* * *
* * *
* * *

End Notes

---

[296] Crucible – a situation of severe trial, or in which different elements interact, leading to the creation of something new

¹ The "children of Israel": God changed Jacob's name to Israel. Ya'aqob – Jacob's Hebrew name literally means "heel catcher" as in one who might trip an opponent in a foot race in order to win; the meaning figuratively is "supplanter" – one who obtains supremacy by taking the place of the rightful winner in any situation. God gave him a name that is a combination of the Hebrew words 'el (God) and Sarah (the masculine form means "prince") which means, "One who prevails with God" or "a prince before God".

² There are no histories intact for any other nations from 4000 BC until the time of the Greeks. Some incidents are sketchily recorded but no sequential tome is to be found. The Egyptians and Hittites only left some monuments with cuneiform descriptions of certain incidents and a few books that have little historical value. Even in the first millennia BC, neither Assyria, nor Babylon nor the Medo-Persian empires left any coherent history. The Bible – the "Book of the People" – is 1500 years of written history – from 1445 BC to sometime around 65 AD and with the oral history from the time of Abraham to Moses committed to writing by Moses one can feasibly add another 700 – 1000 years covered.

³ Harran is said to be in Mesopotamia, Gen. 24:10, or more definitely in Padan-aram, ch. 25:20, the cultivated district at the foot of the hills, a name well applying to the beautiful stretch of country which lies below Mount Masius between the Khabour and the Euphrates. Smith, W. (1986). In Smith's Bible Dictionary. Nashville: Thomas Nelson.

⁴ Terah was Abraham's father. Sarai was Abraham's half-sister and Lot was the son of Abraham's brother Nahor. The clan from Ur had started for Canaan but stopped in Harran. The Bible gives no reason for that move but relates that their journey to Canaan stopped in the city of Harran where Terah died.

⁵ An important city in central Palestine, in the valley between mounts Ebal and Gerizim, 34 miles north of Jerusalem and 7 miles southeast of Samaria. Its present name, Nablûs, is a corruption of Neapolis, which succeeded the more ancient Shechem, and received its new name from Vespasian. On extant coins it is called Flavia Neapolis. Smith, W. (1986). In Smith's Bible Dictionary. Nashville: Thomas Nelson.

⁶ Arameans – named after Abram's nephew Aram – populated the plateau that runs from the northeast of Canaan to the Euphrates River. The languages of Hebrew and Aramaic remained intertwined throughout Old Testament history. It was to Harran that Abram's son and grandson would go to find their wives.

[7] In the racialist classifications of Carleton S. Coon, the Semitic peoples were considered to be members of the Caucasian race, not dissimilar in appearance to the neighboring Indo-European, Northwest Caucasian, and Kartvelian-speaking peoples of the region. https://en.wikipedia.org/wiki/Semitic_people

[8] Genesis 12:14–16; Genesis 20:1–18 God protected Sarai (Sarah) by sending disease to these kings who would have killed Abram to get Sarai. When they and their entire households were in danger of dying, they "appeased the god who afflicted them", learned Abram and Sarai were married and heaped great wealth upon them.

[9] Important for future reference: Faith counted as righteousness. This concept explains how Abraham's descendants – characters from the Old Testament – while deeply flawed, were nonetheless still approved by God. Likewise, under the New Covenant established by Jesus, it is our faith that will save us – our faith is considered the same as our being in complete compliance with God's laws. Righteousness: acting in accord with divine or moral law: free from guilt or sin *Merriam-Webster Intercollegiate Dictionary*

[10] Genesis 15:9–11. Since the Covenant was made according to human customs, it could only be ended according to human customs. The end of such a Covenant required the death of one of the Covenant makers. Since God later made the Abrahamic covenant unconditional it would never come to an end unless Abraham and his descendants died. Paul explained in Galatians 3:15-19 that the Covenant made with Abraham was not abrogated by the covenant God made with Israel at Mt. Sinai 430 years later. Rather God made a conditional covenant with Israel – the "law of Moses" – which became a second reason Jesus had to die. The first reason was His blood was required to sanctify the New Covenant allowing forgiveness of our sins and making the New Covenant for all people and not just Israel. The second reason is that His death negated the Old Covenant.

[11] In their culture, women were chattel and their worth was measured by their ability to provide children and heirs.

[12] *Abraham* is a Hebrew word meaning "father of a multitude" or "father of nations"

[13] *Sarai* or *Saray* means "princess"; *Sarah* means "noblewoman" or "queen"

[14] The Old Testament shows that all of those who were Abraham's descendants

were allotted certain territory by God. Old Testament history is filled with stories of these people harassing Isaac's son Jacob's descendants throughout their history till the time of Jesus. Even today, the Arabs (Abraham's descendants disinherited from the Covenant) are constantly at war with Jacob's descendants.

15 *Mount Moriah.* —The elevation on which Solomon built the temple, where God appeared to David "in the threshing-floor of Araunah the Jebusite." It is the eastern eminence of Jerusalem, separated from Mount Zion by the Tyropœon valley. The top was levelled by Solomon, and immense walls were built around it from the base to enlarge the level surface for the temple area. A tradition which first appears in a definite shape in Josephus, and is now almost universally accepted, asserts that the "Mount Moriah" of the Chronicles is identical with the "mountain" in "the land of Moriah" of Genesis, and that the spot on which Jehovah appeared to David, and on which the temple was built, was the very spot of the sacrifice of Isaac. *Smith's Bible Dictionary* Smith, W. (1986) Nashville: Thomas Nelson

16 This is one of many parallels of this event with God's sacrifice of His Son, Jesus centuries later: Isaac was his only son; Isaac did not deserve death; Isaac was the "son of promise" on which the Covenant depended; Isaac's death was prevented by God but in one sense was likewise received back from death [Hebrews 11:17-19]. Jesus was offered as a sacrifice and yet came back from death after three days and three nights in the tomb.

17 "Possess the gates of their enemies": this *unconditional* promise made to Abraham, Isaac, Jacob and Joseph's sons Ephraim and Manasseh is a physical, birthright promise of political hegemony as opposed to a promise of successful warfare. One who possesses the gates of an enemy is able to *control* the activities of that enemy without having to *conquer* that enemy. Control of the gates of many or all enemies equals political hegemony.

18 Terah was the father of Abraham, Nahor and Haran; he was also the father of Sarai but by a different mother [Genesis 20:12]. Haran was the father of Lot; he was also the father of Milcah. He died in Ur. Nahor was married to his niece Milcah; their children included Bethuel who was the father of Rebekah and Laban [Genesis 22:20-23], Rebekah married Isaac and bore two sons – Jacob and Esau. Laban's daughters and Rebekah's nieces, Rachel and Leah were married to Jacob. Lot had two daughters and one son each by his daughters – Ammon and Moab

19 The blessing of Rebekah's descendants possessing "the gates of their enemies" echoes the *unconditional* promise of God to Abraham as part of the Covenant

20 *Esav* – Esau in Hebrew literally means "hairy"; *Edom* in Hebrew means "red". Esau was born covered in red hair so that was Esau's "nickname" – even more so after he sold his birthright (as the first born) to Jacob for a bowl of red lentil stew and eventually lost the birthright blessing from Isaac. He was the ancestor of the Edomites who often afflicted Israel. *Ya'aqob* – Jacob's Hebrew name literally means "heel catcher" as in one who might trip an opponent in a foot race in order to win; the meaning figuratively is "supplanter" – one who obtains supremacy by taking the place of the rightful winner in any situation.

21 Isaac's blessing of Jacob contained the phrase "Let peoples serve you, And nation's bow down to you." [Genesis 27:29] This too is a promise of political hegemony.

22 Esau tried to regain the good favor of Isaac and Rebekah by marrying Ishmael's daughter. [Genesis 28:6–9] His descendants would be known as the nation of Edom – the Edomites. They blended with the descendants of Ishmael, the descendants of Moab and Ammon and Abraham's children by Keturah – these are the ancestors of the Arabs of today in the Arabian Peninsula and elsewhere. Esau hated Jacob:

So Esau hated Jacob because of the blessing with which his father blessed him, and Esau said in his heart, "The days of mourning for my father are at hand; then I will kill my brother Jacob." Genesis 27:41 (NKJV)

The progenitors of the Arabs held their grudges – Ishmael hating Isaac; Esau hating Jacob; Moab and Ammon being shut out from Abraham's family; Abraham's children by Keturah despising Isaac who inherited everything from Abraham other than the gifts Abraham gave them before sending them away. Those grudges were handed down the generations as their descendants were the main foes of the nation of Israel. Psalm 83 provides a comprehensive list of these people as the continuing foes of Israel at the time of the kings of Israel centuries later. Those descendants are among those trying to destroy today's nation of Israel and the USA today.

23 In the order of their sons' births, from Leah was born Reuben, Simeon, Levi and Judah. When Rachel remained barren and Leah's childbearing appeared to have stopped, the two brides had Jacob sleep with their servant girls, Zilpah for Leah and Bilhah for Rachel. Bilhah gave birth to Dan and Naphtali and Zilpah produced Gad and Asher. Leah then gave birth to Issachar and Zebulon. For all of this time, Rachel was barren but finally conceiving and giving birth to Joseph. Joseph became the 11th son. Sadly a few years later Rachael died giving birth to Benjamin, who survived, becoming the 12th son for Jacob.

[24] Promises of economic and political hegemony in Israel's future.

[15] Then the Angel of the LORD called to Abraham a second time out of heaven, [16] and said: "By Myself I have sworn, says the LORD, because you have done this thing, and have not withheld your son, your only *son*—[17] blessing I will bless you, and multiplying I will multiply your descendants as the stars of the heaven and as the sand which *is* on the seashore; <u>and your descendants shall possess the gate of their enemies.</u> [18] In your seed all the nations of the earth shall be blessed, because you have obeyed My voice." Genesis 22:15–18 (NKJV)

[28] Therefore may God give you Of the dew of heaven, Of the fatness of the earth, And plenty of grain and wine. [29] <u>Let peoples serve you, And nations bow down to you</u>. Be master over your brethren, And let your mother's sons bow down to you. Cursed *be* everyone who curses you, And blessed *be* those who bless you!" Genesis 27:28–29 (NKJV)

[11] Also God said to him: "I *am* God Almighty. Be fruitful and multiply; <u>a nation and a company of nations shall proceed from you, and kings shall come from your body</u>. [12] The land which I gave Abraham and Isaac I give to you; and to your descendants after you I give this land." Genesis 35:11–12 (NKJV)

[25] At this time only a few decades had passed after Egypt had overthrown the reign of the Hyksôs, a collection of 250,000 Semitic nomadic hordes from Syria and Mesopotamia who were forced out of their own territory by the expansion of the Hittite Empire. They overran Egypt and took the reins of government during the 15th and 16th dynasty. The Hyksôs were disparagingly called "shepherds".

[26] The eldest son, Reuben, would have normally received this blessing and if he were dead or disqualified it would have gone to Simeon or then to Levi. Jacob explained to all 12 why those three were disqualified to receive the birthright.

"Reuben, you are my firstborn, my might, the first sign of my strength, excelling in honor, excelling in power. Turbulent as the waters, you will no longer excel, for you went up onto your father's bed, onto my couch and defiled it.

"Simeon and Levi are brothers-- their swords are weapons of violence. Let me not enter their council, let me not join their assembly, for they have killed men in their anger and hamstrung oxen as they pleased. Cursed be their anger, so fierce, and their fury, so cruel! I will scatter them in Jacob and disperse them in Israel." NIV Genesis 49:3-7

Since the first three candidates were disqualified it would seem that the birthright should have gone to Judah. And indeed, a birthright blessing was pronounced upon Judah – a very important blessing.

[27] Till Shiloh comes: the apostle Paul confirms that the spiritual blessings

promised to Abraham but benefiting all of mankind came to fruition in Jesus.

Consider Abraham: "He believed God, and it was credited to him as righteousness." Understand, then, that those who believe are children of Abraham. The Scripture foresaw that God would justify the Gentiles by faith and announced the gospel in advance to Abraham: "All nations will be blessed through you." So those who have faith are blessed along with Abraham, the man of faith.

He redeemed us in order that the blessing given to Abraham might come to the Gentiles through Christ Jesus, so that by faith we might receive the promise of the Spirit.

Brothers, let me take an example from everyday life. Just as no one can set aside or add to a human covenant that has been duly established, so it is in this case. The promises were spoken to Abraham and to his seed. The Scripture does not say "and to seeds," meaning many people, but "and to your seed," meaning one person, who is Christ. What I mean is this: The law, introduced 430 years later, does not set aside the covenant previously established by God and thus do away with the promise. For if the inheritance depends on the law, then it no longer depends on a promise; but God in his grace gave it to Abraham through a promise. NIV Galatians 3:6-9; 14-18

The Bible and history both tell us that Jesus never sat on a throne ruling over Israelites or anyone else.

The (spiritual birthright) "scepter" will not depart from Judah until Jesus comes to sit on that throne. But the (physical) birthright belonged to Joseph and through him to his sons Ephraim and Manasseh.

28 The ability to produce an abundance of offspring or new growth; fertility. https://en.oxforddictionaries.com/definition/fecundity Throughout the Bible, this trait of the Israelites appears over and again – they reproduce quickly and often.

29 HOREB, MOUNT [HOHR eb] (waste) — the "mountain of God" (Ex. 18:5) in the Sinai Peninsula where Moses heard God speaking through the burning bush (Ex. 3:1) and where the law was given to Israel (see Map 2, B–2). "Horeb" is the favored name for Mt. Sinai in the Book of Deuteronomy, where the word occurs more often than in the rest of the entire Old Testament. Youngblood, R. F., Bruce, F. F., & Harrison, R. K., Thomas Nelson Publishers (Eds.). (1995). In _Nelson's new illustrated Bible dictionary._ Nashville, TN: Thomas Nelson, Inc.

30 "I AM WHO I AM" implies eternal being encompassing all tenses – past, present and future – and can also be stated simply as "I AM" cf. John 8:58

31 The Hebrew Tetragrammaton _YHWH_, Yahweh (some call the name Jehovah but neither Hebrew nor Aramaic alphabets contain the letter "J") appears more than

6,000 times in the OT. It is most often translated as LORD (in capital letters) as many translators continued the practice of substituting the Hebrew word *Adonai* (Lord) out of reverence of God's name.

[32] When God "hardened" Pharaoh's heart it was not that God *caused* the feelings and actions of the Egyptian king but rather that He amplified the natural inclination of the Pharaoh so that an event occurred exactly as God planned. The actions would have occurred eventually but needed to occur at a specific point in time to demonstrate God's will.

[33] The oldest firm date in the scriptures is confirmed by virtually every Bible scholar:

KJV 1900 | 1 Ki 6:1 And it came to pass in the four hundred and eightieth year after the children of Israel were come out of the land of Egypt, in the fourth year of Solomon's reign over Israel, in the month Zif, which is the second month, that he began to build the house of the LORD.

Thus, the times for both the Exodus and the beginning of the Temple have been specifically stated in the Bible. Scholars have identified the fourth year of Solomon's reign as 966 B.C. (Gleason, A Survey of Old Testament Introduction, 1974, p. 223). Using this 966 B.C. date, the Exodus took place in 1445 B.C.

[34] It is likely near the point where the Suez Canal ends today. The Suez Canal joins the Mediterranean Ocean to the Red Sea and the Indian Ocean. But on the whole, it is becoming more probable that the place where the Israelites crossed "was near the town of Suez, on extensive shoals which run toward the southeast, in the direction of Ayim Musa (the Wells of Moses). The distance is about three miles at high tide. This is the most probable theory. Smith, W. (1986). In *Smith's Bible Dictionary*. Nashville: Thomas Nelson.

[35] Besides punishing Egypt for enslaving the Israelites, God may have a couple of reasons for displaying His judgement: 1. To demonstrate to the known world His power and that He had chosen Israel to be His people, and 2. To weaken Egypt politically and militarily so that the Israelites in nearby Canaan would not be immediately and/or several times overrun by the Egyptian army. Exodus 13:17–14:31

According to some historians, the Exodus occurred in the third year of the reign of the Pharaoh Amenhotep II. Comparing Exodus 7:7 with Acts 7:23, Moses was in Midian approximately forty years. Assuming the pharaohs mentioned in Exodus 1:8, 22 and 2:23 are all the same person, he would have had to reign for over forty years. Amenhotep's predecessor, Thutmose III, is the only pharaoh within the time specified in I Kings 6:1 who reigned long enough (54 years) to have been on the throne at the time of Moses' flight and to die shortly before his return to Egypt. This would make Thutmose III the Pharaoh of the Oppression and Amenhotep II the Pharaoh of the Exodus.

However, the historian George Rawlinson in The Great Empires of the Ancient East provides a more likely basis for believing that the Pharaoh of the Exodus was Menephthah, the thirteenth son and immediate successor of Ramesses II. Rawlinson suggests that the Passover night resulted in the deaths of "not less than one million" and marks the Exodus as the beginning of the decline of Egypt as the major power in the middle east. Rawlinson writes, "The disaster paralyzed the monarch, and he made no further effort. If the loss was not great numerically, it affected the most important arm of the service, and it was the destruction of the very élite of the Egyptian troops." Rawlinson, George. The Great Empires of the Ancient East: Egypt, Phoenicia, The Kings of Israel and Judah, Babylon, Parthia, Chaldea, Assyria, Media, Persia, Sasanian Empire & The History of Herodotus (Kindle Location 2451). Kindle Edition

History tells us that for several years after 1445 B.C. Egypt was unable to carry out any invasions or extensive military operations.

36 Thus, God introduced the Sabbath as a day of rest even before the 10 Commandments were given [Exodus 16:29–30]

37 Jethro, Moses' father-in-law, learned that Moses and the Israelites had left Egypt and brought Moses wife Zipporah and his two sons to Moses and Jethro visited for a time.

38 Deuteronomy 31:24-26; Hebrews 9:1-4 This is one reason why the Ten Commandments hold such a sacred place in the beliefs and hearts of Christians today – they were spoken by the very voice of God aloud to the million or so Israelites and God added nothing to them. They are the eternal, unwavering, unchanging Laws of God. The other laws and ordinances in the Torah given to the Israelites by God are different from the Commandments and were "added" (as the Apostle Paul explained) for the Israelites because of their sins soon after the Commandments were given [Exodus chapter 32; Galatians 3:19]. Every law in the Torah that is part of the "law of Moses" is prefixed with some form of the phrase "And God said to Moses, 'Tell the children of Israel ....'". The rest of the Torah (the first five books of the Bible), still followed by orthodox Jews, was made of civil and personal conduct law with the religious laws under the auspices of the Levitical priesthood which priesthood was changed by Jesus [Hebrews chapters 6 – 10].

39 Throughout the Old Testament there is the relationship of a "day" for a "year" in prophecy from God. For instance, God punished the Israelites for not going into

the Promised Land when He told them to. The Israelite scouts spent 40 days looking over the land and people and then gave the bad reports – saying that they could not conquer the land. God said:

"For forty years--one year for each of the forty days you explored the land--you will suffer for your sins and know what it is like to have me against you." NIV Numbers 14:34

God told the prophet Ezekiel to demonstrate the sins of Israel and Judah and their upcoming punishment and captivity by Assyria and Babylon using the "day for a year" relationship.

"Then lie on your left side and put the sin of the house of Israel upon yourself. You are to bear their sin for the number of days you lie on your side. I have assigned you the same number of days as the years of their sin. So, for 390 days you will bear the sin of the house of Israel.

"After you have finished this, lie down again, this time on your right side, and bear the sin of the house of Judah. I have assigned you 40 days, a day for each year. Turn your face toward the siege of Jerusalem and with bared arm prophesy against her." NIV Ezekiel 4:4-7

40 Rahab was the mother of Boaz, whose wife was Ruth (a descendant of Moab), the mother of Obed, the father of Jesse, the father of King David. Rahab was a harlot. These examples of the blood line from Abraham to Jesus illustrate the circuitous route during the times of Moses, Joshua and the judges. Moses and Aaron were of the house of Levi, Joshua was of the tribe of Ephraim, the first king (Saul) was of the tribe of Benjamin and the rule did not return to the tribe of Judah until David.

41 A Nazarite vow was for a period of consecration with no product from vines (juice or wine) and no razor touched their hair. Numbers 6:1–21

42 Luke 16:13-15 Jesus said, "You cannot serve God and mammon" and "that which is highly esteemed among men is an abomination in the sight of God". Wealth and power are the things "highly esteemed" by men: wealth and power are the benchmarks of what most people consider "success" in this life. Money by itself is not the object of the desire of most people; it is what the accumulation of wealth can bring — power over others, the ability to control not only one's environment but to control other people. This lust for power permeates all human society: politics, business, and religion. It is these things that are "mammon".

43 The tribe of Benjamin's territory was located between Judah and Ephraim and so appealed to both the northern and southern tribes. He was said to be head and shoulders taller than the other Israelites 1 Samuel 9:1–2

44 5 For the living know that they will die; But the dead know nothing, And they have no more reward, For the memory of them is forgotten. 6 Also their love, their hatred, and their envy have now perished; Nevermore will they have a share in anything done under the sun. Ecclesiastes 9:5–6 (NKJV)

45 https://pjmedia.com/spengler/europes-new-nationalists-love-israel/ David P. Goldman is the columnist "Spengler" for *Asia Times Online*; his latest book is *How Civilizations Die: (And Why Islam Is Dying Too)*. He is the Wax Family Fellow at the Middle East Forum. Goldman insists that throughout the world, the monarchy of David and Solomon represent the pinnacle in all history. Excerpt:

European nationalism from its inception drew inspiration from biblical Israel. Greece was not a nation but a collection of small, quarreling city-states. Rome was not a nation but an empire--as were the Egyptians, Hittites, Sumerians, and so forth. Israel is the only exemplar of a nation in the ancient world, and the Davidic kingdom the only instance of a national monarchy. As I explained in my 2011 book *How Civilizations Die,* the first national monarchies in Europe--the 7th-century Merovingian kingdom in France and the Visigoth kingdom in Spain-- emulated the Davidic model under the tutelage, respectively, of St. Gregory of Tours and St. Isidore of Seville.

46 David's grandfather was Obed, who was the son of Ruth (a descendant of Moab) and Boaz, who was the son of Rahab the harlot, the protector of the Israelite spies who spied on the defenses at Jericho before the attack of the Israelites.

47 A Psalm of David.

1 The LORD said to my Lord, "Sit at My right hand, Till I make Your enemies Your footstool." 2 The LORD shall send the rod of Your strength out of Zion. Rule in the midst of Your enemies! 3 Your people *shall be* volunteers In the day of Your power; In the beauties of holiness, from the womb of the morning, You have the dew of Your youth.

4 The LORD has sworn And will not relent, "You *are* a priest forever According to the order of Melchizedek." 5 The Lord *is* at Your right hand; He shall execute kings in the day of His wrath. 6 He shall judge among the nations, He shall fill *the places* with dead bodies, He shall execute the heads of many countries. 7 He shall drink of the brook by the wayside; Therefore He shall lift up the head. Psalm 110 (NKJV)

48 Abraham, Sarah, Isaac, Rebekah, Jacob, Rachel and Joseph were buried in a plot purchased by Abraham that was near Bethlehem. [Genesis 23:1–20]

49 Youngblood, R. F., Bruce, F. F., & Harrison, R. K., Thomas Nelson Publishers

(Eds.). (1995). In *Nelson's new illustrated Bible dictionary*. Nashville, TN: Thomas Nelson, Inc.

50 7 "Now, O LORD my God, you have made your servant king in place of my father David. But I am only a little child and do not know how to carry out my duties. 8 Your servant is here among the people you have chosen, a great people, too numerous to count or number. 9 So give your servant a discerning heart to govern your people and to distinguish between right and wrong. For who is able to govern this great people of yours?"

10 The Lord was pleased that Solomon had asked for this. 11 So God said to him, "Since you have asked for this and not for long life or wealth for yourself, nor have asked for the death of your enemies but for discernment in administering justice, 12 I will do what you have asked. I will give you a wise and discerning heart, so that there will never have been anyone like you, nor will there ever be. 13 Moreover, I will give you what you have not asked for—both riches and honor—so that in your lifetime you will have no equal among kings. 14 And if you walk in my ways and obey my statutes and commands as David your father did, I will give you a long life." 1 Kings 3:7–14 (NIV84)

51 29 God gave Solomon wisdom and very great insight, and a breadth of understanding as measureless as the sand on the seashore. 30 Solomon's wisdom was greater than the wisdom of all the men of the East, and greater than all the wisdom of Egypt. 31 He was wiser than any other man, including Ethan the Ezrahite—wiser than Heman, Calcol and Darda, the sons of Mahol. And his fame spread to all the surrounding nations.

32 He spoke three thousand proverbs and his songs numbered a thousand and five. 33 He described plant life, from the cedar of Lebanon to the hyssop that grows out of walls. He also taught about animals and birds, reptiles and fish. 34 Men of all nations came to listen to Solomon's wisdom, sent by all the kings of the world, who had heard of his wisdom. 1 Kings 4:29–34 (NIV84)

52 23 King Solomon was greater in riches and wisdom than all the other kings of the earth. 24 The whole world sought audience with Solomon to hear the wisdom God had put in his heart. 25 Year after year, everyone who came brought a gift—articles of silver and gold, robes, weapons and spices, and horses and mules. 1 Kings 10:23–25 (NIV84)

53 The Lexham English Bible and the King James Version are two that translate verse 10 accurately. The NIV and the NKJV use the euphemism "waist" instead of loins as the Hebrew clearly indicates – the ultimate bragging of arrogant youth.

54 *Elijah did not go to heaven in the sense that many believe.* If Elijah or Enoch or any other Old Testament characters had gone to heaven (the abode of God, the Father) they would have seen God.

18 No one has seen God at any time. The only begotten Son, who is in the bosom of the Father, He has declared *Him.* John 1:18 (NKJV) **Jesus said:** "No one has ever gone into heaven except the one who came from heaven--the Son of Man." NIV John 3:13 12 No one has seen God at any time. If we love one another, God abides in us, and His love has been perfected in us. 1 John 4:12 (NKJV)

There is simple, Biblical proof that Elijah did *not* "go to heaven" – the abode of God, the Father. In the book of II Chronicles (the Chronicles repeat a great deal of the information contained in the books of I and II Kings), the fate of Jehoram, king of Judah (849-841 BC), includes a reference to Elijah. Jehoram was a very bad person; among other things, he murdered all his brothers and many others who might have a claim to his throne. He also installed Asherah and other idols in the hills of Jerusalem. **Jehoram received a letter from Elijah in about 843 BC, some 7 – 10 years *after* the "flaming chariot" picked up Elijah.**

55 The story of Jonah and his "three days and three nights" in the belly of the whale was pictured by Jesus as the *only* proof He would give the religious leaders of His day that He was whom He said He was. Furthermore, the 4th chapter of Jonah is a clear example of God's concern for the Gentile people that would be expressed without limits under the New Covenant established by Jesus. As God explained to an angry Jonah:

10 But the LORD said, "You have had pity on the plant for which you have not labored, nor made it grow, which came up in a night and perished in a night. 11 And should I not pity Nineveh, that great city, in which are more than one hundred and twenty thousand persons who cannot discern between their right hand and their left—and much livestock? Jonah 4:10–11 (NKJV)

56 Isaiah 9:8–21; Isaiah 28:1–13; Hosea 7:1–16; Hosea 10:1–10; Hosea 13:1–16; Amos 5:1–17; Amos 9:1–10

57 The descendants of the people from Babylon, Cuthah, Hamath and other places were the despised and shunned "Samaritans" of Jesus' day.

58 Before the split, Israelites were not called "Jews" – that name belongs to those who were part of the Kingdom of Judah. *The people of the 10-tribed nation of Israel were never called "Jews". The 12-tribed Israelite nation was never called "Jews".* That word "Jews" does not even appear in the Bible until the "historical" book of Kings at which time the Israelites were at war with the Jews [II Kings 16:6]. The word "Jews" comes from the name Judah.

As *Easton's Bible Dictionary* explains:

Jew: the name derived from the patriarch Judah, at first given to one belonging to the tribe of Judah or to the separate kingdom of Judah (2 Kings 16:6; 25:25; Jer. 32:12; 38:19; 40:11; 41:3), in contradistinction from those belonging to the kingdom of the ten tribes, who were called Israelites.

I cannot understand why almost all Christian preachers and teachers and even secular Bible scholars continue to refer to the nation of Israel as "Jews", even before the split of the kingdom into Israel and Judah. The Bible never calls them "Jews". Even secular sources like *Easton's* state the above information clearly and yet almost all preachers, teachers and Bible scholars refer to the entire nation of Israel as "Jews".

It is almost impossible to understand the prophecies of Isaiah, Jeremiah, Ezekiel, Daniel and the other prophets without understanding the difference between the Kingdom of Israel and the Kingdom of Judah. All Jews were Israelites but only those of the tribes of Judah, Benjamin and however many Levites and members of other tribes that joined them in the Kingdom of Judah were Jews.

The northern 10 tribes are often referred to by those prophets as Ephraim or Israel while the Kingdom of Judah is called by that name – Judah. On occasion the two kingdoms were called by the names of their two capitols – Samaria for Israel, Jerusalem for Judah. Both nations are occasionally referred to together as Israel but the northern 10 tribes and their kingdom are *never* called Jews.

59 This last historical mention of the "lost tribes" comes from Josephus' Antiquities of the Jews Book XI, Chapter V, in which he relates the Jewish leader Ezra's reading of a letter from Xerxes, the ruler of Persia, at a time when the Jews were about to be released from captivity and allowed to return to Jerusalem.

So, he read the epistle at Babylon to those Jews that were there; but he kept the epistle itself and sent a copy of it to all those of his own nation that were in Media. And when these Jews had understood what piety the king had towards God, and what kindness he had for Esdras *[this is Josephus' name for Ezra, to whom one of the books of the Old Testament is attributed]*, they were all greatly pleased; nay, many of them took their effects with them, and came to Babylon, as very desirous of going down to Jerusalem; but then the entire body of the people of Israel remained in that country; wherefore there are but two tribes in Asia and Europe subject to the Romans, while the ten tribes are beyond Euphrates till now, and are an immense multitude, and not to be estimated by numbers

60 The Talmud is made up of two separate works: the *Mishnah*, primarily a compilation of Jewish laws, written in Hebrew and edited sometimes around 200 C.E. in Israel; and the *Gemara,* the rabbinic commentaries and discussions on the Mishnah, written in Hebrew and Aramaic, which emanated from Israel and Babylonia

over the next three hundred years. There are two Talmuds: the *Y'rushalmi* or Jerusalem Talmud (from Israel) and the *Bavli* or Babylonian Talmud. The Babylonian Talmud, which was edited after the Jerusalem Talmud and is much more widely known, is generally considered more authoritative than the Jerusalem Talmud. [This quote is from https://reformjudaism.org/Talmud]

[61] This custom of the Medo-Persians is one reason by this Empire was so respected among the nations they captured – cities besieged would often open their gates for the Medo-Persian army and thousands upon thousands of lives were saved by this custom. The Empire would allow local rulers to remain in power and the only cost was their loyalty and the tribute they paid to the Medo-Persian rulers.

Even more pertinent to the fate of the people of Judah is that when Cyrus issued his decree returning the Jews to Jerusalem to rebuild their temple and the city [Ezra 1:1–4], it remained in effect even after Cyrus died. When problems arose with the nations around Palestine because of the return of the Jews, Darius searched for and found Cyrus' decree. Then Darius issued additional decree that the treasury of the Medo-Persians *would pay for the reconstruction and relocation of the Jews to Palestine.* [Ezra 6:1–12]

[62] This interpretation is given added veracity by a dream Daniel had some years later related in Daniel chapter 8. The angel Gabriel interpreted that dream for Daniel which only covered the future through the breakup of the Greek empire into four parts[62]. That interpretation verified the two Empires that would arise after Babylon.

The two-horned ram that you saw represents the kings of Media and Persia. The shaggy goat is the king of Greece, and the large horn between his eyes is the first king. The four horns that replaced the one that was broken off represent four kingdoms that will emerge from his nation but will not have the same power. NIV Daniel 8:20–22

[63] The NIV, the KJV and many other translations say the "belly and thighs" are of brass or bronze but they are using "delicate" language in their translations. The "thighs" do not really go with the "belly" as arms go with chest. The belly is part of the torso but the thighs are not. A perusal of *Strong's* Hebrew/English lexicon explains this as a slight mistranslation. The parts representing the third kingdom should be translated as "belly and flank" or "belly and buttocks", or – probably even more accurate – "belly and private parts". This image meshes better with what we know of the decadent culture of the Greek Empire. The Hebrew word *yarka*, translated by most as "thighs", comes from the Hebrew root word *yarek* as does the Hebrew word *yrekah*, which is translated as "rear" in Exodus 26:27, I Kings 6:16 and is translated as "remote parts" in other scripture. It is translated as "loins" in Genesis 46:26 and Exodus 1:5 and according to *Strong's Exhaustive Concordance*

Hebrew-English lexicon is said to be a euphemism for "the generative parts".

[64] The Hebrew word *shaq* related to the Hebrew word *showq* translated as "legs" actually refers to hips and thighs as well as legs. This image also fits the Roman Empire perfectly – being one at the beginning and then splitting into two well-defined parts.

[65] In 330 AD Constantine, who converted to Christianity in 312 AD and convened the Council of Nicaea in 325 AD, opened his second capital city in Byzantium and renamed the city Constantinople. In 395 the Empire was permanently divided into East and West. The Western Empire was beset with strife, assassinations and invasions from the time of Constantine. The Sack of Rome in 410 by the Visigoths and again in 455 by the Vandals accelerated the Western Empire's decay, while the deposition of the emperor, Romulus Augustulus, in 476 by Odoacer, is generally accepted to mark the end of a capitol of the empire in the west. However, Augustulus was never recognized by his Eastern colleague, and separate rule in the Western part of the empire only ceased to exist upon the death of Julius Nepos, in 480. The Eastern capitol and the rise of political power of the Church of Rome retained the control of the Western Roman Empire until the 1400's.

[66] (1.) The gospel-church is a kingdom, which Christ is the sole and sovereign monarch of, in which he rules by his word and Spirit, to which he gives protection and law, and from which he receives homage and tribute. It is a kingdom *not of this world*, and yet set up in it; it is the kingdom of God among men. Henry, M. (1994). *Matthew Henry's commentary on the whole Bible: complete and unabridged in one volume* (p. 1432). Peabody: Hendrickson

[67] The Lord Jesus is the **stone ... cut out ... without hands**. He will destroy the four kingdoms and rule over the whole earth, his **kingdom** standing **forever**. MacDonald, W. (1995). *Believer's Bible Commentary: Old and New Testaments*. (A. Farstad, Ed.) (p. 1080). Nashville: Thomas Nelson.

[68] **34. A stone was cut out without hands** must indicate a supernatural origin for the stone. It is not man-made in any way. Of course, it represents Christ and His millennial kingdom, which succeeds all earthly kingdoms after the Great Tribulation. Hindson, E. E., & Kroll, W. M. (Eds.). (1994). *KJV Bible Commentary* (p. 1633). Nashville: Thomas Nelson.

[69] 29 And you will sing as on the night you celebrate a holy festival; your hearts will rejoice as when people go up with flutes to the mountain of the LORD, to the Rock of Israel. Isaiah 30:29 (NIV84)

¹ "Listen to me, you who pursue righteousness and who seek the LORD: Look to the rock from which you were cut and to the quarry from which you were hewn; ² look to Abraham, your father, and to Sarah, who gave you birth. When I called him he was but one, and I blessed him and made him many. ³ The LORD will surely comfort Zion and will look with compassion on all her ruins; he will make her deserts like Eden, her wastelands like the garden of the LORD. Joy and gladness will be found in her, thanksgiving and the sound of singing. Isaiah 51:1–3 (NIV84)

⁷⁰ Sicily, Sardinia & Corsica, Spain, Illyricum, Macedonia/Cassander, Carthaginian territory, Thrace/Lysimachus (was known as the Province of Asia), Gaul, Syria/Seleucid and Egypt/Ptolemy

⁷¹ Most historians agree that the *official* end of the Roman Empire was May 29, 1453 with the fall of Constantinople as the forces of the Ottoman Empire entered Constantinople and Basileus Constantine XI Palaiologos was killed.

⁷² This is only an enigma when some try to conflate the "woman" in this prophecy with the church Jesus established. The church was established by Jesus and did not give birth to him. The Son born to this woman is to "rule all the nations with an iron sceptre". This can only be Jesus [Psalm 2:9; Revelation 2:27; 19:15] and the woman is Israel ("twelve stars on her head").

⁷³ Not long after John wrote the book of Revelation, the Roman Army slaughtered more than 1,300,000 in their siege of Jerusalem and carried away more than 97,000 as captives. The Romans then razed Jerusalem and the temple.⁷³ The 3 ½ year siege and the end of the nation of Israel was prophesied by Daniel and those who were followers of Jesus – the ones who "hold to the testimony of Jesus" – had heeded His warning and were not penned in Jerusalem like so many of their brothers. [Daniel 12:1, 7; Matthew 24:15–21; Mark 13:14–19; Luke 21:20–23].

Now the number (32)of those that were carried captive during this whole war was collected to be ninety-seven thousand; as was the number of those that perished during the whole siege eleven hundred thousand, the greater part of whom were indeed of the same nation [with the citizens of Jerusalem], but not belonging to the city itself;

End Note 32: The whole multitude of the Jews that were destroyed during the entire seven years before this time, in all the countries of and bordering on Judea, is summed up by Archbishop Usher, from Lipsius, out of Josephus, at the year of Christ 70, and amounts to 1,337,490. Nor could there have been that number of Jews in Jerusalem to be destroyed in this siege, as will be presently set down by Josephus, but that both Jews and proselytes of justice were just then come up out of the other countries of Galilee, Samaria, Judea, and Perea and other remoter regions, to the

Passover, in vast numbers, and therein cooped up, as in a prison, by the Roman army, as Josephus himself well observes in this and the next section, and as is exactly related elsewhere, B. V. ch. 3. sect. 1 and ch. 13. sect. 7. End Note 32 Flavius Josephus *Wars of the Jews*

74 ₃ Then Moses went up to God, and the LORD called to him from the mountain and said, "This is what you are to say to the house of Jacob and what you are to tell the people of Israel: ⁴ 'You yourselves have seen what I did to Egypt, and how I carried you on eagles' wings and brought you to myself. Exodus 19:3–4 (NIV84)

75 Revelation 12:6, 14 Using prophetic symbolism discussed earlier, time, times and half-a-time = 3 ½ years. Bible years are 360 days long; 360 X 3.5 = 1,260 days = 1,260 years.

76 Satan, working his evil through the "beast power"[76] of Rome, pursued the Jews and Christians throughout the empire with no letup until the emperor Constantine came into power in the 300's AD. After the Roman emperor converted to Christianity, the threat was lessened for a few hundred years but the hierarchy of the church soon became corrupt and gained ever more secular power. It wasn't long before those "popes" and religious officials continued the "tribulation" of Christians and Jews who didn't bow down to their authority using the forces of the Roman Empire to do their bidding – the woman's seed and the "commandment keepers".

Over several centuries, thousands of people were slaughtered by the hierarchical church in Rome because they refused to submit to the authority of that church. The most infamous action in this regard was called "The Inquisition" http://en.wikipedia.org/wiki/Inquisition . The carnage of that movement continued into the 15th Century even after the secular power of the Roman Empire came to an end in the 1400's.

God (to whom time has no relevance) was preparing a population, among whom had been sifted the inheritors of the physical Covenant, to inhabit lands far away from the Middle-East. Eventually, these people would wittingly or unwittingly base their *common law* on the 10 Commandments and their morals and ethics on the teaching of Jesus and the church.

When it inherited the wealth and political hegemony promised in Abraham's Covenant, this culture would spread the Gospel and Christianity to the whole world. Because of the Judeo-Christian ethics of this culture those *blessings* would be shared with the whole world, thus fulfilling the last part of the original promise made to Abraham.

77 https://en.wikipedia.org/wiki/History_of_Western_civilization

[78] The British Empire was the most geographically extensive empire in world history and for a substantial time was the foremost global power. It was a product of the European age of discovery, which began with the maritime explorations of the 15th century that sparked the era of the European colonial empires.

By 1921, the British Empire held sway over a population of about 458 million people, approximately one-quarter of the world's population. It covered about 36.6 million km² (14.2 million square miles), about a quarter of Earth's total land area. As a result, its legacy is widespread, in legal and governmental systems, economic practice, militarily, educational systems, sports (such as cricket, rugby and football), and in the global spread of the English language. At the peak of its power, it was often said that "the sun never sets on the British Empire" because its span across the globe ensured that the sun was always shining on at least one of its numerous colonies. *Wikipedia*

[79] Sir Austen Henry Layard, (born March 5, 1817, Paris—died July 5, 1894, London), English archaeologist whose excavations greatly increased knowledge of the ancient civilizations of Mesopotamia.

[80]*Modern discoveries in Assyria.* — (Much interest has been excited in reference to Assyria by the discoveries lately made there, which confirm and illustrate the Bible. The most important of them is the finding of the stone tablets or books which formed the great library at Nineveh, founded by Shalmaneser in 860 B.C., but embodying tablets written 2000 years B.C. This library was more than doubled by Sardanapalus. These tablets were broken into fragments, but many of them have been put together and deciphered by the late Mr. George Smith, of the British Museum. All these discoveries of things hidden for ages, but now comes to light, confirm the Bible. —ED.) Smith, W. (1986). In <u>Smith's Bible Dictionary</u>. Nashville: Thomas Nelson.

[81] Little is known of the reign of Tiglath-pileser's successor, Shalmaneser V (726–722 B.C.), except that he besieged Samaria for three years in response to Hoshea's failure to pay tribute (2 Kings 17:3–5). The city finally fell to Shalmaneser (2 Kings 17:6; 18:9–12), who apparently died in the same year. His successor, Sargon II (722–705 B.C.), took credit in Assyrian royal inscriptions for deporting 27,290 inhabitants of Samaria. Browning, D. C., Jr. (2003). <u>Assyria</u>. In C. Brand, C. Draper, A. England, S. Bond, E. R. Clendenen, & T. C. Butler (Eds.), *Holman Illustrated Bible Dictionary* (p. 135). Nashville, TN: Holman Bible Publishers.

[82] Sennacherib's own account of the invasion provides a remarkable supplement to the biblical version (2 Kings 18:13–19:36). He claims to have destroyed 46 walled cities (2 Kings 18:13) and to have taken 200,150 captives. Sennacherib's conquest of

Lachish is shown in graphic detail in carved panels from his palace at Nineveh. Browning, D. C., Jr. (2003). Assyria. In C. Brand, C. Draper, A. England, S. Bond, E. R. Clendenen, & T. C. Butler (Eds.), *Holman Illustrated Bible Dictionary* (p. 136). Nashville, TN: Holman Bible Publishers.

[83] 6 In the ninth year of Hoshea, the king of Assyria captured Samaria and deported the Israelites to Assyria. He settled them in Halah, in Gozan on the Habor River and in the towns of the Medes. 2 Kings 17:6 (NIV84)

[84] The Assyrian Empire was the first large scale hegemony in the middle-East. Assyria began rose to power around 1300 BC with their power and dominance lasting until 625 BC. A series of military defeats and internecine struggles caused Assyria's power to decline after 1100 BC. This decline was caused at least in part by their defeat by the armies of Israel under King David [I Chronicles 19:17] opening the way for the Kingdom of Israel to be a dominant middle-east power from 1050 to 930 BC reaching the height of its power during the reigns of Kings David and Solomon. The decline lasted until the rise of Shalmaneser III (860 – 825 BC) – during the reign of Ahab, king of Israel. For the following 200 years, as Israel divided into the kingdoms of Israel and Judah and as they sank deeper into idolatry and decadence, Assyria often raided Israel. The most powerful king of Assyria, Tiglath-Pileser, began to cause serious problems for both Israel and Judah around 750 BC. Tiglath-Pileser was succeeded by his son, Shalmaneser V (727–722 BC) who oversaw the complete destruction of Israel in 721 BC. Only divine intervention prevented Shalmaneser V from destroying Judah as well.

[85] War continued between Assyria and Babylon until, in 614 B.C., the old Assyrian capital Asshur was sacked by the Medes. Then, in 612 B.C., Calah was destroyed. The combined armies of the Babylonians and the Medes laid siege to Nineveh. After two months the city fell. An Assyrian general claimed the throne and rallied what was left of the Assyrian army in Haran. An alliance with Egypt brought a few troops to Assyria's aid, but in 610 B.C. the Babylonians approached, and Haran was abandoned. In 605 B.C. the last remnants of the battered Assyrian Empire, along with their recent Egyptian allies, were deferred on The Battle of Carchemish. Assyria was no more. Browning, D. C., Jr. (2003). Assyria. In C. Brand, C. Draper, A. England, S. Bond, E. R. Clendenen, & T. C. Butler (Eds.), *Holman Illustrated Bible Dictionary* (p. 137). Nashville, TN: Holman Bible Publishers.

[86] **Halah** – region in northern Mesopotamia probably today's Republic of Georgia; **Gozan on the Harbor River** is a region included the basin of the Habor (Khabur) River near the borders of today's Iraq and Syria; **towns of the Medes** Azerbaijan, Armenia, Kurdistan and northern Iran *Holman Illustrated Bible Dictionary* (p. 705). Nashville, TN:

Holman Bible Publishers; *Nelson's New Illustrated Bible Dictionary*. Nashville, TN: Thomas Nelson, Inc.

[87] Jewish Historians claim the Medes' progenitor was Noah's son Japeth and ancestor of the Medes through Japeth's grandson Madia [Genesis 10:2].

[88] From *Britannica*: Although Herodotus credits "Deioces son of Phraortes" (probably c. 715) with the creation of the Median kingdom and the founding of its capital city at Ecbatana (modern Hamadan), it was probably not before 625 BC that Cyaxares, grandson of Deioces, succeeded in uniting into a kingdom the many Iranian-speaking Median tribes. In 614 he captured Ashur, and in 612, in alliance with Nabopolassar of Babylon, his forces stormed Nineveh, putting an end to the Assyrian empire. The victors divided the Assyrian provinces among themselves, with the Median king taking over a large part of Iran, northern Assyria, and parts of Armenia. https://www.britannica.com/place/ancient-Iran#ref32108

[89] The Zagros mountains range from southeastern Turkey to southwestern Iran. The western part of that range crosses southern Medea along the path to which the Israelites were deported.

[90] See Esther 4:11 (205) Now the king had made a law, *(Footnote C)* that none of his own people should approach him unless they were called, when he sat upon his throne; and men, with axes in their hands, stood round about his throne, in order to punish such as approached to him without being called. (206) However, the king sat with a golden sceptre in his hand, which he held out when he had a mind to save anyone of those that approached to him without being called; and he who touched it was free from danger. But of this matter we have discoursed sufficiently.

Footnote C. Herodotus says that this law [against anyone's coming uncalled to the kings of Persia when they were sitting on their thrones] was first enacted by Deioces [i.e., by him who first withdrew the Medes from the domination of the Assyrians, and himself first reigned over them]. Thus also, says Spanheim, stood guards, with their axes, about the throne of Tenus, or Tenudus, that the offender might by them be punished immediately.

Antiquities of the Jews Book 11, Chapter 6, 3 Josephus, F., & Whiston, W. (1987). *The works of Josephus: complete and unabridged.* Peabody: Hendrickson

[91] We described this scenario in chapter 4 with the story of Daniel in the lions' den. When the provincial ruler of Babylon, king Darius was convinced to issue an edict that anyone who prayed to anyone but Darius for the next month would be thrown into a den of lions. Daniel prayed to God facing Jerusalem in plain sight and his enemies in the king's court reminded Darius that even he could not reverse that edict. After Daniel lived through the night in the lions' den, those who had trapped

Darius and Daniel paid with their lives. But the edict was enforced.

92 This custom of the Medo-Persians is one reason why this Empire was so respected among the nations they captured – cities besieged would often open their gates for the Medo-Persian army and thousands upon thousands of lives were saved by this custom. The Empire would allow local rulers to remain in power and the only cost was their loyalty and the tribute they paid to the Medo-Persian rulers.

Even more pertinent to the fate of the people of Judah is that when Cyrus issued his decree returning the Jews to Jerusalem to rebuild their temple and the city [Ezra 1:1–4], it remained in effect even after Cyrus died. When problems arose with the nations around Palestine because of the return of the Jews, Darius' son Xerxes searched for and found Cyrus' decree. Then Xerxes issued additional decree that the treasury of the Medo-Persians *would pay for the reconstruction and relocation of the Jews to Palestine.* [Ezra 6:1–12]

Persia was dominated by Media until the time of Cyrus the Great who was founder of the Persian Empire. In 549 B.C. Cyrus defeated Media. Yet under the Persians, Media remained the most important province of Persia. As a consequence, the dual name, "Medes and Persians," remained for a long time (Esth. 1:19; Dan. 5:28). The expression, "The laws of the Medes and the Persians," depicted the unchangeable nature of Median law, which even the king was powerless to change (Esth. 1:19). Youngblood, R. F., Bruce, F. F., & Harrison, R. K., Thomas Nelson Publishers (Eds.). (1995). In *Nelson's new illustrated Bible dictionary.* Nashville, TN: Thomas Nelson, Inc.

93 *Meriam-Webster Online Dictionary* defines Aramaic: a Semitic language known since the ninth century B.C. as the speech of the **Aramaeans** and later used extensively in southwest Asia as a commercial and governmental language and adopted as their customary speech by various non-Aramaean peoples including the Jews after the Babylonian exile.

94 A´RAM (high). 1. The name by which the Hebrews designated, generally, the country lying to the northeast of Palestine; the great mass of that high tableland which, rising with sudden abruptness from the Jordan and the very margin of the Lake of Gennesaret, stretches, at an elevation of no less than 2000 feet above the level of the sea, to the banks of the Euphrates itself. Throughout the Authorized Version the word is, with only a very few exceptions, rendered, as in the Vulgate and LXX, SYRIA. Its earliest occurrence in the book of Genesis is in the form of Aram-naharaim, i.e., the "highland of or between the two rivers." Gen. 24:10, Authorized Version "Mesopotamia." In the later history we meet with a number of small nations or kingdoms forming parts of the general land of Aram; but as Damascus increased in importance it gradually absorbed the smaller powers, 1 Kings 20:1, and the name

of Aram was at last applied to it alone. Isa. 7:8; also 1 Kings 11:24, 25; 15:18, etc. LXX – the Seventy, i.e. the Septuagint Smith, W. (1986). In Smith's Bible Dictionary. Nashville: Thomas Nelson.

[95] Arameans – named after Abram's nephew Aram – populated the plateau that runs from the northeast of Canaan to the Euphrates River. The languages of Hebrew and Aramaic remained intertwined throughout Old Testament history. It was to Harran that Abram's son and grandson would go to find their wives.

[96] Astyages son was Darius (per Josephus); Cyrus the Great was *possibly* the son of Darius (Herodotus says Cyrus was the grandson of Astyages).

Astyages, Akkadian Ishtumegu, (flourished 6th century BC), the last king of the Median Empire (reigned 585–550 BC). According to Herodotus, the Achaemenian Cyrus the Great was Astyages' grandson through his daughter Mandane, but this relationship is probably legendary. According to Babylonian inscriptions, Cyrus, king of Anshan (in southwestern Iran), began war against Astyages in 553 BC; in 550 the Median troops rebelled, and Astyages was taken prisoner. Then Cyrus occupied and plundered Ecbatana, the Median capital. A somewhat different account of these events is given by the Greek writer Ctesias. https://www.britannica.com/biography/Astyages

[97] The first mention of a Persian chieftain refers to his role as an ally aligned against Sennacherib of Assyria. His son was called "King, Great King and King of the City of Anshan." His grandson fathered Cyrus II, also known as Cyrus the Great, who was one of the most celebrated kings of history. He is called by the prophet Isaiah "My shepherd" (Is. 44:28). In another passage he is referred to as "His [the Lord's] Anointed" (Is. 45:1), a term used in the Old Testament of the Messiah. He is the only pagan king to be so designated in the Old Testament.

Cyrus II, founder of the mighty Persian Empire, ascended the throne in Anshan in 559 B.C. He conquered the Median King Astyages. Then he defeated Lydia (about 546 B.C.) and Babylon (539 B.C.), finally establishing the Persian Empire. This last conquest is referred to in Daniel 5. Cyrus' rule was a result of the sovereignty of God. Cyrus was the Persian king who issued the decree restoring the Jews to their homeland, following their long period of captivity by the Babylonians (2 Chr. 36:22–23; Ezra 1:1–4).

Cyrus, following the traditions of Deioces, established an Empire system under which each province, or satrapy, was governed by an official who answered to the great king. However, he allowed a remarkable degree of freedom of religion and customs for the vassal states, including Palestine. He developed roads, cities, postal systems, and legal codes, and treated the subject nations kindly and humanely. The Bible refers to Cyrus in favorable terms (Is. 44:28–45:3).

98 The first phase of Zoroastrian history is defined by the history of Aryans in the sixteen lands or nations listed in the Zoroastrian scripture, the Avesta's, book of Vendidad. It was a history centered on Airyana Vaeja, the Central Asian homeland of the Aryans.

The sixteen lands – the homeland of the Aryans

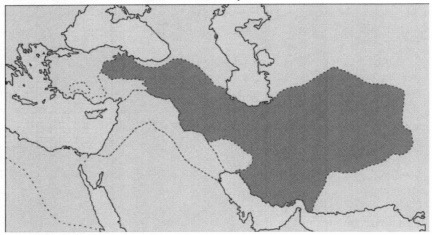

http://www.heritageinstitute.com/zoroastrianism/medians/

99 Any "barbarian" group of people who were involved in battles or revolts were referred to most often by Greek and Roman historians as "Scythians".

100 The Sacaraucae are people that Greek/Roman historians refer to as "Scythians" but they must be distinguished by other historical sources from the Scythians that were attacking the various empires as early as the 8th Century BC from their homeland Scythia located in northern Asia (what we call Russia today) and Eastern Europe. Their most famous leader was named Magog.

The OT refers to those Scythians as Ashchenaz (Gen. 10:3; Jer. 51:27). Earlier scholars identified the Scythians as Jeremiah's foe from the north and Zephaniah's threatened invader of Judah, but such theories rest on weak evidence. Colossians 3:11 uses Scythians to represent the most repugnant barbarian and slave, saying they, too, are accepted in Christ, all social and cultural barriers being abolished in His church.

Thanks to Russian archeologists and other anthropologists that distinction has been made.

Sacaraucae (or Saka) was the name of Iranian-speaking tribes, mostly nomadic, that lived **from the first millennium B.C. to the first centuries A.D.** The name "Saka" is used in cuneiform inscriptions, by classical authors, in Chinese chronicles, and in

Indian sources to denote various tribes; classical sources generally use the term to refer to the Scythians. Ancient Persian inscriptions distinguish three groups of Saka: Saka-Haumavarga ("god-fearing," called Ami-urgii in classical sources), Saka-Tigrahauda ("with pointed hats"), and Saka "who live beyond the sea" (Black Sea Scythians). In modern scholarly literature, Saka is the name given to the ancient tribes of the northern and eastern regions of middle Asia, Kazakhstan, and East Turkestan **to distinguish these tribes from the related Massagetae of the Aral and Caspian regions and the Scythians of the Northern Black Sea Shore.** *The Great Soviet Encyclopedia* (1979)

These Sacaraucae who voted to elect the next ruler of the Parthian Empire were those same people who rebelled against the Medes and Persians, moved to the east to that verdant land where their population could expand virtually without limits. It is *almost certain* that they were Israelites though the Greek/Roman historians called them Dahae.

Daho-Parno-Parthian tribes "chose chiefs for war and princes for peace" from among the closest circle of the royal family. They were famous for their breeding of horses, their combat cavalry, and their fine archers. Alexander encountered them during his Bactrian campaign, and the Greek writers who recorded his reign remarked on their agility and effectiveness as horsemen. They were a people who kept the traditions of patriarchal tribal organization. https://www.britannica.com/place/ancient-Iran/The-Hellenistic-and-Parthian-periods#ref315487

Though the history of the Arsacids is sketchy it is also likely that the line of kings who came from Arsaces were from those same people. It is not unreasonable to speculate that the Parthian Empire was ruled by Israelites who were *elected* by other Israelites

[101] Until the 20th century, most of what was known of the history of the Scythians came from the account of them by the ancient Greek historian Herodotus, who visited their territory. In modern times that record has been expanded chiefly by Russian and other anthropologists excavating kurgans in such places as Tyva and Kazakhstan.

[102] Parthian languages originated in the ancient province of Parthia (the northeastern portion of modern Iran) and became the official language of the Arsacid period of Persian dynastic history (2nd century BCE–3rd century CE). Among the earliest records of the language are more than 2,000 ostraca (inscribed pottery fragments), largely records of wine deliveries dating from the 1st century BCE, which were discovered in excavations (1949–58) at Nisa, an Arsacid capital near modern Ashgabat in Turkmenistan. Parthian is also attested by inscriptions of the first Sāsānian kings (224–303), which were accompanied by a Middle Persian version.

Manichaean Parthian literature is a very rich source for the language and includes the outstanding hymn cycles of the poet Mar Ammo (second half of the 3rd century). **The Parthian script was derived from the Aramaic alphabet.** https://www.britannica.com/topic/Parthian-language#ref11911

[103] Collins is a very good writer and offers a lot of good verifiable information on the Israelite tribes. However, this author he places far too much emphasis on certain sounds of words in the languages of the ancients. For instance, he uses the name of the Scythians from the eastern shores of the Caspian Sea – Sacae Scythians – to infer the "sac" sound refers to Abraham's son Isaac. Almost every time the syllable Sac is found in a tribal or racial name, he infers the name comes from Isaac. A similar practice of looking at the names of landmarks and assigning the origin of their name to the tribe of Dan (Danube, Dniester, and Danmark) seems a bit specious and illogical. These inferences were also used extensively by J. H. Allen in his book *"Judah's Sceptre and Joseph's Birthright"* and by the Worldwide Church of God Founder Herbert W. Armstrong in his book *The US and Great Britain in Prophecy* (which many think plagiarized J. H. Allen). Using such unreliable data along with Irish and other legends and fairy tales and extremely esoteric OT prophecy detracts from otherwise interesting ideas and theories on the fate of the 10 tribes. Furthermore, their insistence (Collins, Allen and Armstrong) on their being able to recognize all 10 of the tribes in their specific countries or territories calls into question the scholarship, logic and conclusions of their books.

[104] The New Sasanian Empire enforced the acceptance of the Zoroastrian religious government that forced most of the Parthians out. Where to migrate was greatly restricted. The Parthians could not go south because of the Arabian Desert and the Arabian Sea. To the east there were huge mountain ranges and Oriental hordes – real barbarians. And to the west was the Roman Empire which remained very inhospitable to Christians in the first part of the 3rd Century AD.

[105] 6 For you are a people holy to the LORD your God. The LORD your God has chosen you out of all the peoples on the face of the earth to be his people, his treasured possession. Deuteronomy 7:6 (NIV84)

4 John, To the seven churches in the province of Asia: Grace and peace to you from him who is, and who was, and who is to come, and from the seven spirits before his throne, 5 and from Jesus Christ, who is the faithful witness, the firstborn from the dead, and the ruler of the kings of the earth. To him who loves us and has freed us from our sins by his blood, 6 and has made us to be a kingdom and priests to serve his God and Father—to him be glory and power for ever and ever! Amen. Revelation 1:4–6 (NIV84)

9 And they sang a new song: "You are worthy to take the scroll and to open its seals, because you were slain, and with your blood you purchased men for God from

every tribe and language and people and nation. 10 <u>You have made them to be a kingdom and priests to serve our God, and they will reign on the earth</u>." Revelation 5:9–10 (NIV84)

6 Blessed and holy are those who have part in the first resurrection. The second death has no power over them, but <u>they will be priests of God and of Christ and will reign with him for a thousand years.</u> Revelation 20:6 (NIV84)

106 One should not be misled by those who interpret the name "Babylon" in Peter's letter to be a euphemism for Rome as it is used, for instance, in Revelation chapter 17. That scenario in Revelation is dated to the end of our age after the falling away of the church in Rome as it solidified its hierarchy just before the "Dark Ages"; after that same church tortured and killed thousands of Christians who refused to bow before the Pope of Rome and after that church has for centuries been allied with various governments and people who have attempting to destroy those who point out the evils that come from men claiming to be the "Vicar of Christ". In Peter's letter, he mentions his wife, who was "chosen together with" the people to whom Peter was writing. He also mentions his son. This author is highly skeptical of the claims that Peter ever visited Rome and suggest that whole scenario is an attempt to give the Catholic Church hierarchy credibility by claiming Peter was the first Pope. The establishment of a religious hierarchy directly opposes the teaching of Jesus:

25 Jesus called them together and said, "You know that the rulers of the Gentiles lord it over them, and their high officials exercise authority over them. 26 Not so with you. Instead, whoever wants to become great among you must be your servant, 27 and whoever wants to be first must be your slave—28 just as the Son of Man did not come to be served, but to serve, and to give his life as a ransom for many." Matthew 20:25–28 (NIV)

107 There are also some related and intriguing questions about the Apostle Paul's relationship with the Galatians – who were located in the Parthian Empire – to whom he addressed one of his letters. Why did the spirit forbid Paul and Silas from going into Bithynia? [Acts 16:7] Why would Paul spend so much time convincing *Gentiles* (non-Israelites) that they should not regress to be under the Law of Moses?

108 The following identification of location and comments are from *Smith's Bible Dictionary* and *Nelson's New Illustrated Bible Dictionary*

PONTUS [PONN tus] — a province in northern Asia Minor (modern Turkey) mentioned in the Book of Acts (see Map 7, D–1). Pontus was situated on the southern shore of the Pontus Euxinus, or the Black Sea.108

As to the annals of Pontus, the one brilliant passage of its history is the life of the great Mithridates.108 (Mithridates VI, king of Parthian Empire)

GALATIA [guh LAY shih uh] — a region in central Asia Minor (modern Turkey) bounded on the east by Cappadocia, on the west by Asia, on the south by Pamphylia and Cilicia, and on the north by Bithynia and Pontus [108]

Although the point is debated, it appears that Paul's Epistle to the Galatians (Gal. 1:2; 3:1) was addressed to the churches founded by him in the southern part of the province of Galatia (south Galatian theory). No evidence exists to show that Paul visited the region of Galatia in north-central Asia Minor. Although Acts 16:6 and 18:23 are sometimes thought to refer to this more remote northern region, the context of these passages seems to point to southern Galatia[108]

CAPPADOCIA [kap uh DOH shih uh] — a large Roman province in eastern Asia Minor (see Map 7, D–2). It was bounded on the north by Pontus and the mountains along the Halys River, on the east by Armenia and the Euphrates River, on the south by Cilicia and the Taurus Mountains, and on the west by Lycaonia and Galatia[108]

BITHYNIA [bih THIN ih uh] — a coastal province in northwestern ASIA MINOR (see Map 7, C–1). Bithynia was bounded on the north by the Black Sea, on the south and east by Phrygia and Galatia, and on the west by Mysia. While at Mysia, Paul and Silas decided to go into Bithynia "but the Spirit did not permit them" (Acts 16:7). Later, however, the gospel reached the province; and many of the citizens of Bithynia became Christians (1 Pet. 1:1–2).[108]

[109] **Jesus' Coming on the Clouds of Heaven:** This happened in 67 – 70 AD when God used the Roman Army to destroy Jerusalem, the temple and the last vestiges of the Mt. Sinai Covenant. "Coming on the clouds of heaven" is an expression used many times in the Old Testament in prophecies of the punishment of nations that were Israel's enemies.

[59] The chief priests and the whole Sanhedrin were looking for false evidence against Jesus so that they could put him to death. [60] But they did not find any, though many false witnesses came forward. Finally two came forward [61] and declared, "This fellow said, 'I am able to destroy the temple of God and rebuild it in three days.' " [62] Then the high priest stood up and said to Jesus, "Are you not going to answer? What is this testimony that these men are bringing against you?" [63] But Jesus remained silent. The high priest said to him, "I charge you under oath by the living God: Tell us if you are the Christ, the Son of God." [64] "Yes, it is as you say," Jesus replied. "But I say to all of you: In the future you will see the Son of Man sitting at the right hand of the Mighty One and coming on the clouds of heaven." [65] Then the high priest tore his clothes and said, "He has spoken blasphemy! Why do we need any more witnesses? Look, now you have heard the blasphemy. Matthew 26:59–65 (NIV84)

Jesus told the high priest and the Sanhedrin that _they_ would see Him "coming on the clouds of heaven." This statement is also recorded in Mark 14:62.

[110] If Parthians, Medes and those residing in Cappadocia, Pontus and Asia were accepted by the Jews in Jerusalem and were not unusual at religious festivals as proselytes, the knowledge of the large presence of Israelites in their home countries would have been discussed at length.

[111] These Jews could not have been speaking of the diaspora that occurred 40 years after Jesus' death. There was a large "dispersion" (*diaspora*) of the Jews after the destruction of Jerusalem and the temple. That diaspora was the result of two causes: 1. the intense persecution of Christian Jews by the Jewish hierarchy (both religious and secular) for decades and 2. The disaster in 67-70 AD when the temple and Jerusalem were razed and the Roman Army took thousands of Jews captive and removed them from Palestine.

[112] The essence of being Christian is not performing any formal religious tasks, rites, or obligations demanded by any particular church sect (perhaps corresponding to Stark's principles?). Instead, the essence of Christianity is invisible, because it comes from the will of a "good" heart and an invisible faith in Christ and his Father—an invisible faith in an invisible God. Secular authorities hostile to Christianity, or the authorities of a competing religion, such as pagan idol worship, do not see into the heart, and do not see what parents may whisper just before bedtime; they do not observe good parents behaving in the home as good hearted Christians. Children brought up in a faith will generally hold on to that faith for life, much as an imprinted chick religiously knows and honors its own Mother for life. So, despite the publicly visible oppression by non-believers in Christ, his message was entirely capable of spreading quietly among good-hearted people who understood that he was the Messiah (i.e., to especially include the members of the lost tribes of Israel). Jack Hiller person communication 04/05/2018

[113] Many Christians at the same time perished, either because they were confounded with the followers of Mani, or because the spirit of persecution, once let loose, could not be restrained, but passed on from victims of one class to those of another, the Magian priesthood seizing the opportunity of devoting all heretics to a common destruction. Varahran I 271 AD Rawlinson, George. The Great Empires of the Ancient East (Kindle Locations 37387-37389)

Cruelties almost as great, but of a different character, were at the same time sanctioned by Sapor in regard to one class of his own subjects—viz., those who had made profession of Christianity. The Zoroastrian zeal of this king was great, and he regarded it as incumbent on him to check the advance which Christianity was now making in his territories. He issued severe edicts against the Christians soon after attaining his majority; and when they sought the protection of the Roman emperor, he punished their disloyalty by imposing upon them a fresh tax, the weight of which was oppressive. When Symeon, Archbishop of Seleucia, complained of this additional burden in an offensive manner, Sapor retaliated by closing the Christian churches, confiscating the ecclesiastical property, and putting the complainant to death. Sapor II ~350 AD Rawlinson, George. The Great Empires of the Ancient East (Kindle Locations 37775-37781).

[114] Tiridates II's resistance to the Sāsānid dynasty after the fall of the Arsacid dynasty in Persia (224) ended in his assassination by their agent Anak the Parthian (c. 238) and in the conquest of Armenia by Shāpūr I, who placed his vassal Artavazd on the throne (252). Under Diocletian, the Persians were forced to relinquish Armenia, and Tiridates III, the son of Tiridates II, was restored to the throne under Roman protection (c. 287). His reign determined the course of much of Armenia's subsequent history, and his conversion by St. Gregory the Illuminator and the adoption of Christianity as the state religion (c. 314) created a permanent gulf between Armenia and Persia. The Armenian patriarchate became one of the surest stays of the Arsacid monarchy and the guardian of national unity after its fall.

[115] Greek and Roman historians refer to any of the people who inhabited the central, eastern and northern parts of Europe as "Germanic". This term does NOT refer to the German people in ancient history but is indicative of the category of the languages they spoke. "The Germanic peoples (also called Teutonic, Suebian, or Gothic in older literature) are an Indo-European ethnolinguistic group of Northern European origin identified by their use of the Germanic languages." https://en.wikipedia.org/wiki/Germanic_peoples

[116] *In the culture of Israel, it was often the mother who taught and bequeathed the religion to the children (see the bishop Ulfilas mentioned in a paragraph below whose grandmother was a Christian in their homeland and obviously brought it with them to their new home.)*

[117] A mountainous country, Media contained some fertile sections; but much of it was cold, barren, and swampy. In the southern area lush plains were used as pastureland for the large herds of horses used in the Median cavalry. Youngblood, R. F., Bruce, F. F., & Harrison, R. K., Thomas Nelson Publishers (Eds.). (1995). In *Nelson's new illustrated Bible dictionary*. Nashville, TN: Thomas Nelson, Inc.

[118] We learn from old traditions that their origin was as follows: Filimer, king of the Goths, son of Gadaric the Great, who was the fifth in succession to hold the rule of the Getae, after their departure from the island of Scandza...found among his people certain witches. Suspecting these women, he expelled them from the midst of

his race and compelled them to wander in solitary exile afar from his army. There the unclean spirits, who beheld them as they wandered through the wilderness, bestowed their embraces upon them and begat this savage race, which dwelt at first in the swamps, a stunted, foul and puny tribe, scarcely human and having no language save one which bore but slight resemblance to human speech (85). https://www.britannica.com/biography/Jordanes

[119]The entomology of the name "Hun" is quite interesting. In languages like Turkic, Mongolian and Tungus the name means "nation, strength, courage" as well as simply, "man". Statues left by the KokTuruks were called "Hun chulu" or "Hun stone" or "stone person".

[120] "New Rome" which eventually became the capital of the Byzantine Empire

[121] After 493, the Ostrogothic Kingdom included two areas, Italy and much of the Balkans, which had large Arian churches. Arianism had retained some presence among Romans in Italy during the time between its condemnation in the empire and the Ostrogothic conquest. However, since Arianism in Italy was reinforced by the (mostly Arian) Goths coming from the Balkans, the Arian church in Italy had eventually come to call itself "Church of the Goths" by the year 500.

[122] 8 "But you are not to be called 'Rabbi,' for you have one Teacher, and you are all brothers. 9 And do not call anyone on earth 'father,' for you have one Father, and he is in heaven. 10 Nor are you to be called instructors, for you have one Instructor, the Messiah. 11 The greatest among you will be your servant. 12 For those who exalt themselves will be humbled, and those who humble themselves will be exalted. Matthew 23:8–12 (NIV)

24 A dispute also arose among them as to which of them was considered to be greatest. 25 Jesus said to them, "The kings of the Gentiles lord it over them; and those who exercise authority over them call themselves Benefactors. 26 But you are not to be like that. Instead, the greatest among you should be like the youngest, and the one who rules like the one who serves. 27 For who is greater, the one who is at the table or the one who serves? Is it not the one who is at the table? But I am among you as one who serves. Luke 22:24–27 (NIV)

[123] Many Roman provincials were Christian higher clergy. Between the legalization of Christianity by Constantine about 313 and the adoption of Christianity as the legal religion of Rome by the emperor Theodosius I in 380, Christian communities received immense donations of land, labour, and other gifts from emperors and wealthy converts. The Christian clergy, originally a body of community elders and managerial functionaries, gradually acquired sacramental authority and

became aligned with the grades of the imperial civil service. Each civitas (community or city), an urban unit and its surrounding district, had its bishop (from the Latin episcopus, "overseer"). Because there had been more Roman civitates in the Italian and provincial European areas, there were more and usually smaller dioceses in these regions than in the distant north and east.

During the 5th and 6th centuries, bishops gradually assumed greater responsibility for supplying the cities and administering their affairs, replacing the local governments that for centuries had underpinned and constituted the local administration of the empire. Two bishops, Ambrose of Milan (339–397) and Gregory I of Rome (pope 590–604), wrote influential guidebooks on episcopal and other clerical duties and responsibilities toward congregations. These works set standards for all later bishops and are still observed in many churches.

124 The influence of the "liberal secularism" of Petrarch still rises from time to time in our culture. For example, a student at Indiana University of Pennsylvania was recently barred from attending a religious studies class that he needed in order to graduate. *The young man had the temerity to argue that there are only two genders!* Furthermore, he questioned his instructor's claims regarding the "reality of white male privilege." Lake Ingle also said he objected to some of the claims made in a video featuring a transgender woman and countered that the "gender wage gap" is a myth. https://www.campusreform.org/?ID=10622

125 Over several centuries, thousands of people were slaughtered by the hierarchical church in Rome because they refused to submit to the authority of that church. The most infamous action in this regard was called "The Inquisition" http://en.wikipedia.org/wiki/Inquisition . The carnage of that movement continued into the 15th Century even after the secular power of the Roman Empire came to an end in the 1400's.

126 According to Chinese historians, the secret of the Huns' military success lies with the invention of the stirrup. This new invention allowed warriors to stand up while riding the horse greatly enhancing the mobility of the rider. The significance of the invention of the stirrup is comparable to the invention of the rocket or the fighter jet in the last century that changed modern warfare forever. http://www.hungarianambiance.com/2013/03/the-invention-of-stirrup-by-huns.html

127 Napoleon Bonaparte (1769-1821), also known as Napoleon I, was a French military leader and emperor who conquered much of Europe in the early 19th century. Born on the island of Corsica, Napoleon rapidly rose through the ranks of the military during the French Revolution (1789-1799). After seizing political power

in France in a 1799 coup d'état, he crowned himself emperor in 1804. Shrewd, ambitious and a skilled military strategist, Napoleon successfully waged war against various coalitions of European nations and expanded his empire. https://www.history.com/topics/napoleon

[128] Here I refer you to the prophecy of the Apostle John in Revelation 12. The people of Israel need to be protected for 1,260 years.

[13] When the dragon saw that he had been hurled to the earth, he pursued the woman who had given birth to the male child. [14] The woman was given the two wings of a great eagle, so that she might fly to the place prepared for her in the desert, where she would be taken care of for a time, times and half a time, out of the serpent's reach. [15] Then from his mouth the serpent spewed water like a river, to overtake the woman and sweep her away with the torrent. [16] But the earth helped the woman by opening its mouth and swallowing the river that the dragon had spewed out of his mouth. [17] Then the dragon was enraged at the woman and went off to make war against the rest of her offspring—those who obey God's commandments and hold to the testimony of Jesus. Revelation 12:13–17 (NIV84)

The woman from Revelation 12 represents the descendants of the 12 tribes – not just the Jews – Israelites who were brought out of Egyptian slavery "on the wings of an eagle". Rather than being pursued by the Egyptian Army, the Jewish and Gentile followers of Christ and the Israelites were avoiding the army of the Roman Empire.

The "river" was swallowed by the "barbarians" who destroyed the Western capital of the Roman Empire and who resisted the efforts of both secular and religious despots who tried to control the people and their culture. It's seems fitting that a secular despot, who thought himself invincible, would put the final nail in the coffin for the plans of a religious world-ruling empire.

[129] The Huns were not nice people when they were opposed. The time line is correct for their visit to Scandinavia and this recent archeological information could have been tied to the Huns if evidence had been sought diligently. https://www.nytimescom/2018/04/25/science/massacre-sweden archaeology.html

[130] Horses were not useful for traveling in Viking ships, crossing oceans and attacking the shores of the lands they wanted to conquer.

[131] Burgess: a magistrate or member of the governing body of a town https://www.merriam-webster.com/dictionary/burgess

[132] There were two major purposes of God's Covenant with Abraham, Isaac, Jacob and the children of Israel:
1 To bring spiritual blessings to the whole world *through* the Israelites. This was

first accomplished by establishing the nation of Israel followed with the gift of the 10 Commandments and God's guidance of the children of Israel through the centuries always allowing anyone to join their nation who would follow their laws. *The most important part was completed in the 1st Century through the advent of God being born as an Israelite, Jesus of Nazareth, who made a New Covenant with the House of Israel and the House of Judah that encompassed every human being on this planet.* Jesus established His church and sent His apostles to convert millions of people beginning with the "lost sheep of the House of Israel" who helped spread that Gospel quickly.

2 To bring physical blessings by the bestowal of the original Covenant's physical, literal promise – that descendants of Abraham, Isaac and Jacob would become a nation and a "company of nations" with political and economic hegemony, "possessing the gates of their enemies" and having "nations bow down to them". *This would mean that the whole world would be blessed again, both spiritually and physically,* with the Israelites' descendants carrying the Gospel to the whole world while distributing technology, knowledge of agriculture, science, medicine and "common law" – the latter including for the first time in history the belief in freedom for the common man.

133 Prior to the archeological discovery of French scholar Félix Marie Charles Texier in 1834 many historians and archeologists denied the existence of the Hittites and cited that as an example of Biblical error. https://en.wikipedia.org/wiki/Hittites Recent excavations at Tel 'Eton in the Judean foothills are being linked to the reigns of Kings David and Solomon. Many biased historians have doubted the very existence of King David. http://www.foxnews.com/science/2018/05/03/king-davids-city-discovered-ancient-site-linked-to-biblical-kingdom-archaeologists-say.html

134 As discussed in previous chapters, the migrants from the East brought with them technologies like the stirrup, the use of the horse in agriculture and transportation, the use of water wheels and windmills as well as their own sense of government which tended to allow much more personal freedom than the feudal systems that permeated Europe before they came.

135 The Black Death (also known as The Black Plague or Bubonic Plague), was one of the deadliest pandemics in human history, widely thought to have been caused by a bacterium named Yersinia pestis (Plague), but recently attributed by some to other diseases. The origins of the plague are disputed among scholars. Some historians believe the pandemic began in China or Central Asia in the late 1320s or 1330s, and during the next years merchants and soldiers carried it over the caravan routes until in 1346 it reached the Crimea in southern Russia. Other scholars believe the plague was endemic in southern Russia. In either case, from Crimea the plague spread to Western Europe and North Africa during the 1340s. The total number of deaths

worldwide is estimated at 75 million people, approximately 25–50 million of which occurred in Europe. http://listverse.com/2009/01/18/top-10-worst-plagues-in-history/

[136] This principle taught by Jesus entered the English lexicon as a quote from Baron Acton: *"Power tends to corrupt and absolute power corrupts absolutely.* Great men are almost always bad men, even when they exercise influence and not authority; still more when you superadd the tendency of the certainty of corruption by authority." John Emerich Edward Dalberg Acton, Baron Acton (1834–1902)

[137] The Catechism of the Catholic Church defines purgatory as a "purification, so as to achieve the holiness necessary to enter the joy of heaven," which is experienced by those "who die in God's grace and friendship, but still imperfectly purified". It notes that "this final purification of the elect . . . is entirely different from the punishment of the damned". https://www.catholic.com/tract/purgatory Many, including this author, find no foundation for the doctrine of purgatory in the Bible.

[138] Luther had rejected the Catholic Church's doctrine of transubstantiation, according to which the bread and wine in Holy Communion became the actual body and blood of Christ. According to Luther's notion, the body of Christ was physically present in the elements because Christ is present everywhere, while Zwingli claimed that entailed a spiritual presence of Christ and a declaration of faith by the recipients.

[139] The book was written as an introductory textbook on the Protestant creed for those with some previous knowledge of theology and covered a broad range of theological topics from the doctrines of church and sacraments to justification by faith alone and Christian liberty. It vigorously attacked the teachings of those Calvin considered unorthodox, particularly Roman Catholicism, to which Calvin says he had been "strongly devoted" before his conversion to Protestantism. https://en.wikipedia.org/wiki/Institutes_of_the_Christian_Religion

The Institutes is a highly regarded secondary reference for the system of doctrine adopted by the Reformed churches, usually called Calvinism

[140] Vulgate, (from the Latin editio vulgata: "common version"), Latin Bible used by the Roman Catholic Church, primarily translated by St. Jerome. In 382 Pope Damasus commissioned Jerome, the leading biblical scholar of his day, to produce an acceptable Latin version of the Bible from the various translations then being used. His revised Latin translation of the Gospels appeared about 383. Using the Septuagint Greek version of the Old Testament, he produced new Latin translations of the Psalms (the so-called Gallican Psalter), the Book of Job, and some other books. Later,

he decided that the Septuagint was unsatisfactory and began translating the entire Old Testament from the original Hebrew versions, a process that he completed about 405.

141 The idea of combining the power of secular government with the religious power, or of making secular authority superior to the spiritual authority of the Church; especially concerning the connection of the Church with government. https://www.britannica.com/topic/Vulgate

142 The Restoration Movement (also known as the American Restoration Movement or the Stone-Campbell Movement, and pejoratively as Campbellism) is a Christian movement that began on the United States frontier during the Second Great Awakening (1790–1840) of the early 19th century. The pioneers of this movement were seeking to reform the church from within and sought "the unification of all Christians in a single body patterned after the church of the New Testament." Especially since the mid-20th century, members of these churches do not identify as Protestant but simply as Christian.

The Restoration Movement developed from several independent strands of religious revival that idealized early Christianity. Two groups, which independently developed similar approaches to the Christian faith, were particularly important. The first, led by Barton W. Stone, began at Cane Ridge, Kentucky, and identified as "Christians". The second began in western Pennsylvania and Virginia (now West Virginia) and was led by Thomas Campbell and his son, Alexander Campbell, both educated in Scotland; they eventually used the name "Disciples of Christ". Both groups sought to restore the whole Christian church on the pattern set forth in the New Testament, and both believed that creeds kept Christianity divided. In 1832 they joined in fellowship with a handshake.

Among other things, they were united in the belief that Jesus is the Christ, the Son of God; that Christians should celebrate the Lord's Supper on the first day of each week; and that baptism of adult believers by immersion in water is a necessary condition for salvation. Because the founders wanted to abandon all denominational labels, they used the biblical names for the followers of Jesus. Both groups promoted a return to the purposes of the 1st-century churches as described in the New Testament.

143 The first notable to move against Copernicanism was the Magister of the Holy Palace (i.e., the Catholic Church's chief censor), Dominican Bartolomeo Spina, who "expressed a desire to stamp out the Copernican doctrine." https://en.wikipedia.org/wiki/Nicolaus_Copernicus

144 The steps of the scientific method are these: 1. Make an observation or observations; 2. Ask questions about the observations and gather information. 3. Form a hypothesis — a tentative description of what's been observed and make predictions based on that hypothesis. 4. Test the hypothesis and predictions in an experiment that can be reproduced. 5. Analyze the data and draw conclusions; accept or reject the hypothesis or modify the hypothesis if necessary. 6. Reproduce the experiment until there are no discrepancies between observations and theory. https://www.livescience.com/20896-science-scientific-method.html

145 Some of the founders of the United States followed this line of thought in their beliefs primarily because they saw the Covenants God made with Israel as having never been fulfilled. These were the very Covenants that we've been tracking in this book. If those Covenant promises were delivered to the British Empire and the United States, we wonder what our founders would make of the concepts in this book.

146 12 "But before all this, they will seize you and persecute you. They will hand you over to synagogues and put you in prison, and you will be brought before kings and governors, and all on account of my name. 13 And so you will bear testimony to me. 14 But make up your mind not to worry beforehand how you will defend yourselves. 15 For I will give you words and wisdom that none of your adversaries will be able to resist or contradict. Luke 21:12–15 (NIV)
45 Then he opened their minds so they could understand the Scriptures. 46 He told them, "This is what is written: The Messiah will suffer and rise from the dead on the third day, 47 and repentance for the forgiveness of sins will be preached in his name to all nations, beginning at Jerusalem. 48 You are witnesses of these things. 49 I am going to send you what my Father has promised; but stay in the city until you have been clothed with power from on high." Luke 24:45–49 (NIV)
147 In prophecy, the "House of Jacob" only refers to the northern kingdom of Israel; likewise, Samaria (the capital) and Ephraim refer only to the northern kingdom while the "House of Judah" and Jerusalem (the capital of Judah) refer only to the Jews.

148 The apostle Paul expounds at great length not only on the phenomenon of the "blinding" of the Jews but also on this subject – Jesus as the eternal "vine" to which His followers must be attached to survive – in his letter to the church in Rome, primarily in chapters 9 and 10.

149 James VI and I (James Charles Stuart; 19 June 1566 – 27 March 1625) was King of Scotland as James VI from 24 July 1567 and King of England and Ireland as James I

from the union of the Scottish and English crowns on 24 March 1603 until his death in 1625. The kingdoms of Scotland and England were individual sovereign states, with their own parliaments, judiciaries, and laws, though both were ruled by James in personal union.

At 57 years and 246 days, James's reign in Scotland was longer than those of any of his predecessors. He achieved most of his aims in Scotland but faced great difficulties in England, including the Gunpowder Plot in 1605 and repeated conflicts with the English Parliament. Under James, the "Golden Age" of Elizabethan literature and drama continued, with writers such as William Shakespeare, John Donne, Ben Jonson, and Sir Francis Bacon contributing to a flourishing literary culture. James himself was a talented scholar, the author of works such as Daemonologie (1597), The True Law of Free Monarchies (1598), and Basilikon Doron (1599).

He sponsored the translation of the Bible into English that would later be named after him: The Authorized King James Version. Sir Anthony Weldon claimed that James had been termed "the wisest fool in Christendom", an epithet associated with his character ever since. Since the latter half of the 20th century, historians have tended to revise James's reputation and treat him as a serious and thoughtful monarch. He was strongly committed to a peace policy, and tried to avoid involvement in religious wars, especially the Thirty Years' War (1618–1648) that devastated much of Central Europe. He tried but failed to prevent the rise of hawkish elements in the English Parliament who wanted war with Spain.

[150] A historiography (noun) or historiographical paper is an analysis of the interpretations of a specific topic written by past historians. Specifically, a historiography identifies influential thinkers and reveals the shape of the scholarly debate on a particular subject. https://uri.libguides.com/historiography

[151] The Aras or Araxes is a river flowing through Turkey, Armenia, Azerbaijan, and Iran. It drains the south side of the Lesser Caucasus Mountains and then joins the Kura River, which drains the north side of Lesser Caucasus Mountains. Its total length is 1,072 kilometres, covering an area of 102,000 square kilometres. The Aras River is one of the largest rivers in the Caucasus. https://en.wikipedia.org/wiki/Araxes

[152] Diodorus Siculus of Sicily was a Greek historian. He is known for writing the monumental universal history Bibliotheca historica, much of which survives, between 60 and 30 BC

[153] Princess Alice, Countess of Athlone, VA, GCVO, GBE (Alice Mary Victoria Augusta Pauline; 25 February 1883 – 3 January 1981) was a member of the British royal family. She is the longest-lived princess of the blood royal of the British royal family and was the last surviving grandchild of Queen Victoria.

¹⁵⁴ Howard Benjamin Rand (June 13, 1889 - August 17, 1991) was a lawyer, inventor, and three-time candidate for Massachusetts state office on the Prohibition Party ticket.

¹⁵⁵ John Arbuthnot Fisher, 1st Baron Fisher, [2] GCB, OM, GCVO (25 January 1841 – 10 July 1920), commonly known as Jacky or Jackie Fisher, was a British admiral known for his efforts at naval reform. He had a huge influence on the Royal Navy in a career spanning more than 60 years, starting in a navy of wooden sailing ships armed with muzzle-loading cannon and ending in one of steel-hulled battlecruisers, submarines and the first aircraft carriers.

¹⁵⁶ John Harden Allen (1847 – May 14, 1930) was an American minister. He was associated with the Church of God (Holiness) and is also heavily associated with British Israelism. He came from Illinois, later moving to Missouri in 1879. Originally a pastor in the Methodist Episcopal Church, he later became a pastor in the Wesleyan Methodist Church in California. He was one of the co-founders of the Church of God (Holiness) in 1883. He "evangelized throughout the West and eventually moved to Pasadena, California, where he died."

Allen is best known for his book titled Judah's Sceptre and Joseph's Birthright, which many have claimed formed the foundation for the teachings on British-Israelism of Herbert W. Armstrong. While the works of Allen and Armstrong are by no means identical, with Allen's work being much earlier, much longer and in hard-back book format, the core of Allen's work does appear to have served as inspiration for Armstrong, and Allen's book was not unknown to Armstrong's students at Ambassador College. There are many similarities between the two works, and in some places, they are nearly word-for-word the same. https://en.wikipedia.org/wiki/J._H._Allen

¹⁵⁷ A closer examination of the context of these scriptures shows that some Israelites did move into Judah but from only two tribes and the numbers were small. Moriel mistakes the incidence of some Israelites preferring to return to Jerusalem to offer sacrifices in the temple with their having become part of Judah.

¹⁵⁸ Moriel cites scriptures that "prove" Israelite and Jew were used interchangeable but the context fails to support that concept. Paul was a Benjaminite – one of the two tribes of the Kingdom of Judah along with most of the Levites – so Paul's statement that he was an Israelite and a Jew has a different meaning from that understood by Moriel. Moriel also fails to deal with Josephus' statement made in 94 AD that the 10 tribes were "beyond the Euphrates" and in numbers too large to count.

[159] Dimont follows the mainstream interpretation that the Israelites of the Northern Kingdom of Israel disappeared or moved into the Kingdom of Judah after the Assyrian deportation. He quotes one Assyrian leader's number of deportees as 27,290 Israelites but failed to research further. The books from the library at the excavation of Ninevah (Assyria's capitol) show Sargon's successors giving the number at more than 200,000. The initial deportation included the entire tribe of Naphtali [2 Kings 15:29]. There was a significant slaughter of the population as well so much that virtually none were left after 721 B. C.

[160] The Church of Christ, the Disciples of Christ and the Christian Church represent a spectrum of 3 organizations that came from the "Restoration Movement". The Restoration Movement (also known as the American Restoration Movement or the Stone-Campbell Movement, and pejoratively as Campbellism) is a Christian movement that began on the United States frontier during the Second Great Awakening (1790–1840) of the early 19th century. The pioneers of this movement were seeking to reform the church from within and sought "the unification of all Christians in a single body patterned after the church of the New Testament".

[161] Tea-Tephi was supposedly the daughter of the last king of Judah – Hoshea – who traveled to Ireland in the company of the prophet Jeremiah. There she married a descendant of King David and reunited the Pharez-Perez schism described in Genesis chapter 38.

[162] Jeremiah 33:14–26 relates God's promise that there would be a descendant of David on the "throne of Israel" so long as "day and night" exist. After His resurrection, as Jesus prepared to leave His apostles: [18] Then Jesus came to them and said, "All authority in heaven and on earth has been given to me." Matthew 28:18 (NIV) This leaves little room for a *human* ruler over "Israel". Furthermore, the same prophecy states that there would be Levites (priests) ministering before God following the same terms as those applied to the descendants of David. Since Jesus has been the New Covenant "High Priest" since His ascension, there is no need for Levite priests. [Hebrews chapters 7-10]

[163] Strangely, McBirnie states that all the Israelites were incorporated into Judah and all became Jews even though his work acknowledges Jesus' command to His apostles to avoid the Samaritans and Gentiles and seek out the "lost sheep of the House of Israel".

[164] Sennacherib's own account of the invasion provides a remarkable supplement

to the biblical version (2 Kings 18:13–19:36). He claims to have destroyed 46 walled cities (2 Kings 18:13) and to have taken 200,150 captives. Sennacherib's conquest of Lachish is shown in graphic detail in carved panels from his palace at Nineveh. Browning, D. C., Jr. (2003). Assyria. In C. Brand, C. Draper, A. England, S. Bond, E. R. Clendenen, & T. C. Butler (Eds.), *Holman Illustrated Bible Dictionary* (p. 136). Nashville, TN: Holman Bible Publishers.

[165] Holy = sacred = "devoted exclusively to one service or use" [Merriam-Webster's Collegiate Dictionary]. One should note that the word "holy" as used in the Bible in our translations of both the Hebrew and Greek does not connote "righteousness" or "in compliance with God's law". Thus, the Israelites were a "holy" nation – devoted exclusively to one service or use. It does not imply that the Israelites were "better" people or a "better" nation than any other people or nation. It only asserts that they were set aside for God's purposes. This is further borne out by the malfeasance and disregard for God's laws and instruction seen throughout the history of Israel. An interesting side note is that the word "sacred" does not appear in the King James or New King James translations of the Bible though it appears often in the NIV and some other translations where it is used interchangeably with "holy".

[166] Some scholars count fourteen or more, directly or indirectly. We know he planted the church at Ephesus, which in turn branched out to plant many others. There were also organic churches in Phillipi and Corinth. Then three churches were planted in Cypress and Crete. There's also Thyatira, Philadelphia, Smyrna, Laodicea, Pergamon, Syria, Arabia, Sardis. Some count up to twenty churches planted by Paul either directly or indirectly. https://www.quora.com/profile/Marie-ODay

[167] 1 When all these blessings and curses I have set before you come upon you and you take them to heart wherever the LORD your God disperses you among the nations, 2 and when you and your children return to the LORD your God and obey him with all your heart and with all your soul according to everything I command you today, 3 then the LORD your God will restore your fortunes and have compassion on you and gather you again from all the nations where he scattered you. Deuteronomy 30:1-3

[168] The Restoration Movement developed from several independent strands of religious revival that idealized early Christianity. Two groups, which independently developed similar approaches to the Christian faith, were particularly important. The first, led by Barton W. Stone, began at Cane Ridge, Kentucky, and identified as "Christians". The second began in western Pennsylvania and Virginia (now West Virginia) and was led by Thomas Campbell and his son, Alexander Campbell, both educated in Scotland; they eventually used the name "Disciples of Christ". Both

groups sought to restore the whole Christian church on the pattern set forth in the New Testament, and both believed that creeds kept Christianity divided. In 1832 they joined in fellowship with a handshake.

Among other things, they were united in the belief that Jesus is the Christ, the Son of God; that Christians should celebrate the Lord's Supper on the first day of each week; and that baptism of adult believers by immersion in water is a necessary condition for salvation. Because the founders wanted to abandon all denominational labels, they used the biblical names for the followers of Jesus. Both groups promoted a return to the purposes of the 1st-century churches as described in the New Testament. One historian of the movement has argued that it was primarily a unity movement, with the restoration motif playing a subordinate role.

The Restoration Movement has since divided into multiple separate groups. There are three main branches in the U.S.: the Churches of Christ, the unaffiliated Christian Church/Church of Christ congregations, and the Christian Church (Disciples of Christ). Some characterize the divisions in the movement as the result of the tension between the goals of restoration and ecumenism: the Churches of Christ and unaffiliated Christian Church/Church of Christ congregations resolved the tension by stressing restoration, while the Christian Church (Disciples of Christ) resolved the tension by stressing ecumenism. A number of groups outside the U.S. also have historical associations with this movement, such as the Evangelical Christian Church in Canada and the Churches of Christ in Australia. It is the author's opinion that of all human religious organizations professing Christianity, the Restoration Movement is closest to following Biblical teaching. Even so, the author believes Jesus' *ecclesia* are likely to be found throughout all Christian organizations [Mark 9:40; Luke 9:50].

[169] Third Reich, official Nazi designation for the regime in Germany from January 1933 to May 1945, as the presumed successor of the medieval and early modern Holy Roman Empire of 800 to 1806 (the First Reich) and the German Empire of 1871 to 1918 (the Second Reich). https://www.britannica.com/place/Third-Reich